The Work of Difference

To Grandma Ceil
and Pappa Eddie –
So happy to share this
with you! all my
love,
audrey

# The Work of Difference

## MODERNISM, ROMANTICISM, AND THE PRODUCTION OF LITERARY FORM

Audrey Wasser

FORDHAM UNIVERSITY PRESS *New York* 2016

THIS BOOK IS MADE POSSIBLE BY A COLLABORATIVE GRANT
FROM THE ANDREW W. MELLON FOUNDATION.

Fordham University Press has no responsibility for the persistence or accuracy of URLs for external or third-party Internet websites referred to in this publication and does not guarantee that any content on such websites is, or will remain, accurate or appropriate.

Fordham University Press also publishes its books in a variety of electronic formats. Some content that appears in print may not be available in electronic books.

Visit us online at www.fordhampress.com.

Library of Congress Cataloging-in-Publication Data

Wasser, Audrey.
  The work of difference : modernism, romanticism, and the production of literary form / Audrey Wasser.
     pages cm
  Includes bibliographical references and index.
  ISBN 978-0-8232-7005-7 (hardback)
  ISBN 978-0-8232-7006-4 (paper)
    1. Literary form. 2. Criticism. 3. Modernism (Literature) I. Title.
PN45.5.W37 2016
808—dc23
                                                                        2015028995

Printed in the United States of America

18 17 16    5 4 3 2 1

First edition

*to Rob*

# CONTENTS

# Introduction

The problem of art in the modern era is the problem of the new. Most of our assumptions and desires about art—that it be creative and thought-provoking; that it be produced by a person of genius; that it be something as yet unseen in the world, let alone unseen in the classroom or the museum—all of these circle around the fundamental proposition that the artwork is the *new* work. Even when we praise a work's timeless or universal qualities, perhaps some "power of imagination" shining through the work, we are liable to agree that if there is not something new about it, perhaps something formally new, it does not really count as art. If we look back to the early twentieth century, to the experimental ethos of literary modernism epitomized by Ezra Pound's exhortation to "make it new," and beyond that to the early nineteenth century, to romanticism's valorization of modernity against neoclassical standards of beauty, we readily see that "newness" has a particular history.

"Newness," in no small way, is our inheritance. This book is concerned with literary modernism from the perspective of this inheritance: with a poetics of the new that belongs to modernism's self-understanding—and which, I will argue, has still not been adequately theorized. Instead, a certain nineteenth-century way of thinking about the new continues to hold sway over the way we read modernist texts. Rather than contest the value of the new, my goal is to consider the terms in which the new has been transmitted to us, terms that end up dragging a whole set of unquestioned, metaphysical assumptions in their wake.

These assumptions find their strongest formulation in the literary-critical writing of the early German romantics. My argument thus begins with a reexamination of the claim made by a number of critics about the decisive importance of romanticism to contemporary ideas about literature. In particular, I show how the experimental writing of early German romanticism, especially as this writing engaged with the system-building philosophy of its time, left us with a legacy that continues to control the way we think about literary newness, literary form, and the relationship between literature and truth. Not only does this legacy dominate popular ways of thinking about literature; it determines in advance even the most critical or searching questions scholars are able to pose, furnishing almost all of the terms we have at our disposal to pose them.

*Romanticism* is the word I use to zero in on this moment in Germany following on the heels of Kantian philosophy, which witnessed an extraordinary imbrication of philosophical ideas and experimental literary and critical practice. *Romanticism* might be one of the most debated terms in literary scholarship, having been used to label a tremendous diversity of texts and trends, but one thing that emerges definitively in this period is a characterization of literature—indeed of art in general—primarily in terms of invention. The turn away from neoclassicism that romanticism represented, and from the value neoclassicism placed on rules derived from classical texts, took the form of an as yet unseen valorization of the modern and the interesting, and perhaps of the new as such. This treatment is prefigured in Kant's third *Critique* (1790), which defined the aesthetic in terms of its autonomy with respect to systems of knowledge and reason. Through Kant aesthetic experience was freed from the domain of the concept, from rational calculation, from the telos of perfection, and from the production of art on the basis of rules of beauty. Romanticism inherited these Kantian assumptions, shifting them from the realm of reception to that of production.

Philosophical and cultural factors have conspired, in short, to bequeath to the present the question of art as, fundamentally, a question of the new. "Newness" names a problem, however, if not an outright paradox. The paradox it presents takes the following form: if, on the one hand, the truly new work must break with its existing context, then, on the other hand, it must still be recognizable in some fashion, and be recognizable as art.[1]

The problem, in other words, is whether the event or rupture that the new work of art supposedly *is* can be apprehended—or even thought—outside of existing institutions and outside of existing systems of determination, expression, and reception. The imperative to grasp art as new confronts the deeper, conceptual difficulty of how one ought to negotiate the relation between system and event, or between history and innovation. How is it that new works or new forms are possible within the determinate orders of history, language use, or the social? How are they in turn recognizable to already-existing institutions? These questions demand careful answers if we hope to move beyond mere assertion in statements of method. Indeed, if we do not have a way of articulating the conceptual relationship between what is and what is not *new*, how can we hope to tackle the question of what is and what is not *literature*?

The question of literature has been posed with the greatest urgency in the postwar French context, from Sartre's *Qu'est-ce que la littérature?* (1947) to the critical writings of Blanchot and Derrida. Within this tradition, the question of literature has served as the occasion for articulating some of the most fundamental problems of twentieth-century thought—the problem of the event, for example, and of the relation between structure and genesis. In fact, I would venture so far as to say that literature became a question for French philosophy in this period above all because *literature* is another name for the problem of structure and genesis, or of system and event. My own project draws on the insights of this tradition, especially on ways of reading that it made possible. But it departs from this tradition in the answers it provides.

So this book addresses an ontological question—*What is literature?*—concerning a historically contingent object and a posing that has itself unfolded historically. But this book is more than a genealogy of the concept of the literary work of art. I work through a diagnosis of present assumptions about the integrity of the work, and about the relationship between the work and the world beyond it, in order to unearth the philosophical basis for these assumptions. Undertaking a critique of these assumptions, with the aid of a different set of philosophical concepts, I attempt to construct an alternative account of literary production. That is, the aim of this book is to articulate a non-romantic theory of literature.

What is the sense of such a question as *What is literature?* The philosophical form of the question "What is . . . ?" takes for granted an essential difference between philosophy and literature, assuming that one kind of discourse is capable of posing a question about the other. In chapter 1, I consider the difficulties that attend posing such a question in the first place. I briefly address the historical separation of the disciplines of literature and philosophy before turning to a very particular historical moment—the moment of the *Athenaeum* journal in Jena from roughly 1798 to 1800—when the critical or philosophical question of what literature *is* is taken up as a problem internal to literature itself.

In the experimental writing of Friedrich Schlegel and the group associated with the *Athenaeum*, a model of literary form as speculation is put in place that, I argue, remains our own. This model emerges in the theory and practice of fragmentary writing. Engaging with the Kantian and post-Kantian problems of system building of the time, the *Athenaeum* fragments aimed to provide an aesthetic solution to a philosophical problem, attempting to invest the literary with the power to overcome the fundamental division of the sensible and the intelligible, the particular and the universal, that emerged from Kant's philosophy, and hence to elevate literature to the status of an effective presentation of the absolute. Literature was invested with a philosophical power, and with a power to speak to philosophy as philosophy's other.[2] This power, I demonstrate, hung on a schema of reflection. The formal delimitation of the literary work was made the occasion for the work's reflection of the absolute as well as for its internal reflection on itself in a structure that resembled self-consciousness. Not only are these notions of reflection perpetuated in the contemporary belief that the purpose of literature is to reveal a higher truth than philosophy alone is capable, but echoes of this treatment can also be found anywhere a literary work is assumed to be formally coherent on the basis of its self-reflection and self-knowledge, so that the work is supposed to be capable of shedding light on itself and of commenting on itself lucidly. Engaged in self-commentary, the work supposedly bridges the gap between literature and criticism, art and knowledge.

I argue that such treatments burden the literary work with a task that is at once too great and too slight. For the very logic that would make the work a privileged point of reflection on the absolute—that is, on truth or Being or the unfolding of history as such—simultaneously condemns the work to the status of *mere* reflection, to the position of a fragment in a process of truth or history that must necessarily overcome it. Individual artworks can then only stage their

own overcoming, dissolving themselves in philosophy or in a movement of thought—thought construed as self-reflection—destined to
fulfill itself in criticism or in a theory of Literature as such. Against
the speculative logic of the fragment, we need a more immanent, and
perhaps more modest, conception of literary thinking.

In chapters 2 and 3, I examine two paradigmatic cases where this
romantic logic is perpetuated in the twentieth century, to the detri-
ment of an adequate account of literary production. Through readings of key texts by the American New Critic Cleanth Brooks and
the French postwar thinker Maurice Blanchot, two writers of decisive influence on contemporary critical practices in the United States,
I demonstrate how the reliance on a schema of reflection prevents
both critics from thinking the genuinely new. Though on the surface
these critics could not appear more different—Brooks's readings of
poetry seek to confirm the organic unity of the literary work, while
Blanchot's aim to reveal the fragmentation at work in poetic language—the very same romantic logic, in fact, is at work in both positions. Each attempts to account for literary creation, either through
an implicit reinstatement of authorial intention, in Brooks's case, or
in a theory of inspiration and sacrifice, in the case of Blanchot. But
each does so by following a retrograde movement of thought, a movement that leads each critic backward from already-given works in his
attempt to think the origin of those works. In each case, I argue, the
logic of reflection demands that a work be grasped as a mirror image
of its conditions of creation. Brooks is thus led to posit an identity
between the work and its animating intention, while Blanchot argues,
conversely, for a theory of total rupture and negation. What these two
seemingly different treatments of literature share, I contend, is the
inability to account for any productive *difference* between form and
intention, or between a work and its causal conditions. If they cannot
account for such difference, it seems to me they cannot account for
the newness they affirm.

Brooks and Blanchot are representative of two entrenched ways
of thinking about literary creation today that, being opposed to one
another, appear to cover the entire field. The former, still relying
on the speculative logic of romanticism, generally assumes that the
cause of a work is an idea, intention, or social-historical reality that
will be reflected or revealed in the work once the work has been
made. The latter suspects that the truly new cannot be articulated
in advance of its creation, that the possibility of a work of art does

not, and cannot, precede its reality the way a sketch precedes an oil painting, and so concludes that the true condition of artistic creation must be the absence of all condition. Thus, for example, Blanchot writes in *The Space of Literature* that the work is born "when the work ceases in some way to have been made, to refer back to someone who made it" (200). In such a view, literature must be characterized by an essential negativity, by a freedom from all of the intentional, programmable, or deterministic structures that belong to the objective world.

This choice between causal determinism and an essential negativity is a false choice, I argue, presented to us by the speculative logic of romanticism. Perhaps most importantly, it leaves us without resources for thinking the *new* as something that might be compatible with a *production* of the new. In chapter 4, I argue that it is possible to diverge from this romantic logic only when we are willing to reconfigure the most basic terms of the problem. Drawing on Deleuze's work, as well as on that of his approximate contemporaries Gilbert Simondon and Pierre Macherey, I work through five propositions for remaking our concept of the literary object on the basis of a different set of ontological claims. My goal is to disrupt the metaphysical assumptions of romanticism—namely, the assumptions of what counts as the unity and integrity of any object, and how causation as such is determined—by marshaling resources from thinkers who do not situate themselves within a Kantian-romantic line. Each of these thinkers, albeit in distinct ways, is engaged in an ontological investigation that privileges repetition over reflection, difference over being, and differential relations over those of identity and negation. My hypothesis is that a work of literature is something that differs from itself as well as from its causes, and thus needs to be theorized on the basis of philosophies that have explicitly articulated a logic and an ontology of difference.

The second half of the book turns to three major modernist texts—Samuel Beckett's postwar trilogy, Marcel Proust's *A la recherche du temps perdu*, and Gertrude Stein's *Making of Americans*—in order to test the implications of this theoretical argument for a practice of reading. I draw a spirit of inquiry from Deleuze here, but I don't replicate his readings of Beckett or Proust, which tend to be aimed at illustrating his philosophical arguments. Instead, I consider whether these arguments might have a greater implication for literary interpretation than Deleuze himself recognized. This implication has to do with the status of literary language as a site for the production and organization of difference.

I turn to three novels or sets of novels as sites for thinking about literary organization rather than to the modernist poem, drama, or critical essay. More than any other genre, the novel is bound to the *novel*, to the new, to the languages and stories of modern life. Its inventiveness, moreover, is bound to its complexity: supported by the apparatus of the book and the forward momentum of narrative, the novel's potential for elaborating times, places, characters, and events, coupled with the capacity of prose for nearly endless syntactical subordination, make the novel a kind of complexity-producing machine.[3] The romantics saw in the novel the possibility of a new thinking of literary organization; specifically, the novel held out the promise of a poetics that might mix and ultimately transcend the classical genres, fulfilling the romantic ambition for a truly "progressive, universal poetry," in Schlegel's words (*Athenaeum Fragments* 116). Conceived as the "romantic book," furthermore, the novel offered (but ultimately failed, for them) to unite a poetics of development with the closure of a system (Schlegel, *Dialogue on Poetry* 101). At any rate, their investment in the novel as a privileged staging of a problem of organization suggests that a real departure from romanticism might best be worked out on this same terrain.

Each of the novels I look at is "major" in terms of its importance for a modernist canon; I've chosen them, in part, in an attempt to reconsider what may be the most distinguishing features of a modernist poetics of the novel. Yet these texts are "minor" in the sense that they pose problems for critical interpretation, challenging entrenched habits of reading as well as basic assumptions about what constitutes the integrity and purpose of a literary work. I turn to these works in order to bring these habits and assumptions to light, for it seems to me that it is our ways of reading, rather than these particular texts, that have been detrimentally overdetermined by a romantic paradigm. If we can dismantle this paradigm, we may finally be open to what is most innovative—and most distinctly modern—in these twentieth-century texts.

Overdetermination is certainly a danger, as is any theory of literature that would run roughshod over individual works, turning them into examples of its master claims. The logic of exemplarity, after all, is a logic of reflection that has everything in common with the romantic treatment of the fragment. While the first half of this book develops an ontology of the literary, the second half does not seek to produce illustrations of this account, nor does it attempt to translate this ontology into a method for criticism. While it should be possible to work out practical considerations on the basis of ontological claims, the former need not be dictated by the latter—indeed they must not be, if what is at issue is precisely the *new*, the new insofar as it falls outside of generalizations and preexisting frameworks. My engagements with Beckett, Proust, and Stein thus unfold primarily as acts of close reading. But these readings are made possible by the ontological commitments detailed in the first half of this book.

Fundamentally, I am committed to the idea that the new, in literature as elsewhere, is defined by its relations.[4] These relations constitute the internal, formal properties of a work no less than they determine the articulation of the work with its outside—with other texts as well as extraliterary contexts. Everything thus depends on the way we characterize these relations. If the closure of the work is not given prior to the work, then it is produced by an operation immanent to the work itself, in which the work articulates some relation of difference with its outside, and articulates this difference as a formal property. One of the things I am interested in is, accordingly, the possibility that a differential operation might be constitutive of literary form.

I am also committed to the idea that the unity of a work is not a necessary ontological thesis. If the formal coherence of a work is neither a foregone conclusion nor a guiding principle of interpretation, if a work is *not* identical with itself, and if it is not in possession of full knowledge of itself—if, instead, it is made up of moments of blindness, excess, contradiction, retraction, and repetition—then the task of criticism should be to ask how these moments of noncoincidence *work*. How are they organized in the service of the production of meaning? And in particular how are they organized in language?

Chapter 5, on Beckett's *Molloy*, *Malone Dies*, and *The Unnamable*, most explicitly addresses these methodological questions, and it does so out of the urgency of an impasse into which Beckett's work tends to lead his readers. These three novels are stories about writing; they thematize the perils of storytelling and the difficulty of maintaining a sovereign relation to one's language, or even to one's own body. But by making the failure of writing the subject of a story of writing, Beckett presents his readers with a paradoxical and potentially abyssal situation, one in which the upshot seems to be a successful expression of expression's failure. Beckett's novels offer us countless figures of failure, loss, and disintegration. Yet any reading that would approach these novels as a series of reflections on the failure of writing—that is, any reading that would turn Beckett's project into an allegory of its own undoing—begs the very question under consideration. To assume that a work is capable of reflecting on itself, commenting on itself, and representing itself by means of its own figures is already to take the work to be coherent and self-sufficient. This reflection of the part in the whole, the fragment in the totality, recalls the speculative logic of romanticism, for self-reflection was the form par excellence in which the romantics attempted to think not only the unity of the literary work, but also the progress of history and the integrity of the moral subject.

Beckett leads us into an impasse, in short, where the reflection assumed in so many critical approaches to his work serves only to reinstate the old forms—totality, unity, the integrity of the subject—that, on another level, his texts are engaged in tearing down. My approach to his novels thus turns away from a representational reading and toward a rhetorical one. That is, following a Deleuzian line of questioning, instead of asking *What does it mean?*, I ask, *How does it work?*[5]

A focus on rhetoric does not entail rejecting thematic meanings but initiating a kind of transcendental inquiry, one that asks *how* such meanings—often multiple and mutually exclusive meanings—are generated and organized in language. Each of my literary chapters thus focuses on a different figure of speech, and specifically on figures that are, in various ways, explicitly figures of noncoincidence. Each of these figures also turns out to be productive of distinct forms of organization. In Beckett's *Molloy, Malone Dies,* and *The Unnamable,* for example, I focus on the figure of epanorthosis, a form of self-correction in which the multiple discourses of the novels engage, which involves going back over what one has asserted, either to add nuance, retract, readjust, or reassert the original statement with greater force. Essentially a figure of repetition and differentiation, epanorthosis works as a hinge between two or more assertions, marking the latter as a repetition of the former while simultaneously differentiating their conceptual content. What this figure helps reveal, in my analysis, is the way that pathos is generated in these texts and mobilized under the guise of necessity.

In chapter 6 I turn to key instances of exaggerated claims in Proust's novel, such claims being another figure of noncoincidence, in this case the noncoincidence between what is said and what is actually the case.

Hyperbole brings into relief an extensive pattern of meaning-making in the novel, from the organization of the Proustian self with respect to its sense impressions, to a narrative strategy of belated revelation, to the transcendent aspirations of the artistic process. What is so revealing about the figure of hyperbole, I argue, is its proximity to both metaphor and irony: like irony, it works in the disjunction between sign and meaning, and indicates the subjective position of the narrator, but like metaphor, it does not surrender its reference to the external world. Proust's novel is caught between these positions and achieves neither the transcendence nor the unity it claims. Instead, turning to hyperbole, it explores a mode of productivity—a productivity of the self and of the artwork—that is neither lucid self-reflection nor ironic dissolution.

Finally, in chapter 7 I examine the intersection between Stein's experimental use of repetition and her attempts at system building in *The Making of Americans: Being a History of a Family's Progress*. What Stein refers to as her "so-called repetition" ends up being a rhetorical strategy of generating and accumulating difference while avoiding the closure of concept formation. Through minute variations in repeating words and phrases, Stein draws attention to the way characters and concepts are produced, and produced cumulatively, while at the same time remaining mutable and receptive to variation. Tautology—a figure of speech that involves a reiteration of words or phrases, as well as a statement of the obvious—becomes Stein's means of exploring the imbrication of lived time and abstraction, phenomenal experience and concept formation. From this exploration emerges a practice of literary form as "composition," which, drawing inspiration from the visual arts as well as from philosophical pragmatism, departs from romantic models of genesis, organic totality, and self-reflection. Stein's system-building novel ultimately elaborates a non-romantic model for the relationship between art and knowledge, one in which art experiments with new ways of knowing, and concepts become the result of a genuinely creative activity.

The legacy of romanticism cannot be broken with by fiat. Each of the novels I explore—and each of my own readings—unfolds in the wake of a literary and critical history that has been well marked by romantic terms and concepts. But these novels can also show us a means of transforming that history, if we let them articulate their own modes of organization. This book joins with them in trying to imagine the forms that this transformation might take.

# CHAPTER I

# Form and Fragmentation

*Romantic Legacies*

A solution always has the truth it deserves according to
the problem to which it is a response

GILLES DELEUZE, *Difference and Repetition*

## THE QUESTION OF LITERATURE

"The Double Session," one of Jacques Derrida's most explicit engagements with the relationship between philosophy and literature, opens
with a series of quotations from texts by Plato and Mallarmé. Yet an
unattributed quotation quickly follows, embedded in Derrida's own
discourse. This is the question "What is literature?," which Derrida
presents without question mark or quotation marks. Referring either
to a line in Mallarmé's *Le Livre* or to the two sessions of the study
group where this argument was first presented, Derrida writes, "The
double session . . . about which I don't quite have the gall to say plumb
straight out that it is reserved for the question *what is literature*, this
question being henceforth properly considered a quotation already, in
which the place of the *what is* ought to lend itself to careful scrutiny,
along with the presumed authority under which one submits anything
whatever, and particularly literature, to the form of its inquisition—
this double session . . . will find its corner BETWEEN literature and
truth" (177). Derrida doesn't answer the question "What is literature?" in this passage, but he does delineate the question's territory.
He characterizes its threshold by a refusal of the directness that would
be required to pose it outright, noting instead that the question has
already been received as a citation. He observes that the question is
bound up with issues of (presumed) authority and with the particular
language of its posing, and that it is not without a certain relationship
to truth. Tacitly, he even links literature to a notion of particularity

or singularity in the phrase *singulièrement la littérature*. He cites the question "What is literature?" in the context of Mallarmé's work, which, he intimates, may be asking this question without quoting it. Derrida, on the other hand, manages to quote it without asking it. In quoting or presenting it this way, in divorcing it from its immediately literal or communicative function, he returns the question to a sort of literary status.

Presenting it without deigning to ask it, Derrida draws attention to the construction of the question itself, to what may already be given in its articulation, to the implications and presuppositions that shape it and allow it to be asked. Likewise, my own argument begins at the site of this question "What is literature?" in order to examine the problems that underlie its formulation, the particular history and plane of suppositions it is made to draw upon, and the kinds of answers it makes intelligible or unintelligible.

There are several reasons the question cannot be posed directly. One is historical: quite literally, the question is a citation of the title of Jean-Paul Sartre's landmark book *Qu'est-ce que la littérature?* (1948), collecting essays that appeared the previous year in *Les temps modernes*. As such it cannot help but recall Sartre's well-known conceptions of "committed" writing and of the essential continuity of literature with political action. Yet Sartre was himself taking up a question that had already been developed with some sophistication in *Les fleurs de Tarbes* (1941) by the critic Jean Paulhan. Paulhan signaled at the time that the question of literature was a "childish question . . . childish, but which we spend our whole lives avoiding" (8). In a similar vein, Maurice Blanchot, at once taking up some of Paulhan's concerns and expressing his own dissatisfaction with Sartre's response to the question, observed in 1949, "It has been noted with amazement that the question 'What is literature?' has received only meaningless answers" (*The Work of Fire* 302).[1]

Paulhan's and Blanchot's dissatisfaction stemmed from a series of foreclosures they perceived in the formulation of the question itself, especially in the assumption such a formulation makes about the nature of literary language and its separability from a language of erudition and truth. The form of the question "What is literature?" is classically philosophical, while at the same time it seeks to identify that which distinguishes literature from other kinds of discourse, among them philosophy. Such a question can only be quoted, as Derrida suggests, because it is already invested in, and invested by, certain decisions about the respective natures of literature and philosophy and what it means to confront one with the other. It operates within an already-given understanding of the distinction between these two discursive fields and their supposedly different uses of language, and decides in advance the terms of their encounter.

The question "What is . . . ?" decides, among other things, that a particular version of philosophy is at stake. Just as Heidegger cautioned in *Being and Time* that the philosophical question "What is being?" involves a certain prior understanding of the "is" (4), so the question "What is literature?" rests on the assumption that literature is the kind of thing to which "being" can be attributed. It involves a prior understanding of what it means to define the essence of something, and of what we mean when we say that something "is." In behaving as if an answer to the question were possible, we suggest that literature is an entity coherent enough to be demarcated and predicated outside of its instantiation in individual works ("Literature is X"), or, as Derek Attridge writes, "This question . . . asks for a statement of the essence of literature, for that which distinguishes literature from all that is not literature" (1).

"What is . . . ?," in other words, is the paradigmatic formula of the metaphysical question of essence. It "announc[es] that which is just as it is," Derrida writes ("Che cos'è la poesia?" 237): not only does the form of the question attribute a predicable being, essence, or presence to literature, but it also attempts to grasp this being as stable and self-identical. Furthermore, it restricts potential answers to those that are intelligible according to a certain set of philosophical presuppositions, one that understands beings as objects present for a subject, and truth as the certainty of representation.[2] Yet what is obscured from the moment the question is posed in this way is the possibility of literature's or the literary work's having a different relationship to being, subjectivity, and truth than the one announced in this interrogation.

The question "What is literature?" implies that literature is answerable to philosophy—and we will see that this answerability has been a definitive feature of the philosophico-literary relation. Furthermore, the apparently timeless form of the question masks the confrontation between these two domains that is presupposed by the question's formulation, as well as covers over the historical process that underlies the possibility of its being asked. For the notion that literature is an activity sufficiently distinct from philosophy that we can even speak of a confrontation between the two is the product of a fairly recent history. An examination of the changing usage of the term *literature* will shed some light on this history, and, what is more, it will draw our attention to a series of constitutive tensions in the concept.

## A CONFLICTED HISTORY OF THE TERM

*Literature* derives from the Latin *litteratura*, with the root *littera*, "letter," likely a translation of the Greek *grammatike*, with the root *gramme*. Its current usage—wherein *literature* refers to a particular body of writing, as opposed to the realm of written culture in general—can be traced back no earlier than the 1730s in France and Germany, slightly later in England, although this modern sense of the term was not consistent until the second half of that century (Escarpit 49).[3] Most scholars cite the publication of Lessing's review *Briefe die neueste Literatur betreffend* (1759) and Mme de Staël's *De la littérature considérée dans ses rapports avec les institutions sociales* (1800),[4] where the sense of literature as an "art of writing" among the other fine arts seems to have been solidified (Escarpit 79). At the same time as the publication of Mme de Staël's work, August Schlegel announced his *Lectures on Art and Fine Literature*, delivered in Berlin in 1801–2, likewise treating literature as a specific kind of fine art, as well as marking the entrance of this literary art into the university as a legitimate object of study.[5]

In what is perhaps the best-known lexicographical approach to the concept of literature, the French journalist and "sociologist of literature" Robert Escarpit notes that, prior to the eighteenth century, the term *literature* designated a realm of general erudition or knowledge of written culture, as today when we refer to a "man of letters," and carried with it implications of belonging to an intellectual elite. By the end of the eighteenth century, the term ceased to designate a general quality of erudition or, by association, a group of erudite men, and came to refer instead to the result of an activity and to a particular object of study. *Literature* no longer named the intellectual quality of written material; it named a particular product. At the same time, a qualitative hierarchy subsisted, Escarpit notes, "but instead of being applied to men, it was applied to works, to the act of writing, to publication" (50, translation mine). Even in this sense of literature as something produced, however, the term continued to encompass both intellectual and aesthetic production; hierarchical judgments were accordingly founded sometimes on the value of intellect, sometimes on the value of art. The notion of literature has continued to bear these two noncoincidental aspects ever since: on the one hand an aesthetic aspect and on the other an epistemological aspect, referring sometimes to the art of writing and sometimes to a body of written, intellectual material (50). That is, embedded in the very development of the concept is an indistinction between literature's aesthetic and epistemological dimensions, between its value as beauty and its value as knowledge.

Prior to the eighteenth century, the term *poetry* was used in a general sense to refer to any writing of the aesthetic sort. As the novel rose to prominence and struggled for legitimacy, the term *poetry* became more restricted, and *literature* became the more useful term for yoking together multiple genres under an umbrella designation. At the same time, it lent those genres, especially the novel, the aesthetic cachet previously reserved for what was designated by the term *poetry*. This turn of events suggests that, insofar as the concept of literature is a modern phenomenon, any serious attention to the question of literature must give prominent place to a consideration of the genre of the novel. For the early German romantics, the novel represented the possibility of overcoming neoclassical divisions of genre altogether. In their theorization and designation of a new concept by the name of "literature"— what Philippe Lacoue-Labarthe and Jean-Luc Nancy have described as the all-inclusive, absolute genre of Literature as such—the romantics aimed at a special kind of aesthetic universality, one open to the inherent generativity of language yet delimited and autonomous with respect to processes of history, society, and philosophy (11).

In the persistence of both terms, *literature* and *poetry*, a marked distinction also persisted between them, so that *poetry*, true to its etymology, could be used to designate creation par excellence, while *literature*, retaining its own "semantic memory," as Escarpit aptly calls it (51), also kept its aristocratic connotation to indicate knowledgeable usage of written language—that is, technique. Finally, the older and more general concept of literature as written intellectual material, so rich at the outset, became increasingly impoverished—like a daisy shedding its petals, Escarpit suggests—as the discourses of the natural sciences, human sciences, and philosophy slowly abandoned it and became more specialized in their own right (50).[6] In this narrative, literature's distinction from philosophy appears as the result of a subtractive operation, and beholden to contingent historical forces.

The semantic memory of the term *literature*, in sum, has served to preserve a number of conflicting values: literature as aesthetic versus intellectual output, as process versus product, as creation versus technique. These distinctions recall disagreements in philosophical treatments of art going back as far as the ancient Greeks, which pitted art's value as craft or know-how (*techne*) against its value as creative making (*poiesis*) akin to natural production (*physis*).[7] And, as we will see, the distinction between *techne* and *physis* inhabited a number of hierarchical oppositions in late eighteenth- and nineteenth-century thinking about art, notably between fine art and handicraft, as well as between "free" beauty and beauty dependent on conceptual determination.[8] Most significantly, this distinction became sedimented in romanticism's elevation of poetry to the highest of the fine arts, and its simultaneous confinement of poetry to the task of speculative philosophy. Indeed, in romanticism the tensions inhabiting the concept of literature reach a certain apex.

## THE MOMENT LITERATURE BECOMES A QUESTION

In the question "What is literature?" the putatively timeless form of the "What is . . . ?" implies that a conceptual discourse can be distinguished in its essence from the creative discourse set up as its object. But can discursive knowledge about literature be neatly distinguished from literature itself? Conversely, is an encounter with literature even possible wholly distinct from an encounter with this (supposedly philosophical) question of its own being? The lexicographical study outlined earlier is itself a discourse of erudition and truth, and a product of the very discursive division of labor it purports to describe. Beyond it lies a literary-critical discourse that has been invested, in a different way, in concepts of literature and the literary. If we cannot decide for certain whether what goes by the name *literature* is merely the object of knowledge and not also, in its own way, *thinking*, then we have to turn to a different locus of the questioning of the concept, namely to the locus of the literary-critical itself.

Derrida does not have the "militant innocence," as he puts it in "The Double Session," either to pose the question "What is literature?" directly or to pronounce it in the place of Mallarmé's text—that is, to unveil this formula as the essential truth of Mallarmé's work—because his own most consistent "place of interest" has been in the confrontation, corner, or fold between literature and truth, or literature and philosophy: two domains so mutually implicated that, as Derrida suggests elsewhere, a "literal" approach to the question would make it a "bad question or an impossible question" (*Demeure* 22–23). Likewise Blanchot, perhaps the most important source of Derrida's own conception of literature, remarks that such a question either lacks seriousness or turns too easily into a prosecution of art and of art's goals (*Work of Fire* 301). His dismissal of the explicit formulation of the question, as we saw, implies that the question is inadequate both to an experience of literature we possess implicitly and to a concern with itself that literature has already demonstrated. That is, Blanchot rejects the explicitly reflective, cognitive, and philosophical form of the question in order to draw attention to literature's ability to "manifest itself from itself . . . to re-emerge as the question itself, and of itself" (Gasché, "The Felicities of Paradox" 35).

"Let us suppose that literature begins," writes Blanchot, "at the moment when literature becomes a question" (*Work of Fire* 300). When he identifies the "beginning" of literature—and this trope of literature's beginning will merit investigation later on—with the moment of its critical questioning, his claim is no less historical than metaphysical. The emergence of the concept of literature and of the literary work as we know them today coincides historically, in fact, with the most radical questioning of these concepts. That is, the notion of literature was, and in its most developed form continues to be, inseparable from a deep-seated questioning of that notion. In this sense, it is more accurate to refer to the formation of an entire literary-critical problematic than to the emergence of a single and self-identical concept of "literature."

The problematic I have in mind is one initially elaborated by the theoretical writings of early German romanticism. *Romanticism* more broadly names both a historical moment and a constellation of concepts and sensibilities nearly universally credited with being perpetuated, to a greater or lesser extent, in assumptions about the nature of literature and criticism today. M. H. Abrams's landmark work *The Mirror and the Lamp* opens with the claim, for example, that "the development of literary theory in the lifetime of Coleridge was to a surprising extent the making of the modern critical mind" (vii). Paul de Man has declared that "the main points around which contemporary methodological and ideological arguments circle can almost always be traced directly back to the romantic heritage," a heritage all the more difficult to demarcate clearly because it originates in "a period of time that we have ourselves experienced" ("Wordsworth and Hölderlin" 48–49). In similarly oracular pronouncements, Blanchot declares that romanticism "inaugurates an epoch" (*The Infinite Conversation* 356), while Lacoue-Labarthe and Nancy, for whom Blanchot's work is an explicit reference, call early German romanticism "our birthplace" (8), arguing that what happened in Jena over a period of only two years "opens the critical age to which we still belong" (xxii, from the original book jacket). All of these authors would claim that a romantic conception of literature is "mirrored" in or at the "root" of nearly all of our literary-critical notions today, if they were not already aware that such metaphors of reflection and generation have been well prepared by a romantic rhetoric, a rhetoric that continues to supply dominant models for thought as well as for the classification and continuity of literary history.

What emerges at this moment of early German romanticism in particular, a moment whose features I outline in more detail shortly, is nothing less than the critical question of literature itself, and with it, literature's self-identification with this question. Literature becomes invested in critical self-reflection, and being put-into-question is disclosed as what is most "proper" to literature. In other words, in early romanticism, literature appears as the privileged form of its own critical question. Theory, moreover, becomes "literary."

My argument thus begins with this (persistent) claim of romanticism's persistence, and I will demonstrate how certain concepts first articulated in early romanticism—of literature and literary form as well as of the task of criticism—pervade twentieth-century formulations and contemporary ways of reading. Yet my aim is neither to rehash a commonplace in acknowledging our indebtedness to the romantic era, nor to embroil myself in nearly century-old debates about the adequate characterization or periodization of the various cultural phenomena that have been grouped under the heading of romanticism. Rather, I focus on a fairly circumscribed moment, early German romanticism, comprising a cluster of texts produced in Jena and Berlin at the very end of the eighteenth century (roughly 1798–1800), a journal (the *Athenaeum*), and a group of collaborators orbiting around Friedrich Schlegel. I take as my starting point the strong claim that concepts first articulated at this moment of early romanticism continue to dominate contemporary literary-critical concerns. If this is true, as I think it is, then we subsequently find ourselves confronted with a very pressing question: How, and under what conditions, might we think otherwise? That is, in what terms is a non-romantic conception of literature possible?

A commitment to this question is crucial if we hope to approach the inventiveness of subsequent literary experiments with anything resembling good faith. Literary modernism characterizes itself as a rejection of previous forms, and in particular those of the nineteenth century. Yet the further we delve into the experiments of the early romantics—the first to take up, aesthetically, the imperative to "be absolutely modern"—the more readily we discover continuities between romanticism and modernism. If romanticism continues to control our major concepts of criticism, however, the issue at hand may be less the similarity that persists between the nineteenth century and the twentieth than the fact that we are not yet equal to—indeed, cannot even recognize—the real divergences.

Ultimately, it is my contention that something else has been thought by certain literary experiments of the twentieth century than what has been or can be apprehended either by the terms of a renewed romanticism, or by notions of literary history that understand modernism as a reaction to romanticism—or, even further, by a self-conscious awareness in the face of a romantic repetition compulsion. Confronting what they alternately call a "romantic unconscious," a romantic "naiveté," or a romantic "repetition compulsion" at work today "in most of the central motifs of our 'modernity,'" Lacoue-Labarthe and Nancy advocate for a "vigilance," or proof of a "minimum of lucidity" (15–17). Yet, as I hope to make clear, the effort to supplant unconscious habits with a heightened vigilance does little to break with a romantic paradigm, as this paradigm was characterized, above all else, by critical lucidity and ironic self-distance. One cannot remain self-conscious in the face of romanticism's contradictions, or adopt a steadfast, critical distance from a romantic "naiveté," without repeating, by these very gestures, those highly sophisticated mechanisms of irony and self-reflection that already characterized romanticism at its most characteristic moment. Nor can one historicize this self-consciousness without repeating the motif of a progressive ordering of history that likewise belonged to romanticism (Derrida, "The Law of Genre" 61). Romanticism and the critique or overcoming of romanticism—as well as the critique *of* overcoming romanticism—tend to be part and parcel of the same problematic.

In place of this problematic, which develops in response to Kantian philosophy and to Kant's subsequent reception in German idealism,

I turn to the resources of an alternative philosophical tradition, one that passes through the rationalism of Benedict de Spinoza and culminates in Gilles Deleuze's reworking of classical notions of system and determination. My interest lies in stepping outside of the realm of aesthetics proper—that is, outside of the discourse on the beautiful that originates with Kant and becomes a theory of art with the romantics and the post-Kantians—in order to examine the metaphysical notions of autonomy and determination that underwrite aesthetic concepts. In this way, I ask whether the constitutive tension at the heart of our received notion of literature, and of the autonomy and integrity of the literary work, cannot be reconceived more productively along non-romantic lines.

## READING ROMANTICISM

*Romanticism* may be the most fraught term in the history of literary scholarship. In 1924 Arthur Lovejoy famously described it as a "confusion of terminology and of thought which has for a century been the scandal of literary history and criticism, and is still . . . copiously productive of historical errors and of dangerously undiscriminating diagnoses of the moral and aesthetic maladies of our age" ("On the Discrimination of Romanticisms" 234). While Lovejoy argued for the fundamental heterogeneity of the various "thought-complexes" that had been labeled romantic, advocating for the use of "romanticisms" in the plural, René Wellek responded in "The Concept of Romanticism in Literary History" (1949) with an argument for the ultimate "unity of theories, philosophies, and style" of European romanticism (129). When, for the sake of a history of ideas, Lovejoy was pressed to attribute some content to the term *romanticism*, he articulated its characteristic features as a "revolt against the finite" and an interest in concepts of "organicism . . . dynamism, and diversitarianism" ("The Meaning of Romanticism" 264, 272). Wellek, on the other hand, named three different features of romanticism: "a view of poetry as knowledge of the deepest reality, of nature as a living whole, and of [poetic style] as primarily myth and symbolism" (161). It hardly seems surprising that Lovejoy, who argued for the plurality of romanticism*s*, ultimately defined romanticism according to concepts and values of diversity and becoming, while Wellek, who has been accused of an excessive "passion for unity" (Crane, qtd. in Wellek, *"Romanticism Re-examined"* 199), focused instead on romanticism's unifying themes and totalizing figures (the poem as form of knowledge, totality as the form of nature, symbolism as the unity of style). In short, it seems the tendency of these scholars was either to determine the content of romanticism according to the measure of their methods or, conversely, to allow their methods to be shaped by what they saw as their object of study.[9] Yet what accounts for the radical divergence in their readings of what is ostensibly the same object? Moreover, what accounts for the intense commitment to definition, and especially to the definition of such an unruly object? The stakes are not negligible, for Wellek claims that to give up on a definition of the term *romanticism* is to abandon "the central task of literary history" ("The Concept of Romanticism" 197).

More than a century prior to Lovejoy and Wellek's debate, in his posthumous "philosophical fragments," Friedrich Schlegel presents a sketch for a new metaphysics that bears on the question of a definition of romanticism: "This metaphysics should proceed through several cycles, ever greater and longer. Once the end has been reached, it should start again from the beginning, alternating between chaos and system, preparing chaos for the system, then a new chaos (This procedure very philosophical)" (*Kritische Ausgabe* XVIII 283, frag. 1048, qtd. in Lacoue-Labarthe and Nancy 121) This "alternation between chaos and system," as Schlegel first described it, turns out to be a feature of romanticism itself, a feature that may extend equally well to romanticism's critical inheritance. If Wellek and Lovejoy can be said to represent two extreme tendencies in romanticism's reception—let us call them a tendency toward unification, on the one hand, and toward dispersal, on the other—we must ask, first of all, whether both of these tendencies are not already found in and made to relate to one another, indeed are prescribed by the earliest activities of romanticism. In the passage from Schlegel just quoted, the alternation is positioned as the outcome or continuation of a cycle or series of cycles, which should lead us to wonder whether what was produced under the retrospective label of *romanticism* was not also romanticism's mechanism of self-perpetuation.

In early romanticism, an investment in reflection as a privileged mode of thinking gave rise to a perpetual dialectic between the positing of a form and the overcoming of that form. This alone has led later critics to a number of definitional problems. "Romantic criticism [today] . . . cannot help but be obsessed with redefining what it admits cannot be defined," Justin Clemens comments in a recent work (14).

Yet it should be noted that the problem of definition was already an explicit concern of the early romantics. "There are classifications that are bad enough as classifications," Schlegel observed in 1798, "but which nonetheless have dominated whole nations and eras" (*Athenaeum Fragments* [hereafter *AF*] 55, qtd. in Lacoue-Labarthe and Nancy 1).[10] Above all, Schlegel and his group sought to classify what was constitutionally unclassifiable, and what was marked by its rejection of neoclassical definitions: the open-ended, unfinished, not-yet-objective character of the present.

The concern with classification manifests itself in Friedrich and August Schlegel's use of the term *romantic* as they sought to characterize the tendency of the age.[11] The romantics did not specifically call themselves romantic, nor use the noun form *romanticism*.[12] They did, however, struggle to bend the term *romantic poetry* toward a new purpose. In 1795 Friedrich Schlegel was still using the term in a sense that had been available for some time, to refer to the romances of the middle ages.[13] By 1798 his use of the word changed, as did his attitude toward modern poetry. Whereas once he railed against the unfinished character of contemporary texts in light of the unity and perfection of ancient works, writing that *"lack of character* seems to be the only characteristic of modern poetry; *confusion* the common theme . . . *lawlessness* the spirit of its history" (*On the Study of Greek Poetry* 20), he only had to invert his valorization, not his essential characterization, of modern literature in order to give birth to romanticism. *Romantic poetry* became a positive term when Schlegel used it to describe any non-classical art that had fully realized its modern vocation.[14]

Schlegel embedded the complex development of his thought in the term *romantic*, using it both in opposition to the products of antiquity and as a rejection of the contemporary taste for neoclassicism, including neoclassical divisions of genre. The term thus mixed evaluative judgment with historical categorization. The oft-cited *Athenaeum Fragment* 116 reveals Schlegel's new understanding of *romantic*: "Romantic poetry is a progressive, universal poetry. . . . Other kinds of poetry are finished and are now capable of being fully analyzed. The romantic kind of poetry is still in the state of becoming; that, in fact, is its real essence" (*AF* 116).[15] Its "essence," in other words, is its nonessential nature; its definition depends on its exceeding definition, and its genre is an overcoming of generic division. A normative claim is embedded in this fragment, as Schlegel concludes by asserting that "all poetry is or should be romantic" (116). Elsewhere he clears up any misunderstanding that he intends the term *romantic* in a simple historical sense, arguing that he would locate "the actual center, the core of the Romantic imagination," with Shakespeare (*Dialogue on Poetry* 101). Paradoxically, he concludes by intertwining the normative sense of *romantic* with the historical, identifying romantic poetry as the only kind that can be considered a "worthy contrast to the classical productions of antiquity" (101).

The romantic "genre"—if we can still call it that—truly invented by Schlegel and his collaborators is the fragment. Just as classical poetry had to be reconstituted on the basis of ancient fragments, Schlegel, who was trained as a classical philologist, dreamed of a restored cultural and poetic unity that would be obtained on the basis of a new production of fragments. Indeed, he envisioned an ethico-poetic project that would take the form of "fragments of the future" and require a forward-looking philology (*AF* 22). Thus a progressive self-definition and a temporal self-understanding is set to work in this mode of writing. "Fragments are definitions of the fragment," Lacoue-Labarthe and Nancy point out (44). That is, in the plurality of the fragment, the very task of definition is refashioned as self-reflexive, paradoxical, multiple, and intentionally incomplete.

Lacoue-Labarthe and Nancy argue that the romantic fragment inaugurates a new model of the literary work, and, at the same time, that the originality of the fragment can be fully grasped only in terms of its philosophical intervention. In what follows, I take up this robust pair of claims, both because the philosophical terrain of analysis reveals the extent to which we are still indebted to romantic patterns of thought, and because this very analysis will lead us to a different set of conclusions than Lacoue-Labarthe and Nancy are ultimately able to offer.

## BETWEEN LITERATURE AND PHILOSOPHY:
## THE FRAGMENT AS CONCERN FOR THE ABSOLUTE

The romantic fragments, to begin with, are born in the context of a philosophical crisis in the concept of system. The crisis was opened by Kantian philosophy, at least as it was received by idealist philosophers of the time—namely by Fichte, Schelling, and the young Hegel.[16] All of them sought to overcome what they saw as a conflict at the heart of the Kantian system, one that divided the mechanical causality of the material world from the freedom of the moral subject. This conflict came to a head in Kant's conception of the subject, which was alternately understood according to the faculty of understanding and its sensible presentation of concepts, and according to the faculty of reason and the unpresentable Idea of freedom. In the most fundamental terms, then, this was a conflict between the subject's form and its freedom, its presentation and the unpresentable as such. In other terms, it was a question of how to guarantee the presence of the moral subject to itself.

The *Critique of the Power of Judgment* (1790) has been described as "a tempest in the depths of the chasm opened up in the subject" (Deleuze, *Kant's Critical Philosophy* xii). Its stated role in Kant's system is well known: it is to "combin[e] the two parts of philosophy into one whole" (*Critique of the Power of Judgment*, introduction §III), to bridge the "incalculable gulf" (§II) between the philosophy of nature and the moral philosophy, the theoretical and the practical. Whether Kant succeeds in bridging the divide, however, or whether he merely aggravates the problem by relocating it to the realm of aesthetics, is difficult to decide. In any case, Kant turns to the power of judgment, or the faculty for thinking the particular under the universal, as the intermediary between reason and the understanding. Judgment has as its a priori principle that what is "contingent for human insight" in a particular, empirical experience of nature nevertheless "contains a lawful unity," that is, is subsumable under universal or necessary laws (§V). This principle, which Kant names the "purposiveness" of nature, asserts the unity and lawfulness of nature, not in itself, but for the purposes of our cognition. We thus behave *as if* the organization of nature were the unified "expression of a creative will" (Cassirer 296)—that is, as if nature were a work of art. Purposiveness, in other words, works on the basis of an analogy with art, because, as Kant explains, "we can be conscious of the [purposiveness of objects] only in the case of products of art" (*Critique of the Power of Judgment*, first introduction §IX).

Like nature, the work of art is produced freely, without concept or end, while its unity is located in the form of its representation, what Kant terms its "purposiveness without purpose" (*Critique of the Power of Judgment* §15). Exhibiting the pleasing quality of purposiveness for the subject that beholds it, yet without being determined by an actual purpose, the work of art is *beautiful*. The beautiful is not, then, grounded in the object but in "the representational state

of the subject," "in the feeling . . . of unison in the play of the powers of the mind" in reflective judgment (§15). Meanwhile, the subject
likewise seeks its unity in the form of the beautiful, "sees itself in
the image [*Bild*] of something without either a concept or an end"
(Lacoue-Labarthe and Nancy 31). In reflection, the beautiful unifies
and totalizes, and in this way serves as the analogon of Ideas, which
otherwise know no sensible presentation.[17] Kant's critical system thus
turns to the beautiful at the moment when reason needs to consider
its own formation. The aesthetic becomes the terrain on which reason
can reflect on itself, and in so doing pose the question of its own form.

The aesthetic, in short, becomes the necessary and privileged terrain of the analysis of reflective judgment, and in turn the linchpin of
the unity of Kant's system. Kant bequeaths the question of art to philosophy *as* philosophy's most proper question, the site of philosophy's
self-realization (Lacoue-Labarthe and Nancy 30). The next generation of thinkers remain in the grips of this question, but they seek to
radicalize the Kantian solution. In their hands, philosophy will have
to grapple with the question of art on its way to the absolute.

The romantics adopt this concern for the absolute characteristic of
German idealism. Specifically, they adopt the imperative to think the
absolute as a means of overcoming what they perceive as the Kantian
divide between the necessity of the lawfulness of nature and the freedom of the subject, an imperative they share with their philosophical contemporaries. Hegel, for example, in *The Difference between
Fichte's and Schelling's System of Philosophy* (1801), describes the
divide in Kant's system as a dualism of subject and object, a dualism
symptomatic of Kant's failure to attain the truly speculative or synthetic thinking that could lead to the thought of the absolute. Effective speculation, on the other hand, would involve the presentation
of the subject's freedom to itself, the self-recognition of the Idea in
the form of an absolute subject-object. Likewise, the romantics seek
an overcoming of the subjective and the objective in an effective presentation of the absolute. Yet what distinguishes romanticism from
idealist philosophy is not merely the mixed terrain of its investigation—the romantics take up literary and art criticism as well as more
"properly" literary and philosophical discourse. More importantly,
romanticism is invested in the unifying function of the idea of the
beautiful, as well as in a concomitant aestheticization of that idea.
"Within the landscape of idealism in general," Rodolphe Gasché
explains, "the very possibility that the unifying idea of the beautiful

can seek presentation as beautiful idea, and that unification hence is always necessarily aesthetic, sensible, and manifold . . . this is what constitutes the Romantic vision and demarcates it from the Idealism of Fichte and Hegel" ("Ideality" xiv).

At the same time, the aims of philosophical idealism help us understand those of early romanticism. Indeed, romanticism can be fully understood only in this context. Recent work by Manfred Frank, Fredrick Beiser, and Elizabeth Millán-Zaibert has been invaluable in arguing for romanticism's philosophical importance, which has long been ignored, especially in Anglophone circles.[18] Yet some of this work goes awry when it attempts to secure the philosophical contributions of romanticism against readings that would relegate it to a "merely" literary tradition.[19] The true innovation of romanticism takes place *in* literature *for* philosophy, to put it crudely, with serious consequences for both fields. Romanticism's invention is to invest questions of literary language and literary form with philosophical importance, and to turn the literary work into the presentation of—if not necessarily the solution to—a philosophical problem. Reading this explosive moment of writing only in terms of its (philosophical) concepts is as much an error as reading it as a "strictly" literary experiment.

"Philosophy . . . controls romanticism," as Lacoue-Labarthe and Nancy argue, insofar as it donates to romanticism the latter's central concern—to overcome the fracture separating nature and freedom— and renders the originality of romanticism's response intelligible (29). At the same time, literature remains the primary medium in which romanticism operates. Play, performance, style, rhetoric, form, and genre: literary modalities are repeatedly instilled with philosophical aims. Consider the following fragment, in which a philosophical striving for system seeks its genre—that is, its aesthetic form: "A dialogue is a chain or garland of fragments. An exchange of letters is a dialogue on a larger scale, and memoirs constitute a system of fragments. But as yet no genre exists that is fragmentary both in form and in content, simultaneously completely subjective and individual, and completely objective and like a necessary part in a system of all the sciences" (Schlegel, *AF* 77). Genre is here envisioned both as aesthetic form and as an exemplary philosophical element, uniting subject and object as in a system of knowledge.

The romantic fragments, in sum, mobilize this philosophical "will to system" in a new mode of literary writing. The *Athenaeum* journal, for its brief duration of two years (1798–1800) and six issues, featured a series of collections of fragments, among other essays and reviews. While *Grains of Pollen* (1798) was attributed to Novalis, and *Ideas* (1800) to Friedrich Schlegel, the *Athenaeum Fragments* (1798) were written and published anonymously in the spirit of a collective enterprise, authored jointly by Friedrich, Dorthea, August, and Caroline Schlegel, along with Novalis and Schleiermacher, or some combination of these. The very concept of the fragment was intimately bound up with that of social and political collectivity, as we can see in an early fragment of Friedrich Schlegel's, which compares the unity of a "motley heap of ideas . . . aiming at a single purpose" to "that free and equal fellowship in which . . . the citizens of the perfect state will live at some future date" (*Critical Fragments* 103).

From a merely formal perspective, conversely, the romantic fragment was hardly novel. Friedrich Schlegel—who was the most obsessed with the form, filling roughly 180 notebooks over the course of his life with his aphoristic jottings (Eichner 5)—was inspired to write fragments not only by his work in classical philology, but also probably by the publication of Chamfort's *Pensées, maximes et anecdotes* in 1796.[20] He was familiar with the earlier English and French moralists—Critical Fragment 59, for example, compares Chamfort's and Shaftesbury's conceptions of wit—and likely Montaigne's *Essays* and Pascal's *Pensées* as well. For this reason, and even if the practical form of the fragment remains indebted to an essayist tradition, the originality of the romantic fragment must be grasped in terms of its philosophical aims.[21] Most importantly, we must not overlook the fact that the very discrepancy between theory and practice was both addressed by and intentionally restaged in the practice of the fragment. The fragment emerged in response to a philosophical problem, but it is precisely as the enactment of an "aesthetic idea"—that is, as the nonconceptual presentation of a conflict between philosophy and art in the domain of art—that the genre attains its true significance. This significance is nothing short of the invention of a new model of the literary work.

The fragments of the Jena romantics are difficult to describe, and even more difficult to quote. As an ensemble (and as an ensemble of ensembles, such as the *Athenaeum* journal) they share certain characteristics: a deliberately fragmentary form, a mixture of objects treated, an obsession with self-reflection, an investment in irony, a straining toward universality, and a valorization of a progressive image of truth. Yet not all of the fragments exhibit all of these features, nor is any one feature adequate to describe all of them; rather this description can serve only as a general characterization of plural and overlapping elements. Moreover, the quality of the fragments is uneven, so that their declarations waver between bold insight and juvenile pretension, and their fragmentary form emerges as much from an engagement with philosophical idealism as from Schlegel's notorious inability to concentrate. Finally, their thematic plurality and use of irony make them troublesome objects to bundle off as quotations in support of another discourse, either in whole or in part. Nevertheless, I will continue to quote from them, while advising the reader to consult the text of the fragments in other available sources.[22]

The romantic fragment is a deliberate and determinate form. This means that its fragmentation is essential, not accidental or extrinsic (Lacoue-Labarthe and Nancy 42). It is bound up with a rethinking of system that is at the same time resolutely antifoundational: rejecting first principles and beginning in media res (Schlegel, *AF* 84), the fragments engage in a process of reciprocal conditioning and mutual confirmation, yet without giving up on the controlling idea of a unified whole.[23] Moreover, the whole at which they aim is not static; they participate in a philosophy of history in which the rift of modernity is overcome only in some past or future age (Szondi 68). It is crucial to understand that, rather than functioning as a mere piece or part of a totality, each fragment participates in a "project" of totalization both by gesturing beyond itself to a whole in which it would take part, and by substituting itself *for* that whole. In this way, the fragment is akin to the historical ruin, which is both a remainder of the past and a monumentalized image of that past, simultaneously recalling and excluding the past through a process of evocation and substitution.

## THE FRAGMENT AS SEED AND MIRROR

For the remainder of this chapter, I will describe this twofold function of the fragment—projection and substitution, recollection and exclusion—as marked by the two metaphors of the seed and the mirror.[24] In *Athenaeum Fragment* 22, describing his notion of "projects" as "fragments of the future," Schlegel writes, "What is essential is to be able to idealize and realize objects immediately and simultaneously: to complete them and in part carry them out within oneself." In other words, "fragments of the future" bear this double task of idealizing or providing an image of—of projecting—the system in which they participate, and simultaneously of realizing that system within them-selves. They are seeds or embryos of systems: "A project is the subjec-tive embryo of a developing object" (22). On the one hand it is their incompletion that makes possible a synthetic overcoming of that very incompletion, their form or limit that makes possible an overcoming of that limit: "Every thinking part of an organization should not feel its limits without at the same time feeling its unity in relation to the whole" (Schlegel, *Ideas* 48). On the other hand, the fragments end up lending an image of incompletion *to* this very whole, so that frag-ment and system mirror one another, as Schlegel notes in the *Literary Notebooks*: "Auch das größte System ist doch nur Fragment [Even the greatest system is only a fragment]" (921). "By combining system and fragment in this fashion," Gasché suggests, "the Romantics were able to avoid the dogmatic and sclerotic connotations that come with the notion of the system, and to ward off the specter of abstraction associated with system building, while supporting at the same time the traditional demand" ("Ideality" xii). Ultimately, Gasché argues, the romantic fragment takes on the Kantian problem of the presen-tation of the Idea—that is, of the presentation of totality—*as* frag-ment, because the Idea as such permits no other possible presentation (xxiv–xxviii).

A notion of the literary work orients the enterprise of the frag-ments, especially in regard to the mutual reflection of fragment and system (fragments are systems, and systems are fragments). This can be seen most clearly in romanticism's most emblematic fragment, penned by Novalis: "A fragment, like a miniature work of art, has to be entirely isolated from the surrounding world and be complete in itself like a porcupine" (Schlegel, *AF* 206). The intrinsic determi-nation of the fragment *as* fragment makes it freely self-positing in its individuality, just like Kant's notion of the purposive artwork, and like the total system of which it would be a part. Fragments resemble little, autonomous works of art. Works, on the other hand, are frag-ments: "The art of writing books, Novalis writes again, "has not yet been invented. But it is on the point of being invented. Fragments of this kind are literary seed-houses. True, there may be many a barren grain among them. But meanwhile, if a few germinate . . . " (Nova-lis, "Miscellaneous Remarks" 104). The books we know in this frag-mented age (or "chemical age," as Schlegel calls it) are but the seeds of a future Work; we are in the position of waiting for a Work to come, for a kind of classicism of the future (Schlegel, *AF* 147, 243). "A work is cultivated," Schlegel writes, "when it is everywhere sharply delimited, but within those limits limitless and inexhaustible; when it is completely faithful to itself, entirely homogenous, and nonetheless exalted above itself" (297). Like the fragment, the work is both limited by its form and finds in its form its occasion for participation in the infinite. Form renders the work at once self-coherent ("homogenous"), incomplete ("sharply delimited"), internally infinite, especially in auto-production and self-reflection ("inexhaustible"), and externally projected ("exalted above itself").

As a seed, finally, the fragment invokes its own plurality and dispersal, just as it seeks an overcoming of this plurality in the universality of a future age and a total Work. There is never one fragment; there are only fragments. Yet "this plural is the specific mode in which the fragment aims at, indicates, and in a certain manner posits the singular of its totality," Lacoue-Labarthe and Nancy suggest (44). Fragments communicate with one another as if in dialogue, in "a chain or garland" (Schlegel, *AF* 77), or according to a model of sociality. For all these reasons, the fragments implicate not only a thinking of literary form but also, in their plurality, a thinking of genre, and ultimately of the genre of Literature as such. Literature as the most inclusive genre becomes "not the sum but the co-presence of [its] parts, the co-presence . . . of the whole with itself" (44). In short, in its plurality, the romantic fragment reveals the intimate relation between the problem of the form of the work, of the identity and ideality of genre, and of the identity of the genre of Literature as such. Each is completely bound up with the other. When we ask "What is literature?" we are entangled with all of these questions at once.

All of this is not to say that the fragments set forth a logic that is entirely coherent. But they do mobilize an economy of production and reflection that draws directly on Kant's third *Critique*, an economy organized by the two figurative poles of the seed and the mirror. In "Economimesis" Derrida analyzes the *Critique of Judgment* as providing two means of reconciling or overcoming the "inherited, ossified, simplified opposition between *tekhnè* and *physis*," or the "play of freedom" that supposedly belongs to art and the "mechanical necessity" attributed to nature. The first reconciliation takes place by means of an analogy between two orders of production: Derrida identifies a *mimesis* or analogy between the production of man, who makes artworks "through freedom, i.e. through a capacity for choice that grounds its actions in reason," whose works "must still seem to be as free from all constraint by arbitrary rules as if it were a mere product of nature" (Kant, *Critique of the Power of Judgment* §§43, 45), and that of nature, to whose productions we cannot ascribe any teleological causality. This is one function of reflection in the third *Critique*, and *analogy*, from the Latin *analogia*, is certainly the right term here, for it indicates the proportionality or correspondence of two processes. Here the processes are those of free productivity, so that we witness a "specular relation between two liberties": that of man and that of nature (Derrida, "Economimesis" 10). Yet, as I described earlier, according to Kant we conceive of the coherency of nature not through any possible experience, but on the basis of another kind of specular relation: this one turns to the integrity of the artwork, to its purposiveness without purpose, for an image of the integrity of nature. Art does not imitate nature in the sense of producing a likeness (for that would make artistic production beholden to the image of an end), but the form of art is the only occasion we have to reflect on or be "conscious of" the purposiveness of nature (Kant, *Critique of the Power of Judgment*, first introduction §IX). Here we should emphasize the distinction between form, or *Bild* (image, representation), and formation, *Bildung*, for there is a double reflection at work in the relation of art to nature. What is formal in a work of art provides an image (*Bild*) of the purposiveness of nature, while nature, conversely, provides the analogy of a process or formation (*Bildung*) of freedom. Between *Bild* and *Bildung*, or form and formation, or product and process lies the entire problematic of the romantic fragment, as well as the conflict of freedom and necessity that constitutes the romantic conception of art.

Let me complete this description of reflection in the third *Critique*. The double reflection between art and nature in Kant is organized by a second instance, that of the gift or seed. What I term "seed" here is the production and donation of genius, nature's gift to man that "blossoms" (*Critique of the Power of Judgment* §47) in artistic production. "Genius is the talent (natural gift) that gives the rule to art" and "Genius is the inborn predisposition of the mind (*ingenium*) through which nature gives the rule to art" (§46) read Kant's well-known lines. As Derrida argues, genius both accounts for the passage between freedoms, and naturalizes artistic production, for it returns artistic production—in fact, it returns the very difference between the two orders of production—to the natural order.

Derrida emphasizes the status of genius as a "gift" in order to draw attention to the paradoxical relation of what is supposedly outside any economic circuit—the gift—to a whole hierarchical economy of labor in Kant's system. Conversely, though, we might emphasize the natural element of genius, its genetic function for art and its origin in natural production. *Genius (Genie)* comes from the Latin, originally from the base form *gen-* and the root *gignere*, "to beget." In the concept of genius, we have the begetting of—the very genesis of—man's productive freedom and thus his difference from the natural order, but only on the condition that this freedom correspond analogically to that of nature's and provide example to future geniuses. In other words, the production of difference between man and nature is based on the system of nature, and (as we saw) is recuperated in a series of analogical reflections of freedoms. That is, while genius entails originality and "is entirely opposed to the spirit of imitation," the product of genius becomes "an example . . . for emulation by another genius, who is thereby awakened to the feeling of his own originality, to exercise freedom from coercion in his art" (*Critique of the Power of Judgment* §§46, 47, 49). I describe genius as a seed because the term enables us to draw a direct connection to the figurative language of the romantic fragments. But most importantly, the notion of the seed encapsulates these two elements of production and reflection, and reveals the ground of their reconciliation: the seed is the productive and donative instance of nature, but more specifically of an *organism*; it is also the organism in miniature, and its development is controlled by this image of the organism, as well as by the very ideality of the organic.

If we return to Fragment 206, we can see this entire figural economy of the seed and the mirror played out in romantic terms. Again, "A fragment, like a miniature work of art, has to be entirely isolated from the surrounding world and be complete in itself like a porcupine" (Schlegel, *AF* 206). Here we can see the specular relation: the fragment is not a work but merely *like* a work. At the same time, specularity threatens to displace rather than to establish unity, as the fragment's claim of being "complete in itself" is immediately belied by its being supplemented with an analogy to the porcupine—an analogy that, drawing its force from the organic or the living organism, in turn offers a new image of the organization of the whole. Everywhere the romantic fragments shuttle back and forth between the mirror and the seed, the specular and the organic, the reflective and the productive. The relationship of fragment and totality takes place under the double aegis of these metaphors; rather than a dialectic of part and whole, we witness the specular reflection of the whole in the form of the fragment, and the formation of these fragments into a whole whose genesis lies in the fragments' excessive and universalizing tendencies—fragments are seeds of systems.

To point out the importance of organicism to romantic thought is, of course, no revelation. Yet a closer look at the effects of this concept is warranted. In the next chapter, I turn to Coleridge and his legacy in the English tradition to demonstrate the stakes of a notion of organic form for a concept of poetry. What I would like to emphasize in the present chapter is the thinking of the organic at work in the romantic fragments. Individual fragments are conceived along the lines of organisms, so that the organicism of the fragments is the basis of the for-itself of their production. While the fragments belong to the horizon of a system, to the exigency of completion and the "will to system," they simultaneously strive to be autonomously self-posited. What constitutes their individuality is the capacity for self-production and self-formation (Lacoue-Labarthe and Nancy 49). Fragments are likened not only to seeds but to self-forming, autonomous subjects. Yet self-formation not only grounds the fragments' individuality; it "incompletes" them by turning their very individuality into something to be constructed—in other words, into a project. Thus in their infinitely incomplete-completion, the fragments again reflect the totality as an infinite work-in-progress.

The flip side of this incompletion is the threat of formlessness or chaos. "The romantic origin becomes the always-already lost of the Organon" (Lacoue-Labarthe and Nancy 50). This is what Lacoue-Labarthe and Nancy call romanticism's most specific gesture, and what distinguishes it from idealism more broadly: "At the very heart of the quest for or theory of the Work, it abandons or excises the work itself—and thus is transformed in an almost imperceptible manner into the 'work of the absence of the work'" (57). The fragments infinitize the completion of their own system, so that, at the limit, they risk doing no more than marking the absence of the whole, and illuminating the contours of their own "infinitely teeming chaos" (Schlegel, *Ideas* 69).

The double exigency of form and formation, reflection and production, undergoes some mutations in the brief years of the *Athenaeum* journal, though it remains governed by the same logic of the fragment. Following the *Fragments* of 1798, the publication of the *Ideas* in 1800, on the eve of the dissolution of the journal and the dispersal of the Jena group, marks the group's reconsideration of the problem of form

(Lacoue-Labarthe and Nancy 61). The *Ideas* revolve around issues of sociality, moral and artistic exemplarity, and the cultural development of mankind; and they illuminate a notion of "religion" as the ultimate fusion of philosophy and poetry, idealism and realism (Schlegel, *Ideas* 46, 96). The *Ideas* appear, then, as a moralization of the genre of the fragment, adopting the style of a series of injunctions directed toward a listener, and figuring the speaker or artist in the form of the "exemplarity" of one who speaks the truth (Lacoue-Labarthe and Nancy 66). In the *Ideas*, Schlegel returns to a certain relation between imitation and creation that was already present in his early evaluation of modern poetry's relation to classicism; only now, instead of decrying imitation, he conceives it along Kantian lines, where what is to be imitated is not the artistic product but the artist's own self-formation. "An artist," he writes, is someone who carries his center within himself. Whoever lacks such a center has to choose some particular leader and mediator outside of himself. . . . Only [another] man's center can stimulate and awaken his own" (*Ideas* 45). Yet the very structure of exemplarity, which leads Schlegel to imagine the absolute in the shape of ellipse with two centers (117), threatens to pull itself apart.

Thus Schlegel seeks a "fulfillment" of the moral tendency of the *Ideas* in the genre of the dialogue (Lacoue-Labarthe and Nancy 86). Schlegel's *Dialogue on Poetry* is split between the last two issues of the *Athenaeum* journal, and it appears to confront the question of literature directly. In so doing, it reveals a thinking of dialogue as a dramatization of the critical question of literature, and thus as the form that can stage the encounter between philosophy and poetry—that is, between critical reflection and sensible presentation. In this way, the dialogue seems to offer itself as a sublation of the distinction between genres, positioning itself as a good candidate for the absolute genre of Literature as such (Lacoue-Labarthe and Nancy 85). Yet what turns out to be missing from dialogue is a presentation of the putting-into-form of its own relations—in other words, a narrative self-presentation. Ultimately, the *novel* will be venerated as the genre capable of overcoming the bifold nature of the dialogue in a truly synthetic form. Only the novel, conceived as a "romantic book"—"romantic" in the sense of progressively unfolding, and a "book" in the sense of attaining the closure of a traditional work (Schlegel, *Dialogue on Poetry* 101)—only the novel will have the capacity to reflect on itself and on its own genre, and to comprehend the law of its self-engenderment (Lacoue-Labarthe and Nancy 90).

But in the end, the novel, too, proves unsatisfactory. It remains a mixed genre, seems artificial, and hence is unable to achieve true organicity. The novel is unable to synthesize, "beyond mixture," the various genres it contains—poetry, prose, drama—because it lacks the possibility of an effective presentation of its own synthetic principle (Lacoue-Labarthe and Nancy 98–99). What it lacks, in sum, is a *theoretical* space that can do the work of reflection and synthesis, that can reflect on the relation between form (poetry) and the idea of the infinite (philosophy), while also maintaining their difference. In the end, the novel's inevitable failure to absolutize itself in self-reflection is what opens the space for literary criticism.

"The critical imperative," write Lacoue-Labarthe and Nancy, "carries the fragmentary exigency to its greatest intensity" (116). The relation of the literary work to criticism is completely bound up with the logic of the fragment. And the economy of the seed and the mirror, production and reflection, helps us understand the central importance of criticism in romanticism; criticism or "theory," after all, is the genre in which the bulk of the Jena romantics' writing takes place. Most significantly, the investment in criticism testifies to the importance of reflection for the early romantics: reflection at once characterizes the form of thinking par excellence and is a structure proper to their notion of the absolute.[25] As Walter Benjamin argued in his own attempt to come to terms with "the concept of criticism in German romanticism," while Fichte sought to unify Kant's system by grounding it in the self-reflection of an absolute subject, the romantics, by contrast, conceived of the activity of reflection itself as "logically first and primary," the originary medium of the absolute (Benjamin 134). Reflection reveals the importance of art for the romantics. Because any object within the absolute can be an occasion for the self-thinking of thought, objects are properly understood as determinants of reflection, and in this way can be said to be "thinking themselves." Following Kant's concern with aesthetics as the locus of a problem of reason, the work of art in romanticism becomes the most privileged determinant of reflection, a site where the presentation of a process in a deliberate and determinate form coincides with the occasion for critical reflection. The form of a work, in other words, is the limitation that makes possible its internal self-reflection (Benjamin 156), as well as what allows it to exceed its limitation in external reflection, where it participates in an idea of genre, and ultimately in the idea of Literature as such.

The "critical imperative" of romanticism, in short, is occasioned by a notion of the literary work as fragment. Criticism seeks simultaneously to complete and incomplete the work with reflective commentary, so that, on the one hand, it aims, in a totalizing gesture, to "seize the whole of the work" (Lacoue-Labarthe and Nancy 116) and to account for its process of formation with a synthetic form, while on the other hand, it seeks to overcome the limits of the individual work in an activity of reflection of which the work would merely be a part or moment. In this way, criticism belongs simultaneously to a totalization of the work and to an infinite project of in-completion. The critical imperative projects the idea of an absolute Work that would be capable of absorbing its own criticism, theorizing itself and reflecting on itself, and thus effectively excluding any supplemental discourse. In self-reflection, the work would become "complete in itself," like the porcupine. At the same time, the work-as-critical-self-reflection would have to remain formed, like a work of poetry. That is, the very mechanism of reflection that calls for a work's critical explication demands that criticism itself be formed like a literary work. This demand seems to lie behind works of criticism that claims to respond "creatively" to works of literature, and its totalizing aspirations can be referred to Schlegel's notion of a "transcendental poetry": a poetry that would "describe itself, and always be simultaneously poetry and the poetry of poetry" (*AF* 239).

Thus criticism turns out to be doubly determined. On the one hand it participates in a literary work's self-theorization, or a self-showing of its operation of forming. But on the other hand, in supplementing the work, criticism marks the absence of a "transcendental poetry," or absolute Work, that would comprehend them both—work and criticism of the work—in an adequate form. In attempting to give form to formation, it marks "the absence of Form in all form, and demands that Form be restored, completed, or supplemented in any given form" (Schlegel, *AF* 105). In this sense, criticism is in the same position as the fragment, acting both as the "part" that incompletes the whole and as the monument to the always-already-lost of this whole.

In sum, the two poles of the self-production and self-reflection of the literary work point the way to the dream of a literary Absolute that resembles an absolute Subject: an organic totality that would be capable of freely producing itself in a form and freely reflecting on itself in self-consciousness—what Lacoue-Labarthe and Nancy also call the critical identity of the work with its own criticism (112). Yet in its reliance on form, and on formal self-overcoming as a necessary component of reflection, this critical identity cannot help but mark the failure of its own project. It would also seem to call for an endless repetition of this failure. We have seen that reflection gives the artwork access to an idea of the infinite. Yet by turning the work into a fragment of the speculative project of thinking the absolute, romanticism burdens literature with a philosophical task it cannot—and should not be asked to—shoulder.

In reflecting on itself and in giving itself to reflection, the work attempts to approach a reconciliation of the philosophical conflict between necessity and freedom, form and formation, that I traced back to Kant's conception of the subject. In fact, this model of the work succeeds only in perpetuating—indeed, in making absolute—the terms of this tension. The romantic literary work is made the locus and privileged icon of an indissoluble metaphysical tension.

In the next two chapters, we will see how this treatment of the literary work is taken up by two major, and seemingly very different, twentieth-century critics, Cleanth Brooks and Maurice Blanchot. Both are at the origin of divergent critical trends, yet I will demonstrate how structurally similar their conceptions of literature are, and how indebted both are to the theoretical paradigm established by early romanticism. Ultimately, the work of these critics will bring into sharper relief the inadequacy of this paradigm, and will point the way to the new set of concepts I am looking for.

CHAPTER 2

# The Book of the World

*Form and Intent in New Criticism, Revisited*

How many contemporary critical approaches to literature continue to be bound by this same romantic conflict between form and formation, necessity and freedom? That is, how many continue to restage, by the very terms of their investigation, the poles of this same opposition? The problem is not that we have retained a romantic conception of literature in any simple way, but rather that the complex economy first articulated in theoretical romanticism continues to control the field of possible questions we can ask about what literature is and can do. The conflict between necessity and freedom characterizing the post-Kantian crisis of system continues to determine the scope and orientation of these questions.

It determines, for example, those questions about literature that assume an alternative—even if they go on to negotiate it—between a work's participation in a causal network of relations and its creative break from any determinate order. This same opposition plays out in treatments that would pit a work's originality against its participation in literary history or everyday language use, or its status as unprogrammable event against its determining social and political circumstances, or social and political consequences. Conversely, it appears in readings that would oppose a work's formal unity to its value for critical activity or, moreover, that would oppose its status as an *object* of study to its characterization as fundamentally *subjective experience*, either of reading or of the inspiration of the writer. Finally, this same tension between necessity and freedom underlies the long-standing opposition between symbol and allegory, where the symbol has been valorized as a necessary identity of idea and image in language, and allegory disparaged as a contingent form, lacking cohesion.[1]

All of these cases, I think, testify to a desire among critics to safeguard the distinctiveness of poetic language, or the originality of the work of art, and at the same time to obtain some critical purchase on it, connecting this originality with other systems of knowledge-making. In this chapter and the one that follows, I examine the ways this conflict between freedom and necessity is brought into sharp relief in discussions of the role of criticism and its treatment of the literary work. My goal is to demonstrate that what appear to be diverse or even opposed critical trends are collaborating in perpetuating the very same romantic problematic.

My first case in point is American New Criticism and the terms in which it attempted to secure the unity of the literary work. In particular, in turning to the organic realm for a metaphor for poetic unity, the New Critics end up reinscribing the speculative vocation bequeathed to literature by romanticism, while at the same time succeeding in excluding the literary from effective or achieved speculation.

## THE NEW CRITICAL OBJECT

The lasting contribution of the so-called New Critics, as well as the basis of their repudiation in the hands of subsequent trends, has undoubtedly been their insistence on the complex unity of the literary work and its autonomy from other discourses, two features that necessitated a practice of close reading as the central activity of literary criticism. They have subsequently been accused of removing the literary object from the domains of history and human psychology, as well as from more comprehensive accounts of language and meaning-production. Consider Terry Eagleton's exemplary remarks in his *Literary Theory: An Introduction* (1983):

> To call for close reading, in fact, is to do more than insist on due attentiveness to the text. It inescapably suggests an attention to *this* rather than to something else: to the "words on the page" rather than to the contexts which produced and surround them. . . . [Close reading] encouraged the illusion that any piece of language, literary or not, can be adequately studied or even understood in isolation. It was the beginnings of a "reification" of the literary work, the treatment of it as an object in itself, which was to be triumphantly consummated in the American New Criticism. (44)

Here Eagleton moves swiftly from the isolation of the literary text to its hypostatization, which he condemns in both Marxist and metaphysical terms, referring to the "reification" of the work and its treatment as an "object in itself."[2] Yet is the hypostatization of a poem the full extent of the problem? What is at stake in treating a text as an object, and, most importantly, what kind of objects were the New Critics dealing with?

According to Eagleton, in New Criticism a poem is made to seem "less like a process of meaning than something with four corners and a pebbledash front" (*Literary Theory* 49): a process is mistaken for a material object, and judging by the use of the term "pebbledash," it is domesticated, made quotidian, and treated superficially.[3] Eagleton likely has Cleanth Brooks in mind, whose predilection for urns—Donne's, Shakespeare's, Keats's, Gray's—is hard to overlook. A moment later, however, Eagleton's comments take on a different cast: "The New Critical poem, like the Romantic symbol, was thus imbued with an absolute mystical authority which brooked no rational argument. . . . New Criticism was at root a full-blooded irrationalism, one closely associated with religious dogma" (49). Here, as Eagleton considers Brooks's "Heresy of Paraphrase," he likens the New Critical poem to a religious or other-worldly object. Yet how can the same object be vulgarly domestic and supernatural at the same time?

Eagleton's remarks are actually quite revealing of the contradictory imperatives at work in New Criticism itself, and he is right to link New Criticism to an investment in the romantic symbol. Frank Lentricchia makes the same connection in *After the New Criticism*, comparing the New Critics' removal of the poem from the domain of ordinary language to the romantic distinction between symbol and allegory: "From Coleridge to Mallarmé, from Yeats to Cleanth Brooks, Philip Wheelwright, and Northrop Frye, a dualism very like that between symbol and allegory is carried through as a distinction between the poetic or literary and the scientific or ordinary kinds of discourses. Brooks told us that it was heretical to paraphrase; within the perspective afforded by the romantic tradition we may come to feel that the urgency in his injunction is motivated by a long-standing romantic need to protect a quasi-religious, ontological sanctuary from all secularizing discourses that would situate literature in history" (6). For both Eagleton and Lentricchia, the romantic symbol itself is the proper "symbol" of the New Critical poem, of its distinct mode of autonomy and integrity. The valorization of symbol over allegory in romanticism is consistent with what we saw in chapter 1 as the post-Kantian attempt to integrate the sensible and the intelligible, the fragment with totality, in a unified presentation. Kant himself invoked the symbol as a means of integrating the sensible and the intelligible in his description of "aesthetic ideas," which seek the presentation of ideas of reason (*Critique of the Power of Judgment* §49). For Goethe and other German writers of the age, the symbol was the poetic revelation of the general by means of the particular (Fletcher 13–17). Similarly, for Samuel Coleridge, who imported this valorization into the English tradition, the symbol was a sensuous object that "partakes of the Reality which it renders intelligible." Allegory, on the other hand, was "nothing but an abstraction" (*Lay Sermons* 30). For both Coleridge and the Germans, the symbol was "founded on an intimate unity between the image that rises up before the senses and the supersensory totality that the image suggests" (de Man, "Rhetoric" 189).

The "intimate unity" of the symbol is the key operator here: the symbol was a necessary union of image and idea, while allegory was an externally and mechanically motivated association. Most importantly for Coleridge, the privilege of the symbol resulted from his notion of organic form, as I will discuss shortly. We can see the connection to the total poem in Brooks's "The Heresy of Paraphrase" in what for Brooks is the marriage of a poem's form and meaning, so that the abstraction of a poem's idea and its translation into logical discourse, or paraphrase, betrays this union and misunderstands "the relation of the poem to its 'truth'" (201). Yet a New Critical poem is not merely a symbol. Let us look more closely now at Brooks's notion of what constitutes the unity of a poem.

"The language of poetry is the language of paradox," begins Brooks's essay "The Language of Paradox," suggesting that the form of a poem might likewise be the form of paradox (3). In fact, this is not the case. Brooks refers instead to paradoxes that "inform" a poem, to "the paradoxical situation out of which the poem arises" (5), and in his discussion of Wordsworth, we see that the term is used to describe the scenes and situations that constitute a poem's thematic content (4–5). Paradox is the matrix of poetry, in short, but not its destination. At the end of the essay Brooks describes the "paradox of the imagination itself" (21)—the imagination being that Coleridgean power of "reconcil[ing] opposite or discordant qualities" (18). Thus the discord of paradox turns out to be relegated to the poem's creative impulse (imagination), to the language on which it draws, and to its prepoetic situations (situations that "give rise" to and inform poetry). In this way, Brooks actually *expels* paradox from poetic form, placing it on a hierarchical continuum of imaginative, heterogeneous process and unified product. He seeks an image of the finished work in the figure of a funeral urn containing the ashes of discordant elements: "the urn to which we are summoned," he writes of Shakespeare's "The Phoenix and the Turtle," "is the poem itself" [20–21]).

Interestingly enough, it appears to be Brooks's valorization of the symbol that inspires his reasoning—and, as we will see, that ends up problematizing it. "The poet has to work by analogies," he writes. "All of the subtler states of emotion . . . necessarily demand metaphor for their expression" ("Language" 9). Here Brooks recalls the romantic notion of the poet's task as that of "mak[ing] sensible rational ideas of invisible entities (Kant, *Critique of the Power of Judgment* §49). The "necessity of the demand" of metaphor is an appeal to the essential unity of an abstraction and its corresponding image. For Coleridge, the necessity of the poetic symbol lay in a kind of vertical union or "translucence": "[A] Symbol," he writes, "is characterized by a translucence of the Special in the Individual or of the General in the Especial or of the Universal in the General. Above all by the translucence of the Eternal through and in the Temporal" (*Lay Sermons* 30). Coleridge's symbol is more than a synecdoche, representing the totality to which it belongs; like the apex of a cone, it is at once the unity of part and whole and a privileged perspective on that whole, the overlapping, condensation and fusion of the special and the general.

Yet we can see how the very intimacy of this union, along with the notion of the symbol as fragment—fragments, remember, are always plural—would complicate the picture of any poem that is greater than a single image. For it leaves open the question of how multiple symbols are to relate to one another laterally, especially within the context of a single poem.[4] If Brooks retains the necessary unity and plurality of the symbol but disregards what may have been a generally nineteenth-century taste for universals, he will have to face this question. In fact, this question seems to be the very basis for "The Language of Paradox." He writes that the poet's only "terms" are metaphors, yet "the metaphors do not lie in the same plane or fit neatly edge to edge. There is a continual tilting of the planes, necessary overlappings, discrepancies, contradictions. Even the most direct and simple poet is forced into paradoxes far more often than we think" (9–10). For Brooks, paradox becomes the poet's "inevitable instrument" because there is no unified plane of metaphorical expression; the poet must continually juxtapose his terms, working "by contradiction and qualification" (9). In this case, what constitutes the form of the poem as a whole—that is, what guarantees the sense of the juxtapositions—must be the intention of the poet, for only a notion of intention can account for the activity of selection and meaningful juxtaposition of metaphors such that one could be said to be "qualified" by another. The notion of qualification, in other words, relies on a presumed intention behind the arrangement. The poet is like a masterful lawn bowler, Brooks suggests, taking another figure from Shakespeare (10), working by indirection but aiming nevertheless. Poetic form is here equated with poetic aim.

It is generally understood that the category of authorial intention was effectively disbarred from literary criticism by William K. Wimsatt Jr. and Monroe C. Beardsley in their landmark essay, "The Intentional Fallacy" (1946), and that the rejection of intention as a standard for critical judgment is a defining characteristic of the New Criticism on the whole. So how do we pass from "The Language of Paradox" to "The Intentional Fallacy"? In fact, Brooks's position, in which the details of a poem must be related to a "total intention" (Brooks and Warren, *Understanding Poetry* 491), is not only reconcilable with Wimsatt and Beardsley's expulsion of intention from poetic form, but leads inexorably to it. Both positions turn out to be consistent with a trajectory that begins with Samuel Coleridge.

## THE BOOK OF THE WORLD

We have seen how, in "The Language of Paradox," Brooks relegates paradox to the space of the creative imagination, drawing on Coleridge explicitly, here as elsewhere in his writing, to define the imagination as what "reveals itself in the balance or reconcilement of opposite or discordant qualities: of sameness, with difference; of the general, with the concrete, the idea, with the image" (18, qtd. from Coleridge, *Biographia Literaria* 2: 12). For Coleridge, the poetic imagination is poetry's "seminal principle," that "vital" power of synthesis that strives "to idealize and to unify" its objects, and to transform these objects in the service of a vision or a passion (*Biographia Literaria* 1: 64, 202).[5] It is a specialized mode of the "primary imagination" at work in all human perception, and seems to be distinguished from the inferior power of fancy by the necessity of its relations. Fancy, by contrast, Coleridge maintains, is not transformative but "must receive all its materials ready made from the law of association" and, in this way, he suggests, is nothing more than a mode of memory (1: 272n18, 202).

In his discussion of the "law of association" in chapters 5 and 6 of the *Biographia Literaria*, we see most acutely what is at issue for Coleridge in distinguishing the imagination from fancy. And it turns out to have less to do with faculty psychology than with the fate of poetry. According to Coleridge's treatment, the law of association, which governs fancy, describes relations that are passive and mechanical (that is, governed by efficient causes). When Coleridge glosses Hobbes by writing, "Whenever we feel several objects at the same time, the impressions that are left . . . are linked together," and "contemporaneous impressions . . . recall each other mechanically" (1: 68–69), he is emphasizing the contingency of these associations, forged in the coincidence of proximity in time and space. Taking issue with David Hartley's philosophy, Coleridge asserts that if association were the sole governing law of our mental life, we would be "divided between the despotism of outward impressions, and that of sense-less and passive memory"; we would find ourselves either in a state of "absolute *delirium*," where our ideas would be strung together in the same order as our lived encounters, or in a condition of total satura-tion, in which "*any* part of *any* impression might recall *any* part of any *other* without a cause present to determine *what* it should be" (1: 77). In the latter case we begin to suspect what the real issue is for Coleridge: the law of association risks leading not only to the delirium of senseless relations, but to the senselessness, or "lawlessness," of an infinity of possible relations given without any principle of selection.

Although Coleridge's discussion is ostensibly about the psychology of associationism, we see in what follows that the stakes are not so much psychological as textual. The poet goes on to tell the story of a young woman who falls ill and, though illiterate, begins raving in Latin, Greek, and Hebrew. She is suspected of demonic possession, but it turns out she is merely recalling scraps of her childhood spent in the care of a pastor who used to pace back and forth in his house reading aloud to himself in these same languages. As the girl speaks in feverish sentences, "coherent and intelligible each for itself, but with little or no connection with each other" (*Biographia Literaria* 1: 78), she rehearses that state of delirium Coleridge described earlier, where ideas are ordered by mere association in memory. The pastor's pacing prefigures the woman's delirium, which plucks sentences at random from his books; the whole scenario suggests to Coleridge the possibility that "all thoughts are in themselves imperishable," and that a more comprehensive intelligence than ours might recall "before every human soul the collective experience of its whole past existence" (1: 79, 80). The terrible aspect of this idea is brought to the fore as Coleridge continues, "And this, this, perchance, is the dread book of judgment, in whose mysterious hieroglyphics every idle word is recorded!" (1: 80).

A world in which nothing perishes is likened to the indelible record-keeping described in Revelations, to God's infinite book that, in containing everything, is utterly unintelligible to us. The book of judgment serves as a compelling figure of unreadability: its "hieroglyphs" invoke the specter of reading that has been replaced by a brute seeing, a "material vision," to borrow Paul de Man's term, "devoid of any reflexive or intellectual complication . . . devoid of any semantic depth" ("Phenomenality" 83).[6] For what would a book be that recorded every human word and deed—a book, in short, that was coextensive with the world? It would be nothing other *than* the material world, a script without semantic depth. When Coleridge concludes, in a moment that recalls his indebtedness to German Idealism, by referring to "that living chain of causes" to which the "absolute self is co-extensive and co-present" (*Biographia Literaria* 1: 80), he confirms this sentiment conjured in the reference to the "mysterious hieroglyphs" of God's book: that a world in which matter and spirit coincided absolutely is one in which no design would be intelligible, at least not to a finite intellect, and one which might, in fact, be indistinguishable from a world without design altogether.

Coleridge's discussion of the law of association, in short, leads him directly to envisioning a world without poetry, for a poem whose "seminal principle" would be passive and contingent association, whose mode of causality would thereby be efficient causality rather than final (*Biographia Literaria* 1: 81), runs this same risk that goes from the possible inclusion of *anything* to the eventual inclusion of *everything*. And like the book of the world, the poem that would include the entire world would not look much like a poem at all. In contrast to the associative power of fancy, then, Coleridge champions the poetic imagination, which he joins to the conscious will.

Much of Coleridge's thinking on the imagination arises from his need to assert the genius and originality of Shakespeare. In his

lecture "Shakespeare's Judgment Equal to His Genius," for example, Coleridge's stated purpose is to upset the "popular notion" that
Shakespeare was a "wild child of nature" operating "by a sort of
instinct," and to demonstrate that his achievements were the result
of conscious design (319–20). In this same short lecture, however,
we also find the most extensive statement of Coleridge's notion of
organic form, which, as de Man points out in "Form and Intent in
the American New Criticism," would seem to run counter to, and
even be imperiled by, the principle of intentionality (28). De Man suggests that, given Coleridge's investment in the organic analogy, his
treatment of intention remains ambiguous and ambivalent. Moreover,
he argues, this "ambivalence reappears among [New Critical] disci-
ples of Coleridge, in a curious discrepancy between their theoretical
assumptions and their practical results" (28). Yet, if I may continue
with Coleridge for a minute, I would like to reconsider the relationship between these two positions in Coleridge's understanding—that
is, to reconsider the relationship between intentionality and organicism—so that we might draw out the logic that links the two together.

In "Shakespeare's Judgment Equal to His Genius," it is clear that the
power of Shakespeare does not run counter to nature. Rather, his power
is something "true in human nature," "founded in faculties common to
all men," and thus to be contrasted with the "accidents of education"
and enslaving "habits of . . . immediate circumstance" (320). This contrast between inborn talent and contingent circumstance repeats the
distinction we have seen between the necessity of imagination and the
contingency of fancy, and it is consistent with Coleridge's definition
of the poetic imagination as a special degree of the "primary imagination" common to all men. The foundation of Shakespeare's genius
in nature is crucial for Coleridge, for only in this way are readers left
with "rules for imitation" and "principles" to which they can refer critical judgment; thus Coleridge will write that Shakespeare is no natural
force but "a nature humanized" (321). Coleridge's arguments here are
clearly indebted to Kant's treatment of genius, which, being the "natural gift that gives the rule to art," as we have seen, functions as the vital
fulcrum between two productions, that is, between the productivity of
nature and the productivity of man. Nature's donation of genius joins
natural and artistic production, or the donative and the exemplary,
together in a comprehensive economy.

The work of genius is not and cannot be lawless, Coleridge continues, broaching the topic of organic unity. It cannot be "barbarous

shapelessness" compensated for only by the "splendor of the parts."
Rather, parts and whole together form a "living body." As the imagination is a "vital power" and not the "lifeless mechanism" of association, so its product is a living organism, one whose form is not
predetermined and imposed from without, but "is innate; it shapes
itself as it develops itself from within, and the fullness of its development is one and the same with the perfection of its outward form"
(*Biographia Literaria* 1: 321). As Coleridge acknowledges obliquely by
referring to "a continental critic," these lines are taken nearly directly
from August Schlegel's *Lectures on Dramatic Art and Literature*.[7]

   "Such is the life," Coleridge writes, "such the form" (*Biographia
Literaria* 1: 321). In accordance with the logic of the organic itself, as
Coleridge develops it, conscious intention and organic unity are not
only practically but, in fact, necessarily continuous. The same notion
of the organic underlies what I referred to earlier as the two poles
of the "economimesis" of Kant's third *Critique*, those of nature's
donation and genius's exemplarity, or production and reflection,
and it unifies them in a single, productive economy. The notion of
the organic *is* the joining of production and reflection on a single
plane of development, and it may in fact have no other purpose than
to address and guarantee the unity of this apparent discrepancy. In
fact, I would go so far as to suggest that "the organic," or "organic
form," or even the "organism," may be no more than a catachrestic
operation for the identification of production and reflection, process
and telos, or rather a process and its culmination in the for-itself of
reflection. When Coleridge refers to the "esemplastic" imagination
in order to highlight the function of the imagination to "shape into
one" (1: 107), he is asserting just this unity of intention and form,
and he undergirds this unity by grounding the poetic imagination in
a natural process (the primary imagination), as we have seen. This is
the same unity that he will alternately assert as that of "genius" and
"judgment," "power" and "beauty," or the "spirit of poetry" and its
"body" ("Shakespeare's Judgment" 321).

   At the same time, and ultimately in keeping with the third *Critique*, the poetic imagination is not itself a natural process, but must
retain its intentional status—it must be a "nature humanized." In
other words, the organic analogy must remain exactly that: the analogical reflection of an artificial process. Likewise, the primary imagination is not continuous with eternal creation but reflects it *"as a
repetition"* (*Biographia Literaria* 1: 202). For what Coleridge risks

in following through on his own assertions that "the fullness of [a work's] development is one and the same with the perfection of its outward form" is a collapse of the very distinctions between form and formlessness, or necessity and contingency, or imagination and fancy, that he has gone to such lengths to establish. He risks returning to the scenario implied by the hieroglyphs of the "dread book of judgment," where a total coincidence of "development" and "form" would render all reading impossible. This is the extreme point to which Coleridge's striving for unity leads him: to a monism in which the absolute unity of matter and spirit in poetry, that is, the absolute coincidence of form and intention, would result in a material script that is no longer legible, or in a poetry that is continuous with, and therefore indistinguishable from, the material world. In this case, the necessity at stake in the poetic imagination actually comes around full circle to meet the contingency of association at its point of greatest saturation.

Coleridge will recoil from the implications of this monism, and will maintain a dualism of consciousness and world. Yet it is the logic of this organic analogy, taken a step further perhaps, that underlies the treatment of intention in New Criticism and allows us to make sense of the passage from Brooks to Wimsatt and Beardsley. For if intentionality is what gives unity to Brooks's paradoxes on the one hand, and if, on the other, Wimsatt and Beardsley appear to banish intention from the poem in order to pay closer attention to "the text itself," both positions are in fact direct consequences of a striving for unity, of a monism that, as James Benziger puts it, "end[s] by limiting this spirit within the confines of the works it creates" (43).

In these consequences we can spot one of the most persistent effects of the organic analogy, which is that in the identification of form and intention that the analogy implies, and in the exchange of qualities effected therein, intention is lent that aspect of unity previously reserved for form. In other words, the consequence of the organic analogy is the unification of intention itself. Intention is made out to be a self-identical and unitary causal principle. We see this move from the form of a work to its intention in the *Biographia Literaria* when Coleridge responds to the question "What is poetry"? with the question "What is a poet?" (2: 12), and when he continually reverts from a discussion of the poem to that of the origin of the poem in genius, imagination, or poetic aim. "A poem contains the same elements as a prose composition," he writes; "the difference therefore must consist in a different combination of them, in consequence of a different object [aim] being proposed" (2: 8). In all of these cases, the object of the poet, the poetic *aim*, is neatly substituted for poetic *form*.

These lines of Coleridge are close to those quoted by Brooks, who likewise tasks the poetic imagination with governing the combination and juxtaposition of poetic elements. In giving priority to the unifying function of intention—indeed, in making the unity of a poem reside solely in the unity of intention, so that the latter is substituted for the former—Brooks can emphasize the paradoxical and complex character of poetic content as much as he wants; the unity of poetic form remains undisturbed. And if Wimsatt and Beardsley appear to excise intention as a criterion for critical evaluation, this is only insofar as they make it wholly immanent to the text itself, so that they can claim, for example, that if an author revises his work to better achieve his original intention, "it follows that his former concrete intention was not his intention" (5).

## A CIRCULAR LOGIC

I read Brooks's "The Language of Paradox," in sum, as exemplary of much of New Critical thinking. For Brooks, poetry draws on paradoxical situations and offers a multiplicity of metaphors, but what guarantees the unity of a poem and the sense of its juxtapositions is ultimately the aim of the poet. This may appear to run counter to the New Critics' well-known exclusion of intention from the standards of literary criticism, but in fact, their exclusion succeeds only in reestablishing intention within the confines of the text itself. In this view of poetry, a unity of form is predicated on the unifying power of intention, while intention, in turn, is made wholly immanent to—indeed indistinguishable from—the finished poem. Intention is supposed to account for the form of the work at the same time as the form of the work is treated as the only possible account of intention.

We have seen that this equating of form and intention is not at odds with an organic view of the work, as one might assume, but is entirely consistent with it, for the metaphor of the organic is what renders intelligible the conflation of process and product, intention and form. And it does so under the sign of necessity, since the notion of organic development invokes a necessary and teleological process, one whose end point is indistinguishable from the integrity of the process itself, which culminates in the being-for-itself of the organism.

The problem with this line of reasoning, though, is its inability to ground itself. What is presented as a genetic or explanatory principle of the literary work, *intention*, is made to depend on what it is supposed to explain, *form*. Even more, the resemblance between this supposedly explanatory principle and its object seems to leave the crucial question unanswered, the question "What is a literary work?" For it offers us no clear guidelines for how to distinguish a work from the work's genetic elements. In other words, how should the passage from intention to form be understood? When our supposedly explanatory principle resembles the object of explanation in this way, it suggests that, underneath this redundancy, something remains entirely unthought. What still remains to be thought is the passage between those elements of form and intention, or form and the genesis of form, that are unique and irreducible to one another. What is the relationship between *those* subterranean elements?

What an examination of the organic metaphor reveals is not that New Criticism reifies a process of meaning, or insists overly on the autonomy of poetry against more complex historical processes, as Eagleton and many others have argued, but that, right or wrong in its concepts, New Criticism fails to deliver on its own promises. What is lacking in this New Critical logic, in particular, is a positive, genetic account of the *difference* between form and intention, or form and its causal context. When, for example, in "The Intentional Fallacy," Wimsatt and Beardsley write that "there is a gross body of life . . . which lies behind and in some sense causes every poem," and that, "for every unity, there is an action of the mind which cuts off roots, melts away context" (12), they are well aware of this difference between the cause of a poem and the poem itself, but they assign it a purely negative status. Intention is charged with excising, with "cutting off" or "melting away" context from the resulting work. But according to what principle? The principle must be sought in the work itself, which can only spring into being fully formed, the spontaneous source of its own sufficient reason. The authors distinguish between what they call internal and external evidence for the meaning of a poem, a distinction that seems to be based on their prior assertion of an internality and an externality of poems themselves, and of the contingent and superfluous nature of what is external. "Poetry succeeds because all or most of what is said or implied is relevant," they write; "what is irrelevant has been excluded, like lumps from pudding and 'bugs' from machinery" (4). But this statement is meaningful only after the fact of the poem: what is irrelevant will have been excluded, because whatever is excluded will have been irrelevant to the poem (that is, assuming we already know what a poem is, and know how to spot one among a morass of other distractions). But what accounts for the exclusion of the irrelevant and for the initial determination of inside and outside, intrinsic and extrinsic? In other words, what accounts for the determination of a poem against this background of supposedly superfluous noise? If we cannot answer this question, I would venture to say that we do not yet know what a work of literature is.

By locating the sufficient reason of a poem in the poem itself, New Criticism can, and does, offer bountiful descriptions of poems that already exist; but it cannot account for the existence of a poem as such. Worse, by making the supposedly decisive feature of a poem—its unity and integrity—dependent on the unity of an animating intention, on the integrity of a "poetic imagination," as Brooks does, this treatment of literature conceals its own lack of explanatory power. In place of an explanation it offers a circular logic supported by a metaphor, the metaphor of organic necessity, and redundant of the very question it purports to answer: Whence the unity of a poem?

# CHAPTER 3

# Tyranny of the Possible
*Blanchot*

If the organic view of literature effects an exchange between the form of a work and its intention, that is, between the origin and the telos of a work in the image of a necessary process, there is another view of the work that, despite radical differences in its content, bears a striking structural similarity to this organicism insofar as it, too, seeks to exchange the origin of the work with its telos. I have in mind the writings of Maurice Blanchot, and their contribution to what will later be identified under the label of French poststructuralism.

No French-speaking writer or critic today invested in literary-philosophical questions can avoid Blanchot's tremendous insights or influence. Compared to American critical practice in the first half of the twentieth century, which even before the New Critics was systematically investigating methods of reading and interpretation, French criticism of the same period was less theoretical, remaining largely in the mode of *explication de texte*, if not biographical study (Cusset 47). Blanchot stands out as one of the first thinkers truly to pose the question of *reading*, though he did so by investigating traces of the writer's experience in the work more than by describing the critic's or reader's experience. And so, Geoffrey Hartman has suggested that "when we come to write the history of criticism for the 1940 to 1980 period, it will be found that Blanchot, together with Sartre, made French 'discourse' possible" (xi). In fact, Blanchot appears to stand at a privileged crossroads in the history of theory and criticism, for on the one hand, in view of his significance for Derrida, he has been called a "crude harbinger of deconstruction" (Clark 78) and a "déconstructioniste avant la lettre" (Nordholt 11), while on the other hand, he has been called "one of the last romantics," at least insofar as his work sustains a mode of questioning that remains "irreducible or excessive with respect to the Enlightenment's unfinished project" (Bruns xv).

In this chapter, I trace out the logic underlying Blanchot's treatment of the literary work, considering the legacy of this logic as well as its limitations. I focus in particular on the concept of possibility Blanchot employs in its supposedly essential relation to literature. If, as I will argue, Blanchot can conceive of the literary work only by both invoking and holding at a distance any possibility that would prefigure it, this account, like that of the New Critics, ultimately remains unable to address the question of the work's passage from possibility to realization. Before I develop the details of this analysis, however, let us take stock of Blanchot's relationship to romanticism.

## THE CLOSURE OF ROMANTICISM

Champion of the incomplete, the impossible, the unsaid, and the non-totalizable in language, Blanchot has devoted his work not only to those practitioners of a formally fragmentary writing—Nietzsche, Mallarmé, René Char, for example—but to a concept of writing that is intimately bound to the fragmentary and the excessive in its very essence. On the question of his relation to and distance from romanticism, and specifically to the fragments of the Jena romantics, his essay "The *Athenaeum*"—a major source for Lacoue-Labarthe and Nancy's *The Literary Absolute*, as I mentioned earlier—proves indispensable. Here Blanchot identifies a tendency toward closure in the romantic fragment and draws out three points that can also be read as a fairly decisive articulation of his own differences from romanticism—or perhaps what will lead him to identify with what he calls "the non-romantic essence of romanticism" (*Infinite Conversation* 357).

For Blanchot, the mode of writing discovered by Schlegel and his group fails to attain, or at least to sustain, its most radical implications. The closure of the romantic fragment hangs on the romantics' tendency to conceive it along the following lines: "1) . . . as a text that is concentrated, having its center in itself rather than in the field that *other* fragments constitute along with it; 2) neglecting the interval . . . that separates the fragments and makes of this separation the rhythmic principle of the work . . . ; 3) forgetting that this manner of

writing tends not to make a view of the whole more difficult or the
relations of unity more lax, but rather makes possible new relations
that except themselves from unity, just as they exceed the whole"
(*Infinite Conversation* 359). Let's examine these points in detail. The
first describes the tendency of the romantic fragment to take on all
the gravity and closure of the aphorism or of the perfect sentence—
whence Novalis's claim that it can be "complete in itself like a porcupine" (359). As Blanchot argues, "The aphorism works as a force that
limits, encloses. A form that takes the form of a horizon: its own"
(152). In place of the self-centered aphorism, Blanchot would propose
an ex-centric discourse, where what is said relates essentially to what
is outside it. In his second point, Blanchot reformulates this idea by
emphasizing the constitutive power of the interval *between* the fragments. In place of a proliferation of centers, he would seek an ex-cen-
tricity belonging to the work or to the discursive field itself; in other
words, he would seek a principle of separation and distance as immanent and necessary to the work rather than extraneous or accidental.

The third point describes the tendency that is perhaps the most
entrenched and most contradictory. By asserting that fragmentary
writing "tends not to make a view of the whole more difficult," Blanchot points to the ease with which the fragments lend themselves to
being re-totalized under the sign of the book, the journal, or the self.
In chapter 1 we saw the tendency of the fragments to appear in collections (such as Schlegel's *Ideas* and Novalis's *Grains of Pollen*), and
I noted the gathering function of the *Athenaeum* journal as a site
of the collection of collections. Moreover, we witnessed the romantics' investment in the novel as the great "romantic book," the genre
capable of swallowing generic distinction, synthesizing dialogue, and
providing the work with its "spiritual central point" (Schlegel, *Dialogue* 101). The romantic notion of the self, however, turns out to be
the most ideal and most tenacious means of bringing a "whole" of the
fragmentary into view. Lacoue-Labarthe and Nancy remark that the
romantic fragments inherit from the English and French moralists—
from the laxity of form in their miscellaneous reflections, essays, and
maxims—a means of centering their discourse "in a certain way outside the work, in the subject that is seen in it, or in the judgment that
proffers its maxims in it" (40). The self, especially the creative or
moral self, serves as the transcendent sign that authorizes and anchors
even the most extreme formal disorder, which in turn becomes an
expression of the merely personal. Thus, as is particularly the case

with Friedrich Schlegel, Blanchot writes, "the fragment often seems a means for complacently abandoning oneself to the self . . . to welcome one's own disorder, to close up upon one's own self in a contented isolation" (*Infinite Conversation* 359).

## THE FRAGMENTARY EXIGENCY

Formal fragmentation alone is thus not equal to what Blanchot calls "the fragmentary exigency of the work [*l'exigence fragmentaire de l'œuvre*]": the demand for/of a mode of writing that would render the very accomplishment of a work problematic, along with the work's concomitant concepts of unity, totality, and continuity (*Infinite Conversation* 348; *L'entretien infini* 510). Blanchot seems to conceive of this writing as the true inheritance of the romantic project, a kind of discovery whose effects have only now become possible. In place of a view of fragmentation that would position the fragment in stark opposition to totality (only, perhaps, to idealize that totality all the more thoroughly), he pursues a mode of writing whose relations would be excepted from or in excess of the very possibility of totalization. The distinction Blanchot draws on here seems to be between two different ways of conceiving of the limits of totalization: as Derrida argues famously in "Structure, Sign, and Play in the Discourse of the Human Sciences," a totality might be undone by an infinite number of instances that are impossible to gather up or account for; or, conversely, it might be logically excluded from a mode of organization. Derrida writes, "If totalization no longer has any meaning, it is not because the infinity of a field cannot be covered by a finite glance or a finite discourse, but because the nature of the field—that is, language and a finite language—excludes totalization. . . . [This field], instead of being too large, [has] something missing from it: a center which arrests and founds the freeplay of substitutions" (289). The field Derrida refers to is, of course, the field of language conceived along structuralist lines as a horizontal system of differences without an anchoring term. Although Blanchot is not operating with the same structuralist conceptions as Derrida is in this essay, he has a comparable sense of literary language as lacking an "anchor" in the world, be it instrumentality or the requirements of truth or faithful representation. For Blanchot, the "fragmentary exigency" of the literary work issues from the particular and privileged nature of literary language; this language demands a rigorous mode of writing that, in its distance from the world, "lets itself speak," and in so doing will let speak or reveal an "ambiguity" at the heart of language in general.

Drawing in part on Mallarmé's conception of poetic language and in part on German phenomenology, what Blanchot calls *writing* is supposed to challenge not only those notions of voice and presence that operate in everyday conceptions of language, and not only the limits of the "work" that such a writing would constitute; it is meant to cut to the heart of all totalizing categories of human knowledge and experience. It is that by which "everything is brought into question—and first of all the idea of God, of the Self, of the Subject, then of Truth and the One, then finally the idea of the Book and the Work" (*Infinite Conversation* xii).

The radicality of Blanchot's claims originates in his notion of language as a transcendental space of negativity: lacking a real anchor in the world, language possesses an "aleatory force of absence" (*Infinite Conversation* xii). "Nothing operates in words [*précisément rien est au travail dans les mots*]," Blanchot writes elsewhere. "Words, we know, have the power to make things disappear, to make them appear as things that have vanished" (*Space of Literature* 43; *L'espace littéraire* 41). This power to make disappear, and thus to make appear the fact of disappearance itself, Blanchot attributes to all forms of representation. And he provides one of his clearest articulations of how representation works in his essay "The Two Versions of the Imaginary" (included in *The Space of Literature*). Following Heidegger's conception of the realm of appearance as that of the concealment of being, where being can be grasped only in its withdrawal, Blanchot pursues the question of phenomenal appearance as covering over the disappearance of being, a covering-over that becomes the very condition of representation.[1] Challenging the notion that the representational image comes "after" the sensory apprehension of an object, appearing in place of that object, Blanchot argues that the image reveals a constitutive displacement at the heart of the object, or at the heart of being itself. The image uncovers "the thing as distance, present in its absence, graspable because ungraspable, appearing as disappeared [*apparaissant en tant que disparue*]" (256; 347). The image points to the void that is its necessary condition, at the same time as it "grazes [*effleure*]" the object (255; 345). These two aspects of representation, according to Blanchot, constitute its "ambiguity."

Representation's ambiguity—its two aspects or "versions"—derive, Blanchot argues, from the double valence of negation. On the one hand, as in the case of communicative language or representational art, the word or image makes meaning possible through a negation of the particular; this is a "life-giving negation, the ideal operation by which man, capable of negating nature, raises it to a higher meaning" ("Two Versions" 260). The particular is negated, we might say, for the sake of the concept. On the other hand, negation might be its own, and only, meaning, the nonrecuperable absence of meaning: "Death is sometimes truth's elaboration in the world and sometimes the perpetuity of that which admits neither beginning nor end" (261). In other words, Blanchot surmises that if finitude is the horizon for human meaning, as Heidegger attests, then there is also a death that is the *death* of death, a night that is the *other* of night, an unfettered negativity serving as the absence of all horizon and all possibility, so that "in death the possibility which is death dies too" (261). Death gives not only possibility but "the horror of impossibility" (261). Here Blanchot is close to his contemporary George Bataille in his pursuit of a nondialectical, utterly nonrecuperable negativity.[2]

The "two versions" of the imaginary come together in ambiguity and neutrality, where negativity is alternately revealed and concealed, or revealed in its concealment as determinate negation. And just as there are two versions of the imaginary, there are two versions of language, which Blanchot tends to address in conjunction with his readings of Mallarmé.[3] While in all language, "the word has meaning only if it rids us of the object it names" (*Work of Fire* 30), communicative language covers over this annihilation with purportedly transparent meaning and instrumental purpose. In communication, language resembles a tool that disappears into its use (*Space of Literature* 258). Literary language, on the other hand, has the potential to "appear": to point to itself, to reveal the illusion of language's immediacy, the void at the heart of its functioning, and the displacement of the void as its most originary gesture. *Writing* is another name for what literature reveals: a displacement of being at the origin of language, and an (effacement of the) inscription of this displacement as language's most intimate operation.

## NOBODY KNOWS THE GREATEST HALLMARK OF LANGUAGE: THAT IT IS CONCERNED ONLY WITH ITSELF

When, in his essay "The *Athenaeum*," Blanchot writes of the "nonromantic essence of romanticism," he seems to designate this notion of *writing* as what was both concealed by romanticism and at the same

time made possible by it, so that it emerges, strangely enough, as romanticism's inevitable conclusion.[4] The aesthetic autonomy that Kantian
philosophy bequeathed to romanticism meant that literature gained the
capacity to become visible for its own sake. Yet in this becoming-visible,
it discovered no task or trait other than its own self-manifestation. As
a consequence, Blanchot writes, "art and literature seem to have nothing other to do than to manifest, that is to say, to indicate themselves
in accordance with the obscure mode that is proper to them: manifest
themselves, announce themselves, in a word, communicate themselves"
(*Infinite Conversation* 355, translation modified).[5] But what does literature "communicate" in communicating itself?

Again Blanchot echoes Heidegger in his assertion that, in literature, "language speaks." This is romanticism's inevitable discovery,
as well as its distinctly "non-romantic essence": "that to speak poeti-
cally is to make possible a non-transitive speech whose task is not
to say *things* (not to disappear in what it signifies), but to say (itself)
in letting (itself) say, yet without taking itself as the new object of
this language without object" (*Infinite Conversation* 357). This non-
transitive language is like the broken tool, which, no longer ready-
to-hand, suddenly becomes visible, writes Blanchot, *as an image*. By
"image," he means both that the tool appears only when it no longer
disappears into its use, and that its appearance is insubstantial—that
it is *mere* appearance. In these terms, language loses its instrumental
character to become its own resemblance. It becomes its own resemblance, double, and reflection, "the pure and simple resemblance
behind which there is nothing" (*Space of Literature* 258–59).

Language as mute image of itself is an image of language as such,
or of the whole of language. But with his conception of writing, Blanchot exposes the displacement of the void as language's non-totalizable
essence. The only possible "whole" of language is thus its own outside:
what Blanchot calls the interval, the displacement, the detour of the void.
As detour, language, as well as the work of literature that would reveal
it, can paradoxically only ever be obscured by the instance of its own
inscription. Conversely, its visibility is like a white light in which all distinction disappears, language become "pure consciousness without content, a pure speech that can say nothing" (*Infinite Conversation* 356).

In chapter 1 we saw how romanticism arose in dialogue with a philosophical demand for the presentation of the absolute. What Blanchot makes clear is the strange dispossession of the literary work at
the very moment it would lay claim to the absolute: "This becoming

self-conscious that renders literature manifest, and reduces it to being nothing but its manifestation, leads literature to lay claim not only to the sky, the earth, to the past, the future, to physics and philosophy—this would be little—but to everything, to the whole that acts in every instant and every phenomenon . . . not every instant such as it occurs, nor every phenomenon such as it is produced, only the whole that acts mysteriously and invisibly in everything" (*Infinite Conversation* 355). In becoming self-conscious, literature gains the whole, Blanchot writes, but "only" the whole: the whole of speech that can say nothing, the whole of consciousness that, as form of the whole, becomes *mere* form of the whole. By the same triumphant gesture with which literature would lay claim to the world in the form of a "literary absolute," it loses the world, the particulars of *this* world, because its claim is premised on the void of its origin. Thus Blanchot can conclude that romantic poetry witnesses "the strange era of its own tautology": a self-eclipse in which literature became "master of everything, but on condition that the whole contain nothing" (356).

## CONCERN FOR THE ORIGIN

The self-eclipse of the literary work finds no better parable than Blanchot's reading of Orpheus in Hades—nor, perhaps, does Blanchot's own treatment of literature. Indeed, Blanchot identifies his short essay "Orpheus's Gaze" as the central point of *The Space of Literature* (i), a book that is itself at the center of his career as well as his theorization of literature.

Orpheus dares to cross the Styx under the protection of a song, pursuing Eurydice, who becomes "the furthest that art can reach . . . the profoundly obscure point toward which art and desire, death and night, seem to tend" (*Space of Literature* 171). At the same time, Orpheus's task, what constitutes his *work*, is not to attain his goal in darkness but to bring it into the light of day, "to give it form, shape, and reality" (171). Orpheus thus finds himself in the grips of contradictory demands: the demand to grasp Eurydice in the obscurity of the night where she essentially appears, and the necessity of turning away from her as his only means of approach— that is, the necessity of approaching his goal by detour.

In this allegory of the artist and the inspiration that drives him, Blanchot uncovers the structure of the artwork as "infinitely problematic movement" (*Space of Literature* 172). The desire to behold Eurydice, not in daylight but "in her nocturnal obscurity, in her distance" (172), is at once the impetus of Orpheus's song and its point of extreme uncertainty, the work's inexorable demand (what Blanchot calls "*l'exigence profonde de l'oeuvre*" [*L'espace littéraire 181*]), and that on behalf of which the work is sacrificed the instant Orpheus turns to look back. This desire, at once the origin of the work and its breaking point, is what Blanchot terms inspiration: "Everything proceeds as if, by disobeying the law, by looking at Eurydice, Orpheus had only obeyed the deep demand of the work. . . . To look at Eurydice, without regard for the song, in the impatience and imprudence of desire which forgets the law, *that* is *inspiration*" (173). Inspiration demands the sacrifice of the artist no less than the sacrifice of his work: it is the imperative to cross the "measureless deep," that condition of the artistic process, and to devote oneself to a project without guarantee. Better, it demands fidelity to a project that, by definition, is the very absence and destruction of all guarantee, insofar as its originality and inventiveness consists in the invention of a new law, one that is both unforeseeable and inaugural of the conditions of its own reception.

The work emerges at a distance from any foreseeable program, from the passion that inspires it, from the world that phenomenalizes it, and from the author that executes it. In the work's distance we find the solitude of the writer, for the activity of writing requires his renouncement of the world (the world of purposeful activities, for example) not only in the prosaic sense, but in an essential sense, in which the writer is bound to the work in his function as writer and yet removed from the work insofar as the work's essence is to exist publicly and independently of his person, his intentions, and his ability to say "I" (*Space of Literature* 26). Hence the paradox of writing "I am alone" (*Faux pas* 2), a phrase that either ceases to refer to *my* solitude uniquely, or else destroys it in making it communicable. Against the flux of the artistic process, the work emerges "the moment when that which is glorified in the work *is* the work, when the work ceases in some way to have been made, to refer back to someone who made it, but gathers all the essence of the work in the fact that now there is a work, a beginning and initial decision—this moment which cancels the author" (*Space of Literature* 200). The structure of the work, in sum, is one of sacrifice; this is its problematic and paradoxical character. In its independence, the work is pitted against everything that gives rise to it. And it must be so (according to Blanchot's line of reasoning), for if it were identical to its conditions it would have no need to come into being.

The writer sacrifices himself for the sake of his work, but on condition that even the work can be risked for the sake of what inspires it. Inspiration both goads Orpheus into action and threatens his ruin, and it compromises the work no less, transforming the work into the search for its own origins—into the search for an expression of the inexpressible cause of the work's realization. The moment Orpheus turns to look at Eurydice shrouded in night, the work attains its inexpressible core and "is lost absolutely" (*Space of Literature* 174). But inasmuch as the imperative to behold Eurydice is the inspiration and the essence of Orpheus's song, the work can be said to take exception to itself in this moment and return to its source in the form of a forbidden, circular movement: "It is only in that look that the work can surpass itself, be united with its origin and consecrated in impossibility" (174). The work is consecrated the moment it is abandoned for the sake of its raison d'être, sacrificed in that "sudden eclipse . . . the nostalgic return to the uncertainty of the origin" (174).

Finally, the instant of Orpheus's gaze reveals the paradoxical temporal structure of the work: a circular time that describes the "space" of literature. Just as the writer is both the author of his work and its product or function, the "origin" of the work is both the work's source and its effect, its hidden central point—a kind of sinkhole: "The central point of the work is the work as origin," Blanchot writes. "One can approach it only by means of the completed work, but one can complete the work only by means of the approach" (*Space of Literature* 54–55). Thus Eurydice in Hades is at once the inspiration behind Orpheus's song, the furthest point his art can reach, and the vortex of its destruction. Here again we come full circle—or perhaps we have gone nowhere—for Orpheus's gaze is both the death and the birth of his art: "Writing begins with Orpheus's gaze. . . . One writes only if one reaches that instant which nevertheless one can only approach in the space opened by the movement of writing. To write one has to write already [*Pour écrire, il faut déjà écrire*]" (176; *L'espace littéraire* 234). Accordingly, the only way to enter literature's space is by means of a "leap" (176).

## BETRAYAL OF THE ORIGIN

We have seen how the New Critics identify the unity of poetic form with the unity of intention, and the integrity of the work with the necessity of the poetic imagination, working in opposition to contingent association. In Blanchot, we encounter a strikingly homologous situation, where the work is alternately identified with its origin ("the central point of the work is the work as origin" [*Space of Literature* 54]), and pitted against it in a relationship of sacrifice, disguise, and betrayal. Both treatments are rendered in the name of an exigency.

How is the work determined specifically as a "disguising of its origin"? Such is the assertion of Derrida's early essay "Force and Signification" (1963), a piece that showcases Derrida's proximity to both Heidegger and Blanchot in his thinking of the literary work, especially in regard to the question of the relation of a structure to its genesis. The determination of the work as a disguising of its own origin is possible on the basis of the double valence Blanchot attributes to the notion of origin. Just as the representational image has one side turned toward the void while the other "grazes" the object, so too does the "origin" have two sides or aspects: one points toward the void as its condition of possibility, and the other toward the work as its proper limit. On the one hand, the work *is its own* origin in the sense that the work simultaneously inaugurates and instantiates a new law in the form of its poetics. In this sense, the origin of a work is what is most essential in the work, in Heidegger's sense of the origin of a thing being "the source of its essence" ("The Origin" 143). On the other hand, the work *is no longer* its origin, for if it were still its origin, it would be nothing more than "an insurmountable problem . . . the impossibility of being written" (Blanchot, *Work of Fire* 305, translation modified). Rather, the work is the limit where the origin ceases. Or we might say that the work's origin is its departure from the origin, just as the origin of writing is a displacement of the void.

The beginning of the work thus lies in the distance that is the work's true condition. Recall that Blanchot criticizes the view of the imaginary in which the image follows the presence of an object, arguing instead that the image reveals an absence that already belongs to the object, "something which it had dominated in order to be an object—something counter to which it had defined and built itself up" (*Space of Literature* 256). The same must be true for the literary work, which originates, as we have seen, "not in another world, but in the other of all worlds" (75). Likewise, Derrida writes in "Force and Signification," "In question here is a departure from the world toward a place which is neither a *non-place* nor an *other* world, neither a utopia nor an alibi" (8).

For Derrida as well as Blanchot, this exit from the world is none other than the opening of a negative space of freedom and possibility. Derrida describes poetic freedom as the work's "blind origin": "the essential nothing on whose basis everything can appear and be produced within language; and the voice of Maurice Blanchot reminds us . . . that this excess is the very possibility of writing and of literary inspiration in general" ("Force" 8). "Everything" is possible in literature, in other words, but only on the basis of a negation of the world, of the world's being held at a distance *as* negated. We know that Derrida remains close to this position throughout his career, testifying, for example, in an interview with Derek Attridge and later in *Passions*, on the essential relation of the "space of literature" to an authorization or principle of "being able to say everything [*tout dire*]" (*Acts* 36–40). The translators of the interview point out that *tout dire* means "both to 'say everything' in the sense of exhausting a totality, and to 'say anything,' i.e., to speak without constraints" (36). I would point out that the ambiguity of this *tout dire* can be referred to a duality in the concept of freedom in Kant's philosophy, alternately construed as the positive freedom *of* self-legislation and the negative freedom *from* external constraint. Thus Derrida can write that the "law" of literature also tends to "defy or lift the law" (36). Most importantly, he observes that a "motif of totality" circulates around the question of literature (36). The literary exhibits a tendency to formalize and totalize at the same time as it involves a kind of essential fragmentation or excess; that is why it is grasped as the "creation of a 'universe to be added to the universe' . . . which articulates only that which is in excess of everything [*création d'un 'univers qui s'ajoute à l'univers' . . . qui ne dit donc que l'excès sur le tout*]" ("Force" 8; "*Force et signification*" 17).

A work of literature does not in itself say "everything," of course, but the promise or principle of the imaginary space that it opens—and this concept of literature's space is explicitly taken up by Derrida—is one of the *possibility* of saying "anything." In other words, the space of literature is the field of the possible. In fact, for both Derrida and Blanchot, literature's space is the *entirety* of the field of the possible, a totalization of the possible that is utterly without content, as its only determination is that of a negation of the whole of the actual.

We know that Blanchot and Derrida do not describe the space of literature as totalizing, but rather the opposite: literature, or literary language, is supposed to upset or exceed totalities such as the Work, the Book, the Self, the World. Yet both thinkers rely on a concept of freedom that is construed negatively as a freedom from constraint, and is predicated upon a prior totalization. *World*, for example, as it has come up in our discussion, is a precise term that refers to the totality of the actual, the whole of what exists in space and time as possible objects of human experience, so that when Derrida writes of an exit from the world and the "'universe to be added to the universe'" which "articulates only that which is in excess of everything" ("Force" 8; *Force et signification* 17), he refers, not to the fictional universe of a novel or epic poem, but to the negative space of imagination construed as freedom from the world, with no determination except that of an excess over the whole. And when he comments, in the interview with Attridge, that literature is "the most interesting thing in the world, maybe more interesting than the world" (*Acts* 47), his seemingly conversational remark has all of the precision of a mathematical formula: literature is the *most* interesting thing in the world because it is possible only on the basis of a totalization of the whole, and *more* interesting than the world because its real origin lies in its negation of and distance from this whole.[6]

In light of Derrida's remark, consider Blanchot's comment in *The Work of Fire*, which emphasizes the essential relation between writing, freedom, and totality: "What does writing care about? To free us from what is. And what is, is everything . . . everything that for us marks the domain of the objective world" (39). Facing the whole of the objective world, we hold it at a distance; in this, Blanchot thinks, our freedom consists. "This liberation," he continues, "is accomplished by the strange possibility we have of creating emptiness around us, putting a distance between us and things" (39).

Everywhere Blanchot celebrates the power of the void, and the power of literature to reveal the void as its proper condition, as well as the condition of human imagination. He draws on Sartre's account of the negativity of the imagination,[7] as well as on Kant's notion of the free play of the faculties in a judgment of the beautiful—the freedom of the imagination to schematize without concepts (*Critique of the Power of Judgment* §35). Blanchot describes the imagination as the "play" that makes fiction possible, again articulating a relation between imagination, negation, and totality: "The very act of imagining supposes that one goes beyond real, particular objects, and orients oneself toward reality taken as a whole . . . in order to hold it at a distance, and in this distance, finds the play without which there would be neither image, imagination, nor fiction" (*La part du feu* 84).[8] Similarly, in "Force and Signification," Derrida cites Kant's treatment of the imagination as generating "inexponible representations . . . in its free play" (7, quoting *Critique of the Power of Judgment* §57), as well as "a powerful agent for creating, as it were, a second nature out of the material supplied to it by actual nature" (*Critique of the Power of Judgment* §49). Between this first and "second" nature we can locate Blanchot's *écart*: the interval, or the negation of and distance from the whole of nature that constitutes the essence of human freedom. This holding at a distance as the essence of freedom, and as the necessary condition of the imagination, remains Blanchot's most conspicuous legacy.

To summarize, Blanchot's reasoning seems to be the following, which I will break down somewhat artlessly into five assertions in order that we may inspect it more closely. (1) The absence of an object is the necessary condition of its representation (in language or otherwise). (2) Literary language has the capacity to point beyond the merely absent object to the fact of disappearance as such, which in turn reveals that (3) absence or "the void" in general is the condition of "the whole of language" or the whole of the imaginary. Derrida reiterates this logic, which travels from determinate negation, or the absence of a thing, to a generalized negativity, or absence as such, attesting that only the latter constitutes the specificity of literature: "Only pure absence—not the absence of this or that, but the absence of everything in which all presence is announced—can inspire, in other words, can *work*, and then make one work. . . . This emptiness as the situation of literature must be acknowledged by the critic as that which constitutes the specificity of his object" ("Force" 8). (4) The essence of a thing can be identified with its condition of possibility. Blanchot's thought is difficult to pin down because it moves with lightning speed from a thing to the condition of that thing, and equates the two as if equating the thing with its essence. In this way Blanchot can proceed as if the essence of language were silence, or the essence of the image were absence. (5) All of the above holds true for the literary work, whose essence is identified with the negation of the world as the condition of its freedom.

It seems that Blanchot would condemn the literary work to an experience of perpetual self-erasure. If what is essentially true of literature is its freedom—and, moreover, if this freedom is construed in purely negative terms as freedom from constraint—then any actually existing literary work will remain the merely negative image of its own freedom, removing itself from the absolutized field of its possibility like a fall from grace. The consequence of Blanchot's reasoning is that the moment of art's phenomenal existence is that of the erasure of its own truth, which in turn can only ever exist as withdrawal from phenomenality. Hence Blanchot's reliance on liminal concepts like betrayal and sacrifice, by means of which traces of freedom can be retained in the work, if only in the form of a loss.

## NEGATIVITY AND LITERARY CREATION

Is there any alternative to Blanchot's understanding of the integrity of a literary work? Is the very notion of a "work" possible only on the basis of the work's extraction from history, human experience, or everyday language use? Can the work's autonomy be thought only in terms of an absence of heteronomy—that is, in terms of the work's freedom from the legislation of all other domains? In Blanchot's terms, must a work come into being on the basis of its distance from and negation of the phenomenal world? Must it be purchased only at the great price of a sacrifice of all of the conditions that gave rise to it?

We have seen that for Blanchot, the structure of the work is one of sacrifice: a sacrifice of the inspiration that gave rise to it, of the flux of the artistic process, of the labor and even the person of the writer, so that the work's very determination is that of a distance from its origin. Underlying Blanchot's account is a concept of negative determination, so that the literary work appears only at the moment of rupture, "when the work ceases in some way to have been made, to refer back to someone who made it" (*Space of Literature* 200). Again, at stake in this account is the question of how to relate an autonomous structure to its genesis, or how to relate the autonomy of a work to the necessity of the causal relationship that produces it. By opposing the one to the other, Blanchot perpetuates the very entrenched romantic and idealist gesture of pitting necessity and freedom against one another, drawing heavily on the high drama of this conflict, and turning the literary work into a testament of its insolubility.

At work in Blanchot's account is a certain conception of literary creation. Negativity is thrust to the fore in this account, I would argue, because of two entrenched ontological suppositions about the nature of creation: that determination can be conceived only negatively, and that creation in particular entails a radical break between the conditions of creation and the conditioned, or between creative process and created product. Blanchot will raise this break to the level of an essential truth, taking negativity as such to be the real condition of creation. The literary work can thus only appear as infinitely paradoxical: it simultaneously depends on negativity for its being, seeks this negativity as it manifests itself as a self-reflexive question, and obscures this negativity in the very fact that it exists at all and still manages to communicate something.

Blanchot assumes that the literary work, or any creative product, must be determined negatively because if it were continuous with its conditions, he reasons, it would not be new. In fact, it would not even be determinate. This reasoning is indebted to Hegelian logic, in which negation is necessary to determination as such. We can see how it inspires a kind of "paradox of the new," in which the conditions of possibility of the new—that the new be unforeseeable, unprogrammable, and, at the limit, unrecognizable—appear simultaneously to be the conditions of its impossibility.[9] What makes the new genuinely possible, in this view, is its rupture with any set of present possibilities, so that impossibility alone remains its true condition. Yet such a paradox collapses without the brace of negative determination.

Against this negative determination of the literary work, I will propose, in the chapters that follow, a positive and differential account of the production of the new. One set of resources we have for developing such an account lies in Gilles Deleuze's work, or at least in a certain reading of Deleuze, one that acknowledges his ongoing engagement with questions of genesis and structure as they have been shaped by the legacy of post-Kantianism. In particular, Deleuze's work, especially as it draws on Henri Bergson's on this question, offers powerful resources for a critique of the concept of possibility. Most importantly, it provides an account of the new that stands as a viable alternative to the Hegelian and Heideggerian aspects of Blanchot's thought—indeed to entire the post-Kantian lineage that continues to control our conceptions of the unity and integrity of literary form.[10] Though neither Deleuze nor Bergson is motivated by the specific question of the mode of being of the literary work,[11] their treatment of creation has much to contribute to theoretical debates about the status of literature.

Returning to the paradox of the new and mobilizing Deleuze's terms, I will note that such a paradox appears only under the assumption that the new must be thought in terms of what can be represented conceptually. Mediated by representation, newness can appear only in the guise of opposition, so that any new creation is grasped in terms of what its conditions of creation are *not*. Or else it is determined as what must lie outside of conceptual thought altogether, so that it is opposed not only to its conditions, but to everything that can appear and be conceived, originating "not in another world, but in the other of all worlds" (*Space of Literature* 75).

Beyond the assertion of an irresolvable paradox, and beyond the pathos that irresolvable paradoxes tend to incite—a paradox that may amount to no more than an oscillation between two unexamined alternatives—what cannot be thought in this representational schema is how something can arise from a given set of conditions and at the same time differ from them. Yet not only is negative determination an imposter for real difference, but it can provide no real account of literary production. We have seen that in Blanchot's parable of Orpheus, Orpheus pursues Eurydice, who is at once the inspiration of his song and that "profoundly obscure point toward which art and desire, death and night, seem to tend" (*Space of Literature* 171). That one approach this obscure point is the work's inexorable demand (*"l'exigence profonde de l'oeuvre"*). But what is the nature of this inexorability? We have seen that the possibility of literature is premised on the negation of the world, which opens up the space of freedom (freedom construed as freedom *from*) necessary to literary creation. To pursue the origin of the work is thus to approach the conditions of possibility of writing.

Yet condition is not causation. Conditions of possibility are not the cause of anything, and certainly not the cause of anything real. And so the question I posed to New Criticism returns: How do we account for the work's passage from its conditions to its realization? For its passage from the possible to the real? Despite Blanchot's rhetorical insistence on the unrelenting obligation of the writer and the "inexorable demand" of the work, there is no logical relation of necessity between the possible and the real, and certainly no necessary passage from the totality of the possible, construed in purely negative terms, to a determinate real whose only function would be to limit this possibility, or to retain a trace of it in the form of a loss.

In his reading of Henri Bergson, Deleuze underscores Bergson's claim that the concept of possibility participates in one of the most notoriously badly posed problems of metaphysics: Why is there something rather than nothing? (*Bergsonism* 18). The possible is supposed to precede the real, but this supposition is based on the domination of thought by representation and representation's need to spatialize and distribute judgments according to preexisting concepts and categories. Representation proceeds as if a given judgment were true for all time, and so, in Bergson's words, "to every true affirmation we attribute thus a retroactive effect; or rather we impart to it a retrograde movement" (*Creative Mind* 22). Thus, of any new product in the universe, we cling to the conviction that "even if it hasn't been conceived before being produced, it could have been, and in this sense from all eternity it existed as possible" (22). But the possibility of a thing does not precede its realization the way a sketch precedes an oil painting, "for the possible," Bergson writes, "is only the real with the addition of an act of mind which throws its image back into the past, once it has been enacted" (62).

The appearance of necessity that belongs to the possible is due to the latter's dependence on the "retrograde movement" of thought that founds it and makes it into an image of the real. The possible appears when an image of the real is projected backward in time in the form of a future perfect (as what will have been possible), and it is supported by the illusion that things can be represented before they are created— "as though," Bergson writes, "the thing and the idea of the thing, its reality and its possibility, were not created at one stroke when a truly new form, invented by art or nature, is concerned!" (*Creative Mind* 13). We can see that the very concept of possibility is antagonistic to a real apprehension of novelty; despite its avowed affinity for notions of origin and inspiration, it in fact privileges the already-made, the given, over "that by which the given is given" (Deleuze, *Difference and Repetition* 222–23). The possible pretends to offer an account of the new on the basis of a retrograde logic and a pregiven image, fashioned on the basis of the already-existent.

It is true that Blanchot argues that the literary work bears an essential relation, not to a positive possibility that would prefigure it, but to a generalized absence that is the space of its freedom. Yet is the thought of this absence not produced by the same additive movement of the mind as the possible? "In the idea of nonbeing," Deleuze argues, "there is the idea of being, plus a logical operation of generalized negation, plus the particular psychological motive for that operation" (*Bergsonism* 17). That is, negation is a derivative operation, and it is inseparable from the psychological interests that motivate it, the desire or expectation that things might be otherwise. The germ of this argument comes, in fact, from Kant's objection to the ontological argument for the existence of God, in which Kant asserts that existence is not a predicate that can be attributed to or subtracted from a concept, but that the concept of a thing is inseparable from the affirmation of its existence (*Critique of Pure Reason* 565). If we accept that the affirmation of a thing is coextensive with its concept, then negation is not an equivalent act of the mind but a second-order operation: an affirmation of the thing *plus the addition* of the thought of its substitution by another object, or by the whole of reality seized *en bloc* (Bergson, *Creative Evolution* 286).

If this is true, and if it is true that the idea of the negation of an object is itself only the truncated idea of the substitution of one particular object for another, together with the direction of our vested interest toward only one of those objects, then does Blanchot's conception of negativity indicate anything other than the subjective direction of his thought coupled with the limitation it encounters there? And is his concept of the whole of the void not, in fact, synthetically produced on the basis of a series of substitutions, so that, in Bergson's terms, "the nought is the limit toward which the operation tends" (*Creative Evolution* 280)? My claim, then, is that the negativity Blanchot discovers is not an essential dimension of the literary work, but a limitation in the very concept of possibility itself. Because Blanchot confronts the imperative to think creation in terms of a difference from what is, and because he cannot conceive of such difference in terms other than negation or opposition, and furthermore, because he likely recognizes the paradox implicit in the concept of the new—the unthinkability of the new before it arrives, and thus the impossibility of its possibility—he comes face to face with the insufficiency of the concept of possibility in accounting for literary creation. He transforms the lacuna he encounters into a radical absence, raising it to the level of a negativity of the whole and bestowing upon it the status of an essential truth. Yet perhaps this lacuna is *not* the origin of the work, but the testament to a blind spot in this logic that is so indebted to German Idealism: a shadow that falls over Blanchot's thought in the form of its inability to account for the productivity and continuity of difference.

Bergson's argument for the subjective dimension of negation, finally, suggests a powerful source of pathos in his work. "The idea of annihilation is . . . not a pure idea," Bergson writes; "it implies that we regret the past or that we conceive it as regrettable, that we have some reason to linger over it" (*Creative Evolution* 295). If Blanchot's interest lies with the negative as a space of possibility, this can only take the form of a regret and appear at the expense of actual literary works. Deleuze points to the two rules of realization with respect to the possible: the real is supposed to resemble the possible, and the emergence of the real is supposed to limit the possible (*Bergsonism* 99). In a conception of literature in which the possibility of the work is not only without representation but wholly unrepresentable, the realized literary work will appear as pure limitation: this will be the "true" meaning or horizon toward which the work tends, and anything else it seems to signify along the way will, at best, be in the service of this horizon and, at worst, appear to be unconscious or illusory.

There is something exceedingly thoughtful in Blanchot's work, something unsurpassably attentive to the precariousness of literary language and the specificity of its experience. Yet, at the same time, there is something resentful in the picture he paints, something that seems to despair in the fact that a thing like literature exists at all. At best, Blanchot bears the burden of this despair with heroic impassivity. I do not mean to deny that his work is also celebratory, but what it celebrates is literature's capacity to reveal the void, its Orpheus-like attempt to bring this nothingness "form, figure, and reality"—even if, by determining the void, it is bound to lose its grip on it and, by manifesting it, it really manifests only an allegory of its own botched attempts at manifestation. It is telling that Blanchot's readings of individual literary works—those of Beckett, Kafka, and Mallarmé, for example—so often seem to be saying the same thing, and to be saying it endlessly. At bottom, for Blanchot, each work is nothing but the site of a greater truth in which literature is overcome—or better, in which literature is revealed as the force of its own self-overcoming, the privileged producer of sad allegories of its own phenomenal and linguistic predicament.

# CHAPTER 4

# A Genesis of the New

*Deleuze*

> The abstract does not explain, but must itself be explained; and the aim
> is not to rediscover the eternal or the universal, but to find the conditions
> under which something new is produced (creativeness).
>
> GILLES DELEUZE AND CLAIRE PARNET, *Dialogues*

Since the birth of Kantian aesthetics, the central question that has had
literature, and indeed all art, in its grips is the question of the new.
How is it that new forms or new works arise within a causal history,
or within an existing use of language, and at the same time effect a
rupture with that history or that language?

In chapter 1, I offered a reading of romanticism that went beyond
characterizing it simply as a will to system, one seeking the organic
unity of mind and nature, form and matter. Nor did I characterize it
solely as a will to fragmentation, paradox, or self-critique. Rather,
what interested me, and what would arguably be most accurately cap-
tured by the term *romanticism*, is the tension constitutive of these
apparently polar interpretations. Specifically, I argued that this tension structuring romanticism stems from the need to address a perceived conflict in Kant's philosophical system between the necessity
of the natural world and the freedom of the moral subject. The enterprise of literature, as it was reimagined in German romanticism, was
charged with the task of addressing this philosophical problem, while
the literary work became the site and manifestation, not of the problem's solution, but of its continual and unresolved reinscription.

Attempting to reconcile necessity and freedom, form and formation, the romantic literary work was to become the new locus of the
self-reflective absolute. Yet the very logic that would bestow autonomy
on literature and grant it privileged access to the absolute guaranteed
precisely the perpetual failure of this project. For the romantics, literature attained the status of the absolute when, in its formal autonomy,

it became the site of its own self-surpassing. Yet this could amount to nothing less than literature's rediscovery of its position as a fragment, or as an exemplary moment within this absolute, and consequently of its true fulfillment in self-annihilation. In other words, the absolutization of literature led directly to the absolutization of literature's status *as fragment*. Perhaps no better example of this logic can be found than Hegel's treatment of the aesthetic, where the artwork (of which poetry serves as the highest example) takes on an explicitly mediating function, negotiating between the immediacy of the sensible world and the infinite, intelligible domain of spirit.[1] For Hegel, famously, "art, considered in its highest vocation, is and remains for us a thing of the past" (*Hegel's Aesthetics* 11).[2] That is, art is necessarily overcome by the movement of the self-unfolding absolute.[3]

I have shown that our received notion of the literary work is born from a clearly identifiable philosophical problem—the conflict of freedom and necessity—one representative of a dominant line in the history of philosophy, namely German Idealism. Even more than this, I have tried to demonstrate that the very terms in which we pose the questions "What is literature?" or "What is a literary work?" have been determined, if not overdetermined, by these conceptual resources. Gilles Deleuze writes that "a solution always has the truth it deserves according to the problem to which it is a response." His point is not that solutions are reflections of pregiven problems, but rather the opposite: that we ought to pose our problems with care, for the way a problem is constructed will determine in advance the parameters or sense of its possible solutions (*Difference and Repetition* [hereafter *DR*] 159). Let us take up this Deleuzian precept, then, that the task of critical thinking is to work on problems and not merely on solutions or concepts, which are epiphenomenal and may obscure their problematical origins (cf. Deleuze, *Bergsonism* 4–5). Such is the case with the concept of the literary work: in confronting the concept, we likewise confront a history that has dictated the terms in which its question can be posed, and which has limited in advance the sense of its possible answers.

In this chapter, I reconsider of some of the basic terms of the question. In the seemingly disparate positions outlined in the previous chapters—namely, in the organic metaphor controlling the New Critics' conception of the literary work, and in the negativity that defines Blanchot's—we discovered that what is lacking in both is a positive, genetic account of the *difference* between literary form and authorial intention, or between form and its causal context. Both positions remain stuck in their attempts to account for the new on the basis of the already-given. Previously, Deleuze's work provided the terms of a critique; now I would like to explore the resources it offers for a positive alternative. Deleuze is, above all, a philosopher of the new who holds fast to the task of thinking the genesis of the new.[4] System and freedom are reconfigured in his work in a way that has much to contribute to a concept of the literary.

While Deleuze is a prolific literary commentator, with important works on Proust, Kafka, and Sacher-Masoch, and essays on Beckett, Melville, D. H. Lawrence, Lewis Carroll, and Pierre Klossowski, it is not to these writings that I turn, but rather to the ontological investigations in his philosophical works, especially *Difference and Repetition* (1968), the major half of his *thèse d'état*, and which draws on arguments he develops in his readings in the history of philosophy. Culling insights from his earlier studies of Hume, Nietzsche, Bergson, and Spinoza, among others, *Difference and Repetition* stands as the most systematic and synthetic presentation of Deleuze's unique itinerary through the history of philosophy; and so, while Deleuze's own formulations will largely be my focus in what follows, it is not without awareness of their embeddedness in much more long-standing philosophical problems.

In his readings of literature, Deleuze tends to draw out those elements that are most useful in illustrating his philosophical concepts. Sensitive and original, these readings nevertheless often leave unaddressed the problematic status of literary discourse, the multiplicity and disparity of the competing claims that constitute the fabric of literary language. My own interest lies in elaborating a Deleuzian ontology of the literary object, which would have different implications for a treatment of literary language, as well as for an understanding of the integrity of a literary work, than might be glimpsed from Deleuze's own reading practices.

Drawing on Deleuze's more explicitly philosophical statements, then, I present my argument in the form of five theses on the literary object. Let me state them in aggregate before I develop each one in detail:

1.  Literary production is conditioned by problems.

2.  Literary production is a differentiating and individuating process.

3.  A work, once produced, remains relative to the problems it articulates.

4.  A work is distinct from the process that gives rise to it.

5.  Literary criticism is conditioned by problems.

## I. LITERARY PRODUCTION IS CONDITIONED BY PROBLEMS

The romantic notion of freedom, largely construed as a negative freedom or freedom from constraint, might be confronted with the notion of a problematic imperative. That is, the idea that an essential negativity must be the source of literary creation can be replaced by a positive conception of a literary problematic field. Consider the idea that literary works arise in response to *problems*.

The critical positions I examined in the previous chapters share a common enemy in what we might call overly deterministic accounts of literary creation. Both Brooks and Blanchot reject a crude historical determinism, as well as any treatment of an author's biography as a horizon for interpretation, all in the name of safeguarding literature's radical power for invention and novelty. Yet both critics' positions betray a common assumption about the nature of causation, and hence about the causal production of literature: since effects must resemble their causes (so they assume), if a literary work is causally determined, it will have to resemble its causes. In biological terms, this is a view of creation as a kind of *preformism*, the eighteenth-century belief that organisms developed from fully formed, miniature versions of themselves (cf. Deleuze, *DR* 251). Whether the cause of a work of literature is located in an idea, an intention, or a social-historical reality, we end up with the same result: a cause is thought to exist and to be mirrored in the work once the work is made. While the New Critics try to tame the messiness of the causal process by purging poetic intention of anything that is not already present in the finished work, Blanchot, on the other hand, avoids preformism by rejecting questions of causation altogether. Holding fast to the conviction that the truly new cannot be articulated in advance of its creation, and that the possibility of a work of art does not, and cannot, preexist its reality, Blanchot seeks the ultimate condition of artistic creation in the absence of all condition. For him, literary production is characterized by an essential negativity, a freedom from all of the intentional or deterministic structures that belong to the objective world. The work is without parentage; it can only be a matter of *creation ex nihilo*.

Yet the choice between preformism and spontaneous creation is a false choice, a choice premised on a reductive opposition between the Being and Non-Being of causation: between causes that must either be located in the realm of the full plenitude of Being, or else be declared wholly absent from the world as it is, so that only a negative power can be responsible for the event of artistic invention. The mis-step here lies in the assumption that Being and Non-Being are the only two possible modalities of creation. But if we reject this either/or in favor of a notion of the reality and productivity of *problems*—that is, in favor of an account of the *problematic genesis of literary works*— then we should discover resources for thinking the question of literary production without passing through the negative.

Deleuze's work will help us develop precisely this account of a problematic genesis. Lamenting the dubious alternative we have received from the history of philosophy with respect to Being and Non-Being, Deleuze pursues a different course: like Heidegger, he affirms the ontological status of questions or problems, and speaks of the "being of the problematic."[5] Problems, in other words, have their own modality.

Most fully elaborated in *Difference and Repetition* and the *Logic of Sense*, Deleuze's positive conception of problems is indebted to the French epistemological tradition, in particular to Henri Bergson's engagement with fundamental questions of metaphysics as well as with the history and philosophy of science.[6] Bergson rejects a posi-tivist account of science as proceeding from ready-made concepts in order to direct his attention to the genetic role of problems in con-cept formation. "Stating the problem is not simply uncovering," Berg-son argues; "it is *inventing*. . . . The effort of invention consists most often in raising the problem, in creating the terms in which it will be stated" (*Creative Mind* 51). Following Bergson, Deleuze seeks to over-turn the priority normally placed on solutions. "We are led to believe that problems are given ready-made," he writes, "and that they dis-appear in the responses or the solution. . . . We are led to believe that the activity of thinking . . . begins only with the search for solutions" (*DR* 158). Instead, Deleuze affirms a problematic register in which solutions acquire meaning and orientation. In problems, he argues, lies the very "genesis of the act of thinking" (158).

In this view, a problem is not the lack of a solution, but the genetic element from which a solution will be constructed. Since problems are formed within existing symbolic fields (Deleuze, *DR* 159), they determine their solutions with respect to those fields, and will remain embedded in their solutions rather than being cancelled by them. Inherence, properly speaking, is the only mode of existence of a prob-lem. "A problem does not exist apart from its solutions," Deleuze writes. "Far from disappearing in this overlay, however, it insists and persists in these solutions" (163). Instead of indicating a negative or merely subjective moment in knowledge, in short, a problem is fully positive and fully objective; it has the objective reality of a structure, "an ideational objectivity or a structure constitutive of sense" (*Logic of Sense* 121). Problems possess the same reality as linguistic or social structures, which inhere in their manifestations but are not exhausted by those manifestations.

What does it mean to say that literary works arise in response to problems? It means that these works articulate local transformations within already-existing ideational, symbolic, and affective fields. The problems to which they respond persist and remain embedded in them; they are expressed by those works without those works resembling them. Rather, certain elements of a problem are selected and "read" in the work that serves as its response. Literary production, in other words, is immanent to the fields of relations that condition a work and preexist it. Within these fields, a work constructs its problematic ground at the same time as it differentiates itself from that ground in the form of a solution. The construction of a problem, then, is a creative act of selection as much as it is of the work's own self-organization. The "expression" of a problem in a work is a reading, by the work, of the work's conditions.

Because problems are indeterminate in themselves and unique with respect to the works that express them, I am hesitant to offer examples in the abstract. But I would at least suggest that the joints of articulation between a work and its problematic field would include those places where the work inserts itself into literary history (but *which* history?), into a social field (but a field populated by *whom*?), into a set of institutional practices, and into an array of material practices (but *which* practices?). It would likewise include those places where the work selects and draws on quantities of sensations, impersonal affects, thoughts, images, linguistic structures, and tropological systems—all of which are determined by the role they play internal to the work, and hence can be accessed by a critic only through an act of assiduous reading.

While all of these orders remain bound to the work for their precise articulation, each can nevertheless be conceived apart from the work, and as constituted in itself by a series of differential relations. A linguistic order, for example, is constituted by the differential relations of ideal units, or phonemes, in addition to the manifestation of these relations in an actual language (Deleuze, *DR* 193). A sensation, to take another example, can be divided into differential "degrees" that allow us to speak of its increase or decrease (so that I might say I am in less pain today than I was yesterday; 223–36). A problematic field is a virtual structure traversed by multiple orders such as these; it is articulated internally (or "differen*ti*ated") by resonances among these orders as well as by their incommensurability.

We might recall Claude Lévi-Strauss's argument that myths arise in response to cultural contradictions. The structural problems of a people motivate the proliferation of stories.[7] Deleuze takes this treatment of structure a step further by arguing that *all* structures are inherently problematic. In his view, structures are not closed systems of binary relations; they are open, dynamic complexes saturated with disparate and mutually exclusive tendencies of multiple kinds. Because they comprise logical contradictions as well as multiple orders that are heterogeneous to one another, such structures cannot be lived, or at least lived all at once. They cannot be sustained by a single body, formed into a unitary work, or represented by a self-identical concept. It is the heterogeneity of a structure with respect to itself, its *excess* of meaning, we might say, that makes it a problem—that gives it the sense of an imperative or a task to be carried out, imbuing it with a dynamism that it transmits to its solution.

## 2. LITERARY PRODUCTION IS A DIFFERENTIATING AND INDIVIDUATING PROCESS

Where in the previous section I focused on the problematic conditions of the literary work, here I want to look more closely at the particular process that leads from the problem to the work. In particular, I will confront the schema of reflection that we found operative in the New Critical approach with the notion of a differential production, one in which the formation of the work from its problematic conditions depends on a process that is internally complex, differentiating, individuating, and nonteleological.

By insisting on the unity of poetic form, and at the same time by locating authorial intention wholly within the confines of the poem, New Criticism, as we have seen, succeeds in turning poetic aim and poetic form into mirror images of one another. Lacking in this approach, as I have argued, is any account of the genesis of the *difference* between form and intention, between what is intrinsic and extrinsic to the work, or between what is contingent and necessary to it. But the metaphysical assumptions of New Criticism—indeed, of any critical approach invested in the autonomy and unity of its object—cannot allow this account to be written. These assumptions have already foreclosed certain philosophical questions that are crucial to the debate at hand, questions such as What is determination? What is the nature of causation? and What is an entity?

Here, my divergence from New Criticism should not be understood as a simple rejection of organic metaphors in favor of structural-textual ones, for even organic processes can be described in terms of the productivity of problems (there are natural problems, biological problems, and so forth). Moreover, structural-linguistic models do not in themselves guarantee any escape from romanticism's metaphysical commitments. My argument does not, therefore, come down to a choice between organic and linguistic models. Rather, what matters is the challenge I wish to bring to the priority normally placed on any existing *product*—be it a work, organism, individual, or idea—over the ontological and transformative *processes* that give rise to it. A priority placed on products operates in any of those accounts that pretend to offer causal explanations while seeking an image of the cause in the already-given effect. Placing the effect back at the origin is the feat of the "circular logic" I identified in chapter 2, which turns form and intention into mirror images of one another. This same logic is also at work in those accounts that would reject any causal explanation. As I argued in chapter 3, negative accounts of creation partake in the same speculative logic that begins with the already-given in order to imagine its absence, thus eschewing questions of real genesis.[8]

In distinction from these positions, Deleuze pursues a genetic account of the real—that is, an account of the production of real effects that truly differ from their causes. Here his work shares concerns with the genealogical projects of Nietzsche and Foucault, each of whom seeks to demonstrate the complexity of historical causation, and so to explain the presence of effects that lie "worlds apart" from their origins (Nietzsche 77). In *Difference and Repetition*, however, Deleuze's interest lies not in the genealogy of historical events but in the genesis of ontological events—that is, in the question of how individual entities and ideas come into being. And it is this interest that leads him to the work of Gilbert Simondon. The importance of Simondon to Deleuze's thought has not fully received the attention it deserves in English-language scholarship, though it is crucial, as I hope to demonstrate.[9]

What Deleuze draws from Simondon is a theory of individuation: an account of how individual entities are differentiated from preindividual elements. For us, this will become a question of how literary works are determined with respect to their problems. To say that a work emerges from already-existing symbolic, affective, and material fields, as I did earlier, and to say that a work articulates a local transformation in these fields, is already to rely on a notion of individuation: works are individuated within existing problematic fields.

Let me begin by addressing Simondon's theory of individuation in more detail. Simondon's work on individuation provides an alternative to traditional accounts of determination; and what is more, it attempts to reverse the hierarchy under which determination is normally thought, a hierarchy that privileges the determined entity over its essential and sustained relation with the indeterminate elements that give rise to it (29). Individuation, then, proposes to think the priority and continuity of a differential process that precedes the constituted individual. Individuation attempts to think the genesis of the individual as well as of individuating differences. Going beyond the diversity of the given, it seeks a reason for this diversity, revealing a process of differentiation as "that by which the given is given" (cf. Deleuze, *DR* 222). As such, individuation signals the possibility of conceptualizing *the genesis of the new as such*. For genesis and the new are not opposed concepts, I want to argue, but demand to be thought together if either is to be thought to its full extent.

Simondon's doctoral thesis, *L'individuation à la lumière des notions de forme et d'information* (*Individuation in Light of Notions of Form and Information*), opens with a critique of the way individual beings have been conceived by the history of ontology.[10] Traditional approaches have privileged given phenomena over the movement of difference that gives rise to them, seeking to account for the being of the individual on the basis of already-constituted individuals. Simondon divides these approaches into two major camps. For one, being is a self-identical and self-sufficient substance, on whose surface individuals appear as precarious and contingent organizations (a view he associates with monism as well as atomism); for the other, being is conceived as a duality of form and matter, whose intersection produces individuals (hylomorphism; 1–2). These apparently divergent approaches are alike in their treatment of the individual: both seek a causal principle that would exist prior to the operation of individuation, one that would explain and govern the process of the

individual's formation. But this common perspective hides a fundamental presupposition, Simondon argues: "To account for the genesis
of the individual with its definitive characteristics, [both perspectives]
have to suppose the existence of a first term or principle, one that
bears within it the reason the individual is an individual and accounts
for its haecceity. But it remains to be shown how ontogenesis can have
a first term or principle as its condition: a term is already an individual, or at least something individualizable" (2, translation mine).[11]
That is, terms, causes, and principles must themselves be individuated
from the field to which they belong. In pretending to be able to pose
the question of the genesis of individual being, then, both monism
and hylomorphism offer a circular logic that proceeds from already-
constituted individuals to explanatory principles that can be thought
only on the basis of, and according to the image of, the individuals
for which they are supposed to account. In the hylomorphic schema,
for example, a principle of individuation is sought either in a form or
in a matter that preexists the form-matter relation, and has already
been isolated from other aspects of being (49). "To a certain extent,"
Simondon writes, "the notion of a *principle of individuation* comes
from a genesis that goes in the wrong direction, from an ontogenesis in reverse. . . . This very notion of 'principle' has the character of
something prefiguring constituted individuality, with the properties
that individuality will have when it is constituted" (2).[12]

We can see how Simondon's critique applies to the logic we discovered in New Criticism, where what was presented as an explanatory principle of literary creation—poetic intention—turned out to
be conceived in the image of the already-finished work. Literary genesis is thought in reverse, in New Criticism, on the basis of works
that already exist. Moreover, this view relies on a particular image
of intention: intention is conceived as a unitary and self-identical
animating principle, one whose formal coherence is a foregone conclusion because it will be mirrored in the formal coherence of the finished work. If the effect is unified, so this reasoning process goes, the
cause must be unified as well. What cannot be conceived here is any
notion of an intention that might be complex or divided against itself,
as, for example, one that drew on unconscious elements or contradictory cultural forces.

To right this account, and to address the conceptual blockage that
comes with according an ontological priority to already-constituted
works or individuals, Simondon argues that we need to conceive the

operation of individuation as anterior to notions of form, matter, or substance (27). As such, this operation must be capable of generating its own principle. That is, rather than thinking the genetic process on the basis of its outcome, the process itself—*individuation*—must be thought on its own terms as a self-conditioning operation (288).

If literary production is a self-conditioning operation, this means that it proceeds on its own terms, and not in the image of any final cause, or in accordance with any model or law that would be imposed on it from without. It determines its own criteria, inventing these criteria by actualizing them in a work of art. In this sense, every act of literary production is an experiment: it works on its problematic conditions at the same time as it sketches the horizon for their solution, staging the transformation between problem and solution in "a veritable theater of metamorphoses" (Deleuze, *DR* 56). Ultimately, in this theory of individuation—and unlike in Kant or the romantics— we find a vision of freedom in which freedom is not opposed to causal systems, but conceived wholly within their bounds. What we might call the autonomy of a work is no more than that work's unique determination of cultural and psychic processes that are wider than itself and that unfold according to their own necessary laws. We might thus seek the originality of a work, not in its rupture from the world that determines it, but in and through its determining problematic, which, in its excess of complexity, transmits to the work its degree of freedom and its event-like character.

### 3. LITERARY WORKS REMAIN RELATIVE TO THE PROBLEMS THEY ARTICULATE

In the preceding section, we saw that Simondon's theory of individuation seeks to account for the genesis of form from within a dynamic system of relations rather than from the imposition of an—already individuated—external model or transcendent principle. Here, I want to emphasize the fact that individuated forms achieve only a relative stability, one that remains bound to their problematic conditions.

First of all, individuation is not a process without remainder. In individuating itself, as Simondon argues, an individual does not divorce itself from its problematic state, but continues to transport certain preindividual potentials and tensions. Preindividual elements persist along with the individual, "because individuation does not exhaust the potentials of preindividual reality in one stroke" (4).[13]

Resolving certain tensions while preserving others in the form of a structure (5), the process of individuation also connects individuals to future problems, of which they will become genetic elements; individuals contain micro-operations of individuation within themselves, as well as participate in collective operations of individuation larger than themselves.

Moreover, individuation gives rise not only to determinate individuals but to dynamic structures that accompany the emergence of these individuals, providing them with sense, orientation, and duration.[14] Individuation always gives rise to relations to a milieu, forming an individual-environmental complex.[15] "What individuation makes appear," Simondon writes, "is not just the individual but the individual-milieu couple" (4).[16] Because the individual constitutes itself in an active exchange with its milieu, the system in which it is articulated cannot be said to be extrinsic to it any more than intrinsic; "it is associated with it; it is its associated milieu" (68).[17] The individual invents its relations as it invents itself as a support for these relations; thus to comprehend the emergence of the individual is to comprehend "the genesis or constitution of relation itself" (Toscano 138). In Simondon's terms, "what is truly and essentially the individual . . . is the active relation, the exchange between the extrinsic and the intrinsic. . . . The intrinsic, the interiority of the individual would not exists without the continuous operation of relation which is continuous individuation" (68).[18] The individual is not a self-sufficient term participating in a form-matter relation that preexists it, but "the theater and the agent of a relation" (68),[19] actively constituting itself as it actively relates itself, and sheltering its relations with a relative degree of consistency and a residue of problematic potential. In this way, an individual cannot even be said to abide within its own limits, but rather "to constitute itself at these limits" (68, italics mine).

Following these arguments, we might replace the romantic conception of literary form, which depends on the interiority, self-reflection, and closure of the work, with the notion of a relative consistency that constitutes itself at its own limits. We know that the critical tradition has invented myriad ways to account for the integrity of literary form, many of them contradictory, and that it has attempted to explain the coherence of the literary work with metaphors that range from the organic to the structural. Yet what the majority of these accounts have in common is their reliance on a metaphysics that has decided in advance the nature of determination and its priority over the creative processes that give rise to it, thus remaining stuck in oppositions between Being and Non-Being, autonomy and heteronomy, freedom and necessity. A differential ontology—that is, an ontology that privileges constitutive relations over entities—can offer an alternative account of a work's organization because it entails a different conception of organization as such. Namely, the self-identity presumed to be the only possible basis for a work's cohesion can be replaced with a notion of form as a synthesis and a structuring of differential relations. Here differences are not annihilated or overcome but perpetuated and made to communicate, so that they can also be said to open up the work to its own non-difference with its outside. In this view, the work is neither an autonomous subject, as the romantics imagine it, existing in and for itself, nor is it a heteronomous object, complying with an external law or a causal system that would determine it. Rather, the work marks the process of differentiation and transformation that gives rise to it. Its consistency is an effect among other effects; its coherence is not a principle of composition but "the 'effect' of [its] multiplicity and of its disconnected parts" (Deleuze, *Proust* 163).

Literary production entails the production of the new from within an immanent field of differences, which means that the process is not only genetic (productive) but *heterogenetic* (its production is differential).[20] A heterogenetic system is an open system, one in which "structure is not at all defined by an autonomy of the whole, by a preeminence of the whole over its parts," as Deleuze writes; "structure is defined, on the contrary, by the nature of certain atomic elements which claim to account both for the formation of the wholes and for the variation of their parts" (*Desert Islands* 173). This is a view of structure that avoids the abstract opposition of the one to the multiple, unity to plurality, stasis to genesis, conceiving instead of relations that cohere only insofar as any division would entail a qualitative change of state (cf. Deleuze, *Bergsonism* 38). Its consistency, in other words, is relative to its transformations and determines their threshold. Thus we can refer provisionally to what is "internal" and "external" to a literary work only to the extent that the work—insofar as every work is *reading* its problems and will in turn be *read* as a problem in its own right—is the site of an active negotiation and exchange between its own internality and externality. Because of this exchange, what is relevant to a given reading will always be subject to argument, to the particular arguments that constitute the activity of criticism.

Consider, in particular, the example of genre as a "heterogenetic" element of a literary work. Is it properly internal or external to the work? Properly, neither: it may be grasped as an "internal" problem that the work transforms into a solution, just as it may function as a set of "external" constraints or conventions, themselves subject to change on the basis of an accumulation of repeated elements, or a shift in institutional investments. This example of genre should also help illuminate the significance for my argument of a theory of reading. From one point of view, a work (Beckett's *Endgame*, for example) might be understood to respond in its unique way to a problem of genre (tragedy, let us say). For another reading or another point of view (for a contemporary critic writing a theory of tragedy), the same genre might be grasped as an individual in its own right, while the genre's problematic element might be identified as the tensions among the cultural conventions and particular works (Beckett's included) that the genre emerges to resolve.[21] In either case, the object in question is not given, but must be constructed. A genre's external milieu (for example, an institution, a journal, or a critical practice), moreover, is likewise not an indifferent, homogeneous space in which the genre comes to be inscribed, but an emergent dimension of the genre itself, that which provides the genre with dimensionality and sense.

In "The Law of Genre," Derrida similarly describes genre as being neither wholly "internal" nor "external" to a work, but the emphasis of his argument departs from my own. In his essay, which claims to be at once a reading of Blanchot's *The Madness of the Day*, a response to Lacoue-Labarthe and Nancy's *Literary Absolute*, and a meditation on problems of literary genre and sexual difference, Derrida reveals a series of constitutive paradoxes informing traditional conceptions of genre. On the one hand, genre is thinkable only according to notions of purity, law, and participation, he argues, while on the other hand, genre is always marked by impurity, exception, and nonbelonging ("Law of Genre" 59). No text instantiates the law of its genre perfectly; no text is without genre; and no genre belongs to itself as a member (in other words, a theory of the novel is itself not a novel, despite what Friedrich Schlegel hoped; 65). Derrida's emphasis on impurity and nonbelonging is aimed at dismantling genre as a totalizing concept or a priori category; the thrust of his argument is critical. My own argument diverges from Derrida's by taking this so-called nonbelonging as a point of departure in order to seek the positive, differential, and ultimately ontological process that gives rise to it. What I describe as the active exchange of inside and outside is not a "contamination," in the terms of my argument, but a positive and necessary condition of production, one in which what is essential to a work includes its generic and social-historical outside. My argument will thus not conclude with the assertion of an impossibility of classification—an assertion that, I fear, is too easily mistaken for a merely empirical problem (in other words, mistaken to mean that the concept of genre holds in theory but presents problems in practice). Rather, I am seeking a positive account for the way things hang together in the first place—works, genres, and institutions alike—an account of classification that can describe the minimal consistency of an individual for a certain amount of time.

We might say, in sum, that literary production should be grasped not only genetically but "ecologically," in the sense that the individuation of a work from its preindividual problematic defines its external relations no less than its internal dynamisms (see Deleuze, *DR* 216). A literary work distinguishes itself from its problematic field, selecting linguistic, sensory, and ideational elements, but at the same time it articulates itself with respect to external environments, such as genres, institutions, markets, and literary histories. It individuates the literary-historical space in which it turns, casting light on the features of this space as a means of throwing itself into relief.

## 4. A WORK IS DISTINCT FROM THE PROCESS THAT GIVES RISE TO IT

I have described literary production as a heterogenetic process. Such a process does not coincide with itself but is traversed by exteriority, and results in the existence of determinate works. In other words, what ends up being produced will be heterogeneous not only to its causal conditions but also to the very process that gives rise to it. Earlier, I examined the complex genesis of a literary work from its problematic conditions, and I emphasized the priority of this process over the works that result from it, arguing that literary production needs to be grasped as a self-conditioning process. In this section, I want to make a corollary point, one that may seem obvious at first but that I think is important: literary production results in the existence of determinate works. That is, the particular notion of production I am interested in here does not entail the mere celebration of process over product, flux over fixity. Rather, it must be able to grasp the transformation that *differentiates* process and product in the first place. Let us look more closely, then, at that particular aspect of this process that articulates, demarcates, and distinguishes.

In chapter 3 we saw how Blanchot and his inheritors seek to account for the newness of literary creation by invoking the category of possibility, in order then to hold the work at a distance from any possibility that would prefigure it. According to this logic, creation is either dominated by an already-given representation, or else must appear as a radical break with representation, falling outside of all conceptual determination. At best the work is determined negatively, while the genesis of the illusion of representation—that is, the illusion of the work's possibility—is never explained to us. The impasse in Blanchot's argument may well be the category of possibility itself, as I have argued, and the opposition between the possible and the real that this category requires. "Every time we pose the question in terms of possible and real," Deleuze argues, "we are forced to conceive of existence as a brute eruption, a pure act or leap which always occurs behind our backs and is subject to a law of all or nothing" (*DR* 211). The problem is that the zero-sum game of opposition and reflection on which the possible depends attributes no power of invention to existence itself.

But existence, not idea, is the domain of the aesthetic. In place of the conceptual pair "possible/real," then, the notions of problem/solution allow us to think a causal process that ultimately entails an experimentation in the real, not the adherence to an idea or preconceived model. In experimenting, literary production "breaks with resemblance as a process no less than it does with identity as a principle," in Deleuze's terms (*DR* 212). The existence of a work does not resemble its possibility; its coming-into-appearance is a genuine act of creation (cf. *DR* 212).

To focus on existence as the domain of creation, we need a notion of the production of works that have determinate existence in space and time. Literary production is not an infinite activity or limitless experience, but one that culminates in actual works. Here we might draw inspiration from an apposite essay by Pierre Macherey, "Philosophy as Operation," in which Macherey makes a similar point about the production of works of philosophy. He distinguishes between "operative" and "inoperative" philosophical activity—between activity that ends up producing works and activity that does not. Macherey traces the "inoperative" back to Aristotle's treatment of *praxis* in the *Nicomachean Ethics*, where Aristotle opposes *praxis* not to *theoria*, as one might assume, but to *poeisis*, where *poeisis* involves "the production of a work . . . a technical activity exercised with a view to a goal external to the procedure that it pursues" (Macherey, "Philosophy as Operation" 28).[22] *Praxis*, on the other hand, whose privileged example is the very activity of living, is defined as activity for its own sake. *Praxis* is "inoperative," in these terms, because it does not produce an object outside of itself.

We have already witnessed this opposition between *poeisis* and *praxis* in the romantic treatment of the literary work, which thrived on the tensions between form and the overcoming of form, poetry and process, conscious intention and natural development. Indeed, the notion of the absolute subject in post-Kantian philosophy, or the notion of organic form, so crucial to the romantics as well as the New Critics, was meant to reconcile such oppositions. The metaphor of the work as organism treats the work as both subject and object of its own development, a totalizing process whose end lies in itself, a form that "shapes itself as it develops itself from within," so that "the fullness of its development is one and the same with the perfection of its outward form" (Coleridge, "Shakespeare's Judgment" 321). Analogous to a natural process, the work is supposed to be the source of its own value and necessity.

Like the exercise of practical reason in Kantian ethics, however, *praxis*, or an activity that exists wholly in and for itself, tends toward an extreme formalism (Macherey, "Philosophy as Operation" 29–30). Measured only against an internal principle, such activity is freed from the material interests and causal relations of the world, and is thus untroubled by the constraint of any external determination or condition, so that "in its action, [it] relates to nothing except itself" (33, translation modified; "La philosophie comme opération" 73). This notion of an activity freed from constraint likewise lies at the heart of the romantic treatment of the literary work: external conditions are subordinate to the interminable unfolding of the work's meaning; literature is made into a kind of infinite interiority or absolute subject.

In lieu of this putatively free activity that coincides only with itself, that is, in lieu of this romantic attempt to overcome the duality of *poeisis* and *praxis* through the metaphor of the organism or the absolute subject, I am arguing for a notion of organization that is traversed by objectivity and exteriority, one that determines, and is determined by, external entities. Such an organization is "operative" insofar as it produces objects, and insofar as its own objective status allows it to be articulated with respect to wider processes. It does not emanate from a transcendent principle or intentional subject, but it articulates itself within a structure. The fact that a heterogenetic process results in determinate *works* is what allows this process to effectuate itself with respect to other already-existing works; heterogenesis gives rise to actual, determinate beings that interact with and respond to other actual, determinate beings. Moreover, such a process does not realize some potential that is already given at its origin. It invents solutions and acts retrospectively on its own conditions, "transforming itself and modifying its conditions at the same time as it carries out its effects," as Macherey writes. This process "is by no means prefigured and somehow pre-established in the system of its conditions. . . . But it effectuates itself," producing works whose existence in turn "radically transforms the . . . field within which they have been produced." It "takes part" in an objective system of relations ("Philosophy as Operation" 34, translation modified; "La philosophie comme opération," 74).[23]

This transformative process of production that acts on its conditions no less than its effects ultimately derives from what Deleuze calls a "heterogeneity in the production mechanism" of being (*DR* 212). Such a heterogeneity extends from the contradictory imperatives of a problem, to the transformative processes that work on this problem, to the actual solutions that respond to the problem without resembling or reflecting it. Heterogenesis is what ensures that there is no emanation of beings from an originary principle, no ontological preformism (Toscano 179). It produces a nonresemblance between cause and effect, while yet linking the two inextricably. This is a differential process culminating in works that are neither reducible to, nor even reflective of, the process that gives rise to them.

To underestimate the differential nature of this process is to make a mistake common to novice writers no less than to poor critics: the former think they can convey joy or doubt, for example, by writing about a joyful character or a doubtful event, while the latter think they can access a writer's experience or a set of historical circumstances through their own experience of a work. Both cases entail a confusion of cause and effect, for what goes into a work does not resemble the effect it will have on a reader. What I mean to say is that literature is transformative; it transforms the very elements that constitute it, so that the important thing is not, or not only, to recognize its effects, but to follow the asymmetrical and transformative process that produces these effects. As Proust observes on the resemblance of writing to life, "Certain comparisons which are false if we start from them as premises may well be true if we arrive at them as conclusions" (*Remembrance of Things Past* 3: 936; *A la recherche du temps perdu* 2288). All literature is Proustian in this sense: it records the dynamic production of meaning, and demonstrates the distance between its own premises and its conclusions.

## 5. LITERARY CRITICISM IS CONDITIONED BY PROBLEMS

"The modern work of art has no problem of meaning, it has only a problem of use," Deleuze writes provocatively in the re-edition of *Proust and Signs*. "To the logos, organ and organon whose meaning must be discovered in the whole to which it belongs, is opposed the anitlogos, machine and machinery whose meaning . . . . . . depends solely on its functioning" (146). Literature as machine: this characterization relocates the site of literary truth from the level of cause to the level of effects. In a view of literature as machine, truth or meaning—the object of literary criticism—is neither waiting to be discovered, nor created ex nihilo, but produced on the basis of a problematic encounter.[24]

In his collaborations with Guattari later in his career, Deleuze gives us a specific term for an individuated, literary multiplicity that constitutes itself at its own limits: an assemblage (*un agencement*). I would like to turn briefly to the notion of the assemblage here, because the pragmatic terrain on which it is articulated can help us approach the question of the literary object from another direction. As we shift from questions of production to those of reception, the assemblage can show us a path from ontological concerns to epistemological ones—that is, from the question "What is a work?" to "How is it apprehended or known?"

In their introduction to *A Thousand Plateaus*, Deleuze and Guattari contend that books are multiplicities of the order of "assemblages," "rhizomes," or "little machines." From Deleuze's revision of *Proust and Signs* (1964, revised 1973) to Deleuze and Guattari's *Kafka* (1975) onward, machines and assemblages come to characterize the activity of writing as well as the apparatus of the book. Specifically, they characterize the production and organization of signs on the basis of problematic encounters. Assemblages can thus give us a way to think about interpretation as a productive activity, one constitutive of literary works no less than of works of criticism.

Assemblages entail the double articulation of a form and a content, as well as a form and a substance, both with respect to a milieu that Deleuze and Guattari qualify as a "territory":[25] "On a first, horizontal axis, an assemblage comprises two segments, one of content, the other of expression. On the one hand it is a machinic assemblage of bodies, of actions and passions, an intermingling of bodies reacting to one another; on the other hand it is a collective assemblage of enunciation, of acts and statements of incorporeal transformations attributed to bodies. Then on a vertical axis, the assemblage has both territorial sides, or reterritorialized sides, which stabilize it, and cutting edges of deterritorialization, which carry it away" (A Thousand Plateaus 88). Assemblages "assemble" (agencer) with other assemblages, and can be broken down into multiplicities of smaller assemblages. Regarding the activity of writing, Deleuze asserts that the assemblage is in fact the minimum unit of reality, which is to say that there is no simple unit because the "minimum" is already complex and relational: "The minimum real unit is not the word, the idea, the concept, or the signifier, but the assemblage. It is always an assemblage which produces utterances. Utterances do not have as their cause a subject which would act as a subject of enunciation, any more than they are related to subjects as subjects of utterance. The utterance is the product of an assemblage— which is always collective, which brings into play within us and outside us populations, multiplicities, territories, becomings, affects, events" (Deleuze and Parnet, Dialogues 2: 51). That is, a statement is individuated from a collective linguistic field, that field being the real cause of the statement as well as of the statement's subjective (or expressive) dimension. Likewise, its objective (or content) dimension is a product of the trajectories of populations, affects, and events that traverse it.

The components of any assemblage are, in sum, a battery of variables individuated from multiple fields simultaneously: linguistic, material, social, territorial, emotional, evental. Thus "an assemblage, in its multiplicity, necessarily acts on semiotic flows, material flows, and social flows simultaneously (Deleuze and Guattari, A Thousand Plateaus 22–23). The notion of the assemblage ultimately disrupts the traditional division of subject and object imposed by representational schemas. "There is no longer a tripartite division between a field of reality (the world) and a field of representation (the book) and a field of subjectivity (the author),"

Deleuze and Guattari write (23). Rather, "objective" and "subjective" become reciprocally determining. They are internal dimensions of the work-assemblage, produced on the basis of its variables, just as we saw earlier that the individual and its milieu are *both* dimensions of individuation, produced on the basis of a preindividual problematic.

We might say that an assemblage not only comprises preindividual germs of subjects and objects *in itself*, but also produces a subjective and an objective dimension *for itself*. The categories of subject and object are not errors for Deleuze, to be tossed aside once and for all in favor of the truth of pure multiplicities. Rather, they are transcendental illusions. The only so-called error is the priority of these categories, for subjects and objects are produced by multiplicities as features of the extensive world; they persist alongside these multiplicities as their effects, and ask to be analyzed as such. The assemblage is that unit of analysis: its subject and object do not preexist the operations that produce them and that bind them to the particularities of these processes.[26]

This notion of assemblage means that the author does not preexist a work, but is constituted as the subject of something that she experiences as a problem, and thus belongs to the problem as its function or emergent element (Deleuze, *DR* 199). The author does not merely put the problem to work, but is herself put to work by the problem; the two can be understood to be reciprocally determining on the basis of common genetic elements. The same may be said about the "objective" world represented in the work: the world is constituted as an object only insofar as it is read as a problem. And just as literary works construct the problems to which they respond, so does criticism construct its literature. Reading, in this view, is always an act of creation.

Conceived along these lines, criticism is a form of writing that constructs the literary object to which it responds. This is not to say that the reader is the "true" author of a literary work, as in some exaggerated version of reader-response criticism. Rather, it is to advocate for the distinctiveness of critical knowledge. We can find a version of this argument in Macherey's *A Theory of Literary Production* (1966), in which Macherey identifies the productivity of acts of knowing: "The act of knowing is not like listening to a discourse already constituted, a mere fiction which we have simply to translate. It is rather the elaboration of a new discourse. . . . Knowledge is not the discovery or reconstruction of a latent meaning, forgotten or concealed. It is something newly raised up" (6). Criticism, then, does not seek to reiterate or reproduce its object, but to produce it in the first place, manifesting this object in a new discourse. "Literary criticism," Macherey continues, "is a certain form of knowledge, and has an object, which is not a given but a product of literary criticism" (7).

The irreducible difference between writer and work ultimately rests on a more profound difference, one that lies not between two different literary works, nor even between two different points of view, but between two aspects of the selfsame object. The work is already different from what it is; it draws on the disparate trajectories that make up its problematic element, and it makes the disparate communicate, organizing it in a work of difference. Criticism is secondary to this difference that is already there.

The critic may bring out the difference in a literary work, in sum, but this is possible only if the work already differs in itself, exists as something essentially constituted by self-difference (cf. Macherey, *Theory of Literary Production* 7). Constitutive difference in the work is what makes it possible for the work to be grasped in continuity with its historical or linguistic context, yet without its being reducible to that context. And it is what allows the critic to produce an object of critical knowledge that is at once continuous with its literary original, and at the same time distinct from it.

In the chapters that follow, I take up a series of readings inspired by this theory of the work of difference. Looking at three major twentieth-century novels or sets of novels—Beckett's trilogy *Molloy, Malone Dies* and *The Unnamable*, Proust's *A la recherche du temps perdu*, and Stein's *The Making of Americans*—I show how each text constitutes a unique response to the problem of literary production after romanticism. Each offers a unique way of thinking about the form of difference, and about the productivity of differential relations. Focusing in particular on rhetorical figures as examples of such relations—on figures of disjunction, noncoincidence, and excess, from the figure of self-correction in Beckett's work, to the exaggerated claims in Proust's novel, to the productive repetition in Stein's prose—I seek to uncover the potential these figures have for generating distinctive forms of systems, forms irreducible to those prescribed by a still regnant romanticism.

I begin with Beckett's texts, for the question of how to "go on," in his terms—or how to write after the monumental and exhaustive works of Joyce and Proust that came before him—puts Beckett in the position of speaking starkly about the possibilities of late-mod-. ernist innovation.

# CHAPTER 5

# From Figure to Fissure

*Self-Correction in Beckett's* Molloy, Malone Dies, *and* The Unnamable

C'est notre image—au miroir de l'absolu littéraire—qui nous est renvoyée. Et cette vérité massive qui nous est assénée: nous ne sommes pas sortis de l'époque du Sujet.

PHILIPPE LACOUE-LABARTHE AND JEAN-LUC NANCY,
*L'absolu littéraire*

"On n'a pas besoin d'essayer, ça va tout seul."

SAMUEL BECKETT, *L'innommable*

"Where now? Who now? When now?" Samuel Beckett's *The Unnamable* begins. "Unquestioning. I, say I," or in French, simply "Dire je" (291; *L'innommable* 7).[1] In this interrogative opening that acknowledges, at least formally, the traditional requirements of beginning a novel with place, time, and character (Clément 125), the question "Who?" is underscored by what is proposed as its "unquestioning" response. But what does it mean "to say I" in the context of Beckett's trilogy? Who says "I"?

This question of "saying I" will guide my approach to Beckett's *Molloy, Malone Dies*, and *The Unnamable* (1951–53). It is a question that needs to be referred to both a literary and a philosophical history, as well as one that marks a point of entry into a set of texts that has been treated as a "work" and at the same time, like all works, constitutes its own response to the question of what a work of literature is. The text's self-presentation and self-allegorization is another sort of "saying I," a "saying I" dominated by themes of failure, silence, passivity, and ignorance.[2] Yet in this work that explicitly thematizes the perils of writing, I would argue that what is at issue is precisely the referentiality and self-referentiality of the discourse. In what follows, I demonstrate how and why the trilogy's actual functioning cannot correspond to the compelling images it offers of itself, and I argue, ultimately, that it is in the very discrepancy between the two—between what the text says and what it does—that the text's most productive operation lies. In particular, I turn to a study of Beckett's rhetoric to show how the trilogy's noncoincidence with itself is organized in language and imbued with meaning and emotion.

Both formally and thematically, as the majority of its critics acknowledge, Beckett's trilogy raises questions about the classical conception of the subject, about the aesthetic aims of writing, and about what constitutes the stable, coherent contours of a literary work. The traditional goals of the novel as a genre—let us say, an accumulation of knowledge about human life, a creation of realistic characters, and a display of linguistic or literary-cultural prowess—are thwarted from the outset. Yet what is less apparent is that those readings that attempt to explore a negative or critical relation to the concepts of the "subject" and the "work" through Beckett's texts risk reinstating these very concepts through their own processes of reading. Readings that approach Beckett's trilogy as a kind of critical allegory for its own undoing—or as governed by what we might call an "aesthetics of failure"—might be appealing, but they are ultimately unsatisfactory. They are unsatisfactory both because they reinstate at another remove those totalizing concepts of subject and work that they seek to criticize, and because they neglect the very operation by which this aesthetics is produced. Before confronting the limitations of these readings and considering an alternative, let us begin by examining the images that the text offers as characterizations of itself.

FIGURE

Written first in French in 1947–50, and subsequently translated by the author into his native English (*Molloy* with the help of Patrick Bowles), *Molloy*, *Malone Dies*, and *The Unnamable* belong to the most intensely productive period of Beckett's life—"the siege in the room," as Beckett called it (Bair 346)—where from the end of the Second World War to the winter of 1950, the fairly unknown Irish writer produced four *nouvelles* ("La fin," "L'expulsé," "Premier amour," "Le calmant"), four novels (*Mercier et Camier*, *Molloy*, *Malone meurt*, *L'Innommable*), and two plays (*Elutheria*, published posthumously, and *En attendant Godot*), in addition to several poems, translations, and a critical article on the painting of the van Velde brothers for *Cahiers d'Art* ("Le monde et le pantalon"). This is the period in which Beckett first began to compose entirely in French, a decision that coincided with a full-fledged pronominal shift: for the first time, Beckett began to write in the first person.

Maurice Blanchot directs his attention to this first-person narration when he asks, in his seminal 1953 review of the postwar trilogy, "Who is speaking in the books of Samuel Beckett? What is this tireless 'I' that seemingly always says the same thing?" ("Where Now? Who Now?" 210). The answer changes depending on which portion of which text we are reading. *Molloy* is in two parts: in the first, Molloy says "I," narrating his confused and increasingly crippled movements toward his mother's room, where he is now writing his story; in the second, Jacques Moran, Molloy's uncanny twin, says "I," narrating his obscure pursuit of Molloy and eventual degeneration. In *Malone Dies,* we discover that both Molloy and Moran, along with characters from Beckett's other works, may be mere fictions invented by the aged Malone, who lies dying in a room—likely an asylum or old-age home—telling himself stories to pass the time and populating them with characters whose condition seems to mirror his own. In *The Unnamable,* we move into the narrative voice of the one who seems to be responsible for inventing Malone as well as Molloy and all the rest—someone or something that says "I" but occasionally "we," someone named (or naming) Mahood, or Basil, or something named Worm, if Worm is even capable of words. This narrative is partly about the impossibility of speaking of oneself ("Strange task, which consists in speaking of oneself" [Beckett, *Three Novels* 311]), of having to mingle a pure narrative of self-expression with references to things and people in the world ("Me, utter me, in the same foul breath as my creatures?" [300]), and partly about the impossibility of ceasing to speak, though the speaker seems to want nothing more ("strange hope, turned towards silence and peace" [311]). To continue is the problem, but ceasing is impossible: the narrator bears witness to "this obligation, and the quasi-impossibility of fulfilling it" (320). And the trilogy ends this way, with a three-page-long and lurching sentence, seeking some termination point but culminating instead with the stuttering formula "You must go on, I can't go on, I'll go on" (414).

The trilogy has been described as a poioumenon, a work that narrates its own process of creation,[3] but even as it speaks of such creation, its speakers see their bodies and personalities gradually disintegrate. The precariousness of the "I" is foregrounded, in sum, through speakers whose bodily and psychological integrity remains uncertain, and whose discontinuous narratives are punctuated with ignorance, silence, and ellipses. In the first novel of the trilogy, Molloy is nearly blind and mute, struggling with memory. On the way to his mother's room, the toes of either his left or right foot go missing, one of his legs is gradually shortening, and even his pneumatic bicycle horn is "suffocating." His legs are bad, stiffening like his crutches; his teeth are bad; his eyes are bad; he "bristle[s] with boils," sweats foully, drools, and "oozes urine, day and night" (at least uremia won't be the death of him, he reasons; 81). His memory is bad, so that he confuses the woman Lousse (or Sophie, or Mrs. Loy) with the only woman he has ever "rubbed up against" (Ruth, or Edith, or Rose), and both of them with his own mother (whose name he cannot remember). Yet he seems to desire a more profound disintegration still, longing for the earth to swallow him up (81); on sleeping in Lousse's garden, he writes, "And there was another noise, that of my life become the life of this garden as it rode the earth of deeps and wildernesses. Yes, there were times when I forgot not only who I was, but that I was, forgot to be. Then I was no longer that sealed jar to which I owed my being so well preserved, but a wall gave way and I filled with roots and tame stems" (49). With the eruption of roots and earth into the "sealed jar" of his person, Molloy certainly suggests an apt metaphor for the fragmentation of the modern subject.

Molloy is no more fixed for his pursuer Moran, for he might also be "Mollose," "Mollote," "Molloc" (the English text even proposes "Malone"). Pursuing his quarry, Moran gradually comes to resemble Molloy in his increasing mental confusion and physical disintegration—so much so that a few early critics have concluded that the pair must constitute two continuous halves of the same person whose journey is narrated out of order, so that Moran is the original protagonist and Molloy the "subconscious, antithetical self" into which Moran slowly deteriorates (Kern 10).

In *Malone Dies* we find that Malone shares certain infirmities with these previous protagonists, as if some free-floating parasite were traveling from one book to the next, and recalling Beckett's *Proust*, where a feature's passing from one of Proust's characters to the next is described as the metamorphosis of some "atavistic embryon" that has broken through its chrysalis (39)—terms more befitting a horror story, it would seem, than *A la recherche du temps perdu*. The breakdown of the physical self seems to be mirrored by a breakdown of identity and by a strange passage between selves. Malone, who like Molloy finds himself confined to a room without remembering his arrival, writes, in phrases nearly identical to Molloy's, "I do not remember how I got here. In an ambulance perhaps, a vehicle of some kind certainly" (*Three Novels* 183). He charts his deterioration, and, like Molloy, who felt himself merging with the garden soil, Malone too testifies to "times when I go liquid and become like mud," when his thoughts are "streaming and emptying away as through a sluice, to my great joy, until finally nothing remained" (225, 224). Waiting to die, Malone tells himself stories in the meantime, stories "neither beautiful nor ugly . . . calm . . . almost lifeless, like the teller" (180).

The characters of the trilogy present some awareness of the abyssal nature of these repetitions. Malone frequently refers to an "other," which might be the principal character of his stories, Macmann (formerly Saposcat), about whom Malone writes with the same stub of a pencil and in the same exercise book as he writes about himself (*Three Novels* 207). In fact, Beckett himself composed *Malone Dies* in just this sort of notebook.[4] Malone highlights the recursivity of this situation when he says, "I write about myself with the same pencil and in the same exercise-book as about him. It is because it is no longer I . . . but another whose life is just beginning" (207). Macmann turns out to have much in common not only with Malone but also with Beckett's other characters: like Molloy he is a wanderer and has the same trick of tying his hat to his overcoat with a piece of string (as the narrators in "La fin" and "Le calmant" do before them); like Murphy he has "gulls' eyes" (29). Such nightmarish recurrences of plot and character give one the sense of Beckett's having created a kind of alternate universe, where events are generated from the combination and recombination of a fixed set of narrative elements.

Among the mutations and repetitions in Beckett's works, however, the character who reoccurs with the most consistency is the narrative "I" (Clément 84). Simon Critchley describes Malone as "an identity minimally held together by a series of stories" (193), but it seems rather that the opposite is true: that the only thing uniting Malone's stories—fragmented, discontinuous, overlapping, and at times a little boring ("What tedium," even their author laments [*Three Novels* 189])—is the presumed continuity of the self of their narrator, which sustains interest in the narratives for the reflection they might cast on his person and situation. Malone suggests that he will tell stories in order to "pay less heed to himself," but this seems only to reinforce the sense that when Malone tells tales of other people and things, what he is "really" talking about is himself. More importantly, where bodies are broken and failing, the narrative "I" becomes the site of continuity, reassemblage, and synthesis.

Unlike the uncanny duo Molloy-Moran, whose relationship remains indeterminate within the confines of the first book, the reflection of Malone in his principal character Macmann ("son of Man") can be understood as the expression of the writer in his characters, an incarnation of the creator in his creation. Yet halfway through *Malone Dies*, Malone exclaims, looking forward to his demise, "Then it will be all over with the Murphys, Merciers, Molloys, Morans and Malones" (*Three Novels* 236), suggesting that not only Molloy and Moran but characters from Beckett's earlier novels (are these all "other Malones"?) may be mere fictions sprung from the mind of this ageless and impotent writer.

The character of Malone in the second book thus solves a problem set up in the first—that of the uncanny symmetry between Molloy's and Moran's respective journeys and degenerations—by relocating the narrative of both books in a space of interiority, Malone's mind, and by guaranteeing the narrative's coherency through recourse to the form of the subject, here the writer-hero. It is well known that the development of the individual and the historical form of the novel have long been intertwined, and that the concept of both emerged in roughly the same literary-historical period.[5] Yet perhaps even more significant than the novel's ties to the individual are its ties to interiority: both the French and the English novels have their beginnings in sustained psychological explorations, where the action of the plot is grounded in the mental space and narrative voice of their heroes and heroines.[6] Moreover, the form of the novel mirrors the conditions of its reception. Rising to prominence with the increased literacy rates of the middle class, the novel is distinct from other literary genres in that it has no historical ties to performance, only to solitary inscription and silent contemplation.[7]

In Beckett's trilogy, *Malone Dies* appears to alleviate the ambiguity of the origin of Molloy and Moran's strange relationship. It provides a supplemental point of reflection and serves as the middle term in a series of abyssal retreats into a mental space that can absorb and account for what came before it. But no sooner does Malone suggest, "You may say it is all in my head" than he adds, "and indeed sometimes it seems to me I am in a head and that these eight, no, six, these six planes that enclose me are of solid bone. But thence to conclude the head is mine, no, never" (*Three Novels* 221). Is Malone, too, the product of another's mental machinations? Just as Malone appears ex post facto as the author and originator of Molloy, the unnamed hero of *The Unnamable*, in turn, seems to take credit for authoring Malone and all the rest, whom he calls "these sufferers of my pains" (303).

In this way, *The Unnamable* represents a culmination of the narrative logic established in the first two books, in this series of monologic meditations where "each successive volume . . . consumes its predecessor, swallowing and negating it" (Banville 20). Moreover, the motif of physical degeneration reaches new lows here. The narrator, who may or may not be Mahood, is at first short of an arm and a leg, managing on his crutches only because he has "retained sufficient armpit" (*Three Novels* 321). Later, nothing remains of him but a head, torso, and defunct penis, together "stuck like a sheaf of flowers in a deep jar" (327), adorned with lights and posted outside a Paris restaurant. Ultimately this character is reconceived as Worm, a shapeless heap, naked, hairless, with a giant head grown out of an ear, faceless but for "a wild equine eye, always open" (356–57). Here the character doubling and self-reflexive narration seem to fuse into nearly total indistinction, the distance between narrator and narrated collapses, and the possibility of an endless generation of new speakers disturbs our sense of closure and our reliance on the "I" as a principle of this closure.

In short, on the one hand, we seem to waver between a successive series of points of reflection and an ever-widening field of elements to be subsumed. Yet, on the other hand, how do we explain the nature of Beckett's images: not consumption and mastery, but expulsion, uncertainty, and inability; not generation and proliferation befitting the creation of such a cast of characters and series of worlds, but images of enclosure, diminishment, deterioration, and disintegration?

In *The Unnamable,* as in *Malone Dies,* the idea of some continuity of the narrative voice, like the notion of Malone's authorship, not only logically holds together a series of fragmented stories by giving them a common origin, but also offers a figure or series of figures to represent the status of their integration. Beckett suggests an interchangeability between Malone's person and his "tepid" stories, "almost lifeless, like the teller" (*Three Novels* 180); and in all three novels, the activity of the central character's writing or speaking is thematized to the extent that each narrative, which more or less follows the novelistic tradition of taking its title from the name of its principal character, becomes a stand-in for its fictional author.[8] Malone, as first-person narrator, has no apparent existence outside of his own "saying I"—these "few lines to remind me that I too subsist" (283). The narrator of *The Unnamable*, who compulsively recites stories and compulsively comments on his own recitation, and even Molloy, whose story supposedly comes to us on sheets of paper exchanged for weekly sums, are likewise inseparable from the act of self-narration.

But what does it mean for figures like these to represent the act of writing or storytelling? More precisely, what does it mean for Beckett's work to seek—in this cast of confused, degenerate, and degenerating characters, this band of "miscreated puppets" (*Three Novels* 325) approaching their end or functioning somnambulistically in pieces, parts, and heaps, in some limbo beyond—images of the status of its own integrity and autonomy? The frustrated movements of these characters' broken-down adventures cannot be taken unproblematically as allegories of the work's composition. True, these novels are constructed from scenes of impoverishment, deterioration, dismemberment, and literal decomposition that suggest a metaphorical de-composition. They feature a hallucinatory series of M-named personalities that bleed confusedly into one another, a sequence of uncertain forms that suggest, perhaps, as Malone muses, "the forms are many in which the unchanging seeks relief from formlessness" (197). Yet it is not enough to assert that the dissolution of character is mirrored in problems of narrative form. We must ask: By what means is this allegory of writing produced?

## FAILURE

The notion that Beckett's work is representative of something like an "aesthetics of failure" has become a commonplace among Beckett's critics, with the majority drawing on his *Three Dialogues with Georges Duthuit* (1949) to support this reading.[9] The *Three Dialogues* is easily read as a companion piece to the trilogy, as it was written in the interval between the trilogy's second and third books; in fact, it has been treated as "the nearest thing we have to an explicit statement of [Beckett's] esthetic tastes or program" (Bersani, *Balzac* 301), even as constituting "a highly suggestive preface to the trilogy itself" (Trezise 7). And yet, such treatments are not at all certain, given the stated subject of the text and its theatrical presentation: the *Three Dialogues* stages a fragmentary conversation between Beckett and friend Duthuit on three contemporary painters, and is written in the form of a dramatic vignette.

In the *Dialogues* Beckett's persona announces a "fidelity to failure" in the work of Bram van Velde, by which he means that van Velde is "the first to admit that to be an artist is to fail, as no other dare fail" (125). Similarly, in Tal Coat's work he finds a "preference" for "the expression that there is nothing to express, nothing with which to express, nothing from which to express, no power to express, no desire to express, together with the obligation to express" (103). These statements have been used to support the argument that the aesthetic telos of Beckett's own work is some sort of failure, whether the failure of novelistic conventions, of literary form, of knowledge, of the mind-body relation, of life itself, of the referential function of language, or of language's general expressivity. In the French reception of Beckett, this reading coincides with the author's first emergence on the literary scene, where review articles by Blanchot and Georges Bataille heralded the work of the unknown Irish writer by praising, for example, the "absence of human feature" and "formless character of Molloy. . . . Only an incontinent flux of language could accomplish the feat of expressing such an absence" (Bataille, "Molloy's Silence" 132). Note that Bataille links the formlessness of a character directly to the formlessness of the language that describes him.

Major statements in English and German have been made in much the same vein. "Solitude, emptiness, nothingness, meaninglessness, silence—these are not the givens of Beckett's characters," Stanley Cavell writes of *Endgame*, "but their goal, their new heroic undertaking" (156). For Theodor Adorno, famously, "Meaning nothing becomes the only meaning" (252), and in a recent article, Terry Eagleton writes in powerful terms, "Beckett's art maintains a compact with failure. . . . Against fascism's megalomaniac totalities, he pits the fragmentary and unfinished" ("Political Beckett?" 70). In much the same way as these authors, a great deal of secondary literature tends to read Beckett's trilogy as an exercise in the successive impoverishment of language and meaning, a straining toward silence, absence, and formlessness—as if to take Beckett at his word when he states in a 1956 *New York Times* interview, "At the end of my work there's nothing but dust—the namable. In the last book—*The*

*Unnamable*—there's complete disintegration. No 'I,' no 'have,' no 'being.' No nominative, no accusative, no verb. There's no way to go on" (Shenker 148). But of course Beckett did go on, producing short prose pieces, radio plays, theater plays (including *Endgame*, *Krapp's Last Tape* [1958], and *Happy Days* [1961]), television plays, four more novels, and a film. I do not mean to be flippant here, but rather to point out that we do not have to read Beckett's remarks literally in order to take them seriously. They may better be taken, not as a statement on the finished work, but as a window onto the work's motivating problematic. This problematic turns out to be connected to Beckett's self-positioning in a history of modernism, as Beckett repeatedly brings up a notion of impotence in the context of his relationship to both Joyce and Proust.[10] "With Joyce the difference is," he continues in the *Times* interview, " . . . the more Joyce knew the more he could. He's tending towards omniscience and omnipotence as an artist. I'm working with impotence, ignorance. I don't think impotence has been exploited in the past" (Shenker 148).[11] Earlier, in 1930, drafting his essay on Proust, Beckett bluntly characterizes his ambition in a letter to Thomas MacGreevy to "pull the balls off the critical and poetical Proustian cock" (Ackerley and Gontarski 460). In sum, Beckett figures his positive difference from Joyce and Proust, as well as his affinity with certain contemporary artists, in terms of impotence, which suggests that one of the problems he faced in his work was, as Mark Pedretti aptly puts it, how to "mark a difference without positing *either* a break or a continuity with the modernist legacy" (586). The problem of how to "go on" after the monumental works of high modernism, framed in terms of impossibility, powerlessness, and failure, paradoxically opened up for Beckett a singularly productive path of writing.

It is true that the language of the trilogy seems to echo Beckett's metacritical statements about impotence and failure. The theme of the "ablation of desire" (*Proust* 10) returns in *Molloy* when Beckett puts in Molloy's mouth the same lines from Leopardi that appear in the *Proust* essay: "*non che la speme, il desiderio* [*è spento*] [not only hope, but desire . . . has vanished]" (*Three Novels* 35). And Molloy occasionally waxes philosophical on the negative nature of writing: "Not to want to say, not to know what you want to say, not to be able to say what you think you want to say, and never to stop saying, or hardly ever, that is the thing to keep in mind, even in the heat of composition" (28). Since we read Molloy's comments in the context of his own struggling acts of narration, they necessarily take on a recursive dimension. Moran perpetuates this recursivity when he ruminates, "Stories, stories. I have not been able to tell them. I shall not be able to tell this one" (137). Is this a narrative about the difficulty of telling stories, or about the difficulty of telling about the difficulty of telling stories? (Repeat question ad infinitum.)

Yet to turn toward Beckett's "gallery of moribunds" (*Three Novels* 137), as he calls them, for figures of the failure of language, or of the formlessness of Beckett's art, would be problematic on at least two counts. On a basic level, any fishing for figures of the failure of language in Beckett's text is simply logically contradictory. To argue that Beckett constructs images of impoverishment and failure in order to signify the impoverishment and failure of his own language is to make a case for the successful expression of (the) failure (of expression) in Beckett's art, a reading that, at the very least, the author explicitly rejects in the context of his *Three Dialogues*. Here, when Beckett suggests the possibility that van Velde's art is entirely inexpressive, Duthuit asks, "But might it not be suggested . . . that the occasion of [van Velde's] painting is his predicament, and that it is expressive of the impossibility to express?" To which Beckett replies, "No more ingenious method could be devised for restoring him, safe and sound, to the bosom of Saint Luke. But let us, for once, be foolish enough not to turn tail" (143). The phrase *to turn tail* might hint at the recursivity involved in turning a failed language into the expression of its own failure; the imperative in Beckett, however, is always to "go on," not to double back. To be fair, most critics make an effort to avoid the fairly apparent contradiction that this reading entails; but what they end up proposing in its place is that Beckett necessarily fails in his attempt to express failure, a proposition that only places Beckett's "success" at another remove.[12] In other words, if his aesthetic telos is failure, and he fails to fail, does he not still fail (that is, succeed)? To put it still another way, the real "referent" of Beckett's language is identified here as the authorial intention to fail to express, which is in turn unexpressed (hence expressed) because language continues to be expressive (hence unexpressive). I find these readings a bit dizzying as well as unsatisfactory; we should be wary of mistaking a structure of oscillation for one of profundity. Ultimately, these readings continue to propose a contradictory pair of assertions. They propose, on the one hand, that the expressivity of language fails in Beckett's work and, on the other, that this failure can be thematized by means of a set of figures, which in turn makes failure the new object of expression of Beckett's art.

The second count by which a study of Beckett's "gallery of moribund" metaphors is problematic is perhaps only a more developed version of the first. Any question we pose about the form, integrity, or autonomy of Beckett's work in terms of the disintegrating identities and failed expeditions we find there begs the very question under consideration, namely the status of the form, integrity, or autonomy of the text. That is, any time we seek the reflection of formal problems in the figures that make up the novels' thematic content, we take for granted the very same formal unity we are supposed to be investigating. The text that produces images of its own status, that represents itself, comments on itself, and is able to comment on itself, is already understood to be coherent and self-sufficient. It turns to itself as its referent, and perhaps has only its own content to say. The most self-reflexive text is also the most autonomous, a self-enclosed orb totally divorced from the world. This is the fantasy of a neat retreat into the interiority of a text and, ultimately, the fantasy of language itself as a space of pure interiority.

Moreover, even the secondary literature that does not address the self-reflexivity of Beckett's work explicitly, but argues rather that his trilogy "deconstructs" the modern concept of the subject or challenges prevailing notions of subjectivity, runs into a similar problem as long as it deals with the thematic content of Beckett's work and neglects the question of reading.[13] That is, the tendency of the literature is to rely on interpretative strategies that continue to lend a referential function to Beckett's figures. For even given the argument that Beckett's work is non-mimetic in the sense that it does not reflect actual situations in the world (itself a debatable claim), we continue to attribute a function of reference to elements of the text when we treat them as metaphors for philosophical concepts. And whether we read these elements as figurations of a critique of the subject or as figurations of a crisis in the concept of the work, we perpetuate a structure of reflection that merely serves to reterritorialize the very "subject" in question: we map it either onto the philosophico-literary relation or onto the text as a whole. In the latter case, the work becomes the new subject: insofar as the reader relies on interpretative strategies that relate a part of the text to the whole by means of a metaphorical and, in the end, totalizing gesture, she reconstitutes the text as a space of interiority structured by a very recognizable operation of self-reflection and synthesis.[14]

When I characterize this operation as "recognizable," I mean both that it is familiar and that it is itself born from the specular activity of self-recognition in the form of reflection. For it should not be overlooked that self-reflection constitutes the form of the modern subject par excellence. In what follows, I outline the conceptual stakes of reading according to a schema of reflection and situate these stakes in the context of the romantic literary inheritance that I described in chapter 1. We will see that the supposition that Beckett's text is capable of reflecting on itself not only runs into conceptual contradictions but also remains indebted to an essentially romantic notion of subjectivity.

REFLECTION

Ever since Descartes's *cogito me cogitare*, in which the activity of thinking is reflected in a second act that grasps the first as its object, thinking has been characterized as a fundamentally reflexive and reflective operation. As such, it has served as the paradigm of subjectivity as well as the cornerstone of certainty on the basis of which knowledge of the world is made possible. With Johann Fichte's rewriting of Kantian philosophy, the conjunction of reflection and subjectivity reached a kind of apex. Fichte aimed to found his theoretical project of *Wissenschaftslehre*, or *The Science of Knowledge* (published in 1794–95 but revised throughout the philosopher's life), on the absolute first principle of the freely self-positing "I," from which a philosophy of the natural world could subsequently be deduced. This "I" is constituted by an act of positing that immediately takes the form of a knowledge of itself as self-positing; as such Fichte identifies the "I" as an originary unity of consciousness and self-consciousness, subject and object, form and content, agent and product of its own action.

The early German romantics, and principally Friedrich Schlegel, responded to Fichte in a way that has had major consequences for the Western conception of art and its relation to subjectivity. In "The Concept of Criticism in German Romanticism" (1919), Walter Benjamin argues that whereas for Fichte, the two distinct moments of reflection in the self-positing of the "I"—that is, the positing and the knowledge of that positing—are immediately united in intuition and limited by the concept of the "I" so that an infinite regress of reflection is avoided, Schlegel, in contrast, attempts to hold on to both an immediacy of intuition and an infinity in reflection. It was precisely the romantics' "cult of the infinite," as Benjamin calls it, that "divided them from Fichte and lent their thinking its most peculiar and characteristic direction" (126).

For Fichte, then, reflection constitutes the essence of subjectivity and must be referred to the positing "I"; for the romantics, reflection refers to the formal character of thought as such. Insofar as any act of reflection may give rise to a subsequent reflection of which the previous will serve as the object, the romantics observe a kind of ceaseless becoming-form of the content of thinking, where thinking becomes a thinking of thinking, which in turn becomes a thinking of thinking of thinking. At this third (and every subsequent) level lies the romantics' originality, as Benjamin explains: "The thinking of thinking of thinking can be conceived and performed in two ways. If one starts from the expression 'thinking of thinking,' then on the third level this is either the object thought of, thinking (of the thinking of thinking), or else the thinking subject (thinking of thinking) of thinking. The rigorous original form of second-level reflection is assailed and shaken by the ambiguity in third-level reflection" (129). The self-contained reciprocity of the "thinking of thinking," in other words, is torn open by the addition of a third "thinking," which may be understood either as the subject or as the object of the previous reflection, and thus establishes an ambiguity between the two. According to Benjamin, third-level reflection witnesses the becoming-object of the subject of reflection and a becoming-subject of the object, such that reflection reveals a "disintegration of original form" and a "peculiar ambiguity" (126). This ambiguity of the subject and object of reflection yields an infinity of "connectedness," in Benjamin's terms: an infinite connectedness of multiple centers of reflection that together constitute the "medium of the absolute" (132).

If, for Fichte, the activity of reflection is essentially characteristic of subjectivity, for the romantics reflection is an originary medium, "logically first and primary" (Benjamin 134). Reflection constitutes the medium of the romantic absolute, the form of the interconnectedness of the real (132). In this way we can understand the importance of art for the romantics. Because any object within the absolute can be an occasion for the self-thinking of thought, objects are properly understood as determinants of reflection and, in this way, can be said to be thinking themselves. Following Kant's treatment of aesthetics as a philosophical problem, the work of art becomes a privileged— indeed, the most privileged—determinant of reflection, a site where the self-presentation of a process in a determinate form coincides with the occasion for critical reflection in a structure that looks a lot like self-knowledge. The formal quality of the artwork is the limitation that makes its internal self-reflection possible (156), as well as what allows it to exceed its limitation in external reflection, where it participates in an idea of genre and ultimately in the idea of art as such. This treatment of art, and of literature in particular, as a privileged center of reflection is romanticism's explicit concern. Schlegel dreamed of a "transcendental poetry," in which "in all its descriptions poetry should describe itself, and always be simultaneously poetry and the poetry of poetry" (*AF* 238). Ultimately he heralded a "progressive, universal poetry" that would "reunite all the separate species of poetry and put poetry in touch with philosophy and rhetoric," this poetry alone being "like the epic, a mirror of the whole circumambient world, an image of the age" (116).

Although the romantic conception of reflection purportedly refers to the self-reflexivity of thought rather than to the self-consciousness of an "I," this conception nevertheless succeeds in mapping onto the work of art, and onto the world, the same Enlightenment image of subjectivity, only construed along more expansive lines. What it secures once again is an image of thought in which thought's constitutive essence is both its coincidence with itself and its grasping of that coincidence. As such, a "self" of thought emerges, even if this is no more than the pure form of consciousness grasping itself as self-consciousness. But this pure form in turn becomes substantial, in a typically romantic inversion, once it is made to serve as the content of reflection for the self-thinking absolute.[15] Ultimately, while the absolute self as self-consciousness is affirmed "in the shadow or in the wake of Fichte," as Lacoue-Labarthe and Nancy write, the artwork is affirmed as the corollary of this self, as well as the privileged site of its production (48).

Now let me bring this story of reflection back to Beckett's trilogy, and to what I criticized earlier as a way of reading by means of schemas of reflection. Specifically, I took issue with an approach to Beckett's work that would treat it as an allegorical critique of the notion of the subject, in the service of an aesthetics of failure. What such a reading should not neglect to take into account is that this very notion of allegory relies on a mechanism of reflection that reproduces the formal structure constitutive of the very subject in question.[16] In other words, what Beckett's text is supposed to critique at the level of its content is reinstated at the level of form. And the same can be said for readings that would mine the trilogy for figures of the dissolution of the boundaries of the work or of the integrity of the traditional novel. Such arguments rely, paradoxically, on the integrity of the work's ability to reflect on itself by means of its figures, thus reproducing the very concept under consideration (the work's integrity) in the form of the investigation (the work's self-reflection). Bringing this paradox to the fore by looking explicitly for something like a "representation of unrepresentability" in Beckett's trilogy—indeed, making such a paradox the principal tool by which one would proceed—would be an improvement on a mere disregard for such contradictions, but certainly nothing that we have not already seen in early German romanticism. For Schlegel's conception of art par excellence is that of form as constitutive paradox, or, to echo Benjamin, form as "disintegration of form" and "peculiar ambiguity." This ambiguity is precisely what in the work (and "out" of the work, for romantic reflection upsets the boundary between inside and outside) trembles between representation and unrepresentability, form and freedom, object and idea—what already belongs to the work as the seeds of its own *désoeuvrement*, as Blanchot calls it.[17]

If we hope to exit from the abyssal nature of this problem of reflection, we have to turn to another way of reading, one that would suspend the question of what Beckett's text says about itself by means of its figures, in favor of an examination of the *way* it has of saying and the means by which it constructs these figures. In other words, we need to leave behind the questions "What does it say?" or "What does it mean?"—which will always drag us back, one way or another, into the specular formula "I = I"—in favor of the question "How does it work?"[18] That is, we need to turn to an examination of how the trilogy's auto-allegorizing dimension is produced.

DISJUNCTION

*Molloy, Malone Dies,* and *The Unnamable* not only witness Beckett's shift to first-person narration, but also mark the emergence of an explicit thematization of the act of narration, unprecedented in Beckett's earlier works. As I mentioned earlier, all the narrators of the trilogy are writers or storytellers in one way or another, under obligation to blacken pages with text or to fill the silence with a series of stories. This thematization is brought to the fore and managed by Beckett's narrators, who overlay their abject tales with a kind of neurotic and nearly constant, self-disparaging metacommentary, which functions in tension or even in direct contradiction with the embedded discourse. Molloy, for example, punctuates his descriptions with remarks of self-approval, disapproval, or doubt: "It was on a road remarkably bare, I mean without hedges or ditches or any kind of edge. . . . Perhaps I'm inventing a little, perhaps embellishing. . . . [The cows] chew, swallow, then after a short pause effortlessly bring up the next mouthful. . . . But perhaps I'm remembering things" (*Three Novels* 8); remarks of self-erasure: "a pomeranian I think, but I don't think so" (11); and of self-revision: "I got to my knees, no that doesn't work, I got up" (29). These foreground the precariousness of the act of writing and lend a sense of uncertainty, even defectiveness, to the resulting narrative. Malone, likewise, interrupts his stories with evaluations of his own writing process: "What tedium" (189), he protests, "This is awful" (191); later, "We are getting on" (193), or "No, I can't do it" (196). In *The Unnamable*, the alternation of discourses increases in speed until this alternation constitutes the very fabric of the narrative, which proceeds much as it begins: "I seem to speak, it is not I, about me, it is not about me" (291).

The denial and doubt of the metaremarks, and the repetition of evaluations like "What tedium" and "This is awful" to the point of their seeming inevitability, play what is probably the largest role in the temptation to read Beckett's work in terms of an aesthetics of failure. One of the peculiarities of the trilogy—which Bruno Clément points out at the start of *L'oeuvre sans qualités: Rhétorique de Samuel Beckett*, outlining an approach to Beckett to which my own reading is much indebted—is "to propose both a fiction and a discourse on that fiction, or rather to impose, surreptitiously, the idea that it contains these two instances, and that one depends on the other" (24, my translation).[19] What we must not lose sight of, however, is that both this fiction and the discourse on this fiction issue from one and the same work, and both are equally constitutive of its fictional universe. Furthermore, Clément describes a certain uniformity of the critical literature and a lack of detachment in its approach to its object (referring to Beckett's French reception, although his remarks are pertinent to the English context as well). This attitude stems from critics' taking up and perpetuating a particular metadiscourse of failure and of the inadequacy of language—as well as a particular pathos—that is already contained in the text. But if the two discourses are equally comprehended in and equally constitutive of Beckett's fiction, why do we end up privileging the metadiscourse as a source of truth? As an instance of reflection, its formal status as "meta" is enough to grant it a superiority of insight where its object is in turn supposed to be blind, and its location within the work establishes it as a privileged point of reflection on the very aesthetic process that gives rise to it. In the grips of this formal reflection, conversely and paradoxically, the aesthetic process appears all the more uncertain; in the reflective knowledge that metadiscourse purports to bear, the constructive process appears all the more immediate and unreflective.

I am not suggesting that critics have naïvely confused the biographical author with his narrators, or his actual work with the narratives and statements presented therein. I am suggesting, though, that there is a very strong tendency to assume that the tasks and struggles of the one are analogous to or representative of the tasks and struggles of the other. In one of the first full-length studies of Beckett's work, for example, Hugh Kenner comments obliquely on what he knew of Beckett's depression and solitude while writing the trilogy, making an obvious connection between the author and his writer-characters, speaking on Beckett's behalf. "All you can do with your novels is write them, alone in a room, assembling what memories you can of experiences you had before your siege in the room commenced, all the time secretly a little ashamed of the genre you are practicing. How can all these lies be taken seriously, and all this local color?" (17–18), Kenner writes with inimitable elegance, yet guided by the assumption that remarks in *The Unnamable* such as "this voice that speaks, knowing that it lies" (*Three Novels* 307) refer to Beckett's own experience as a novelist.

The disjunction Beckett establishes between the fictional and metafictional discourses gives rise to two distinct attitudes toward the work. The differentiation of discourses in the trilogy generates a distance between the work as it seems to be and as it ought to be, between what it seems to attain and what it laments as its unattainable goal. On the one hand, Beckett's work appears to be defined by what I referred to as an "aesthetics of failure": that is, it appears to be thoroughly infused with and governed by its relation to failure, and ultimately by a telos of silence and formlessness, which indicates the irremediable absence of an ideal. On the other hand, a negative image of the work emerges at the level of that ideal, where it persists as an unattainable and inexpressible truth. Beckett's work systematically upholds the image of an essential truth, or of an ideal work capable of presenting this truth, through what it constructs as its own eternal inability to disclose this truth, exhausting itself instead in rendering this inability sensible.[20] To this end, Beckett's narrators tend to present their own language as "lying," "blathering," "babbling," or "prattling."[21]

If we turn instead to an analysis of Beckett's rhetoric, however, we can find a language to describe the mechanism that propels the narrative forward, forward in a way that does not depend on the idealism of a specular or teleological logic that we saw in the romantic figures of reflection and generation (such as the seed and mirror we saw in chapter 1). Following Clément, we might identify the most characteristic rhetorical gesture of the trilogy as one of *epanorthosis* (423). From the Greek roots *epi*, "on"; *ana*, "marking a return"; and *orthos*, "right" or "correct," epanorthosis is a figure of speech that entails going back over what one has just asserted, either to add nuance, to weaken or retract, or to reassert the original statement with greater force (Morier, *Dictionnaire*).[22] This figure is often associated with correction (*correctio*), but I prefer the term *epanorthosis* as it underscores the element of repetition at work in this figure. Its function is to generate discourse without regard to logical coherence, so that it serves as a hinge between what would otherwise be mutually exclusive assertions, marking the latter as a repetition of the former while simultaneously differentiating their conceptual content. In Beckett's work, it is worth noting, epanorthosis rarely involves direct contradiction, but puts into motion a kind of nervous adjusting, adding, displacing, or diminishing. All of these gestures are forms of repetition, as is the schema of reflection I criticized earlier. But unlike reflection, epanorthosis does not entail synthesis in a consciousness, but seeks only to perpetuate itself in a series of endless displacements.

The mechanism of productive repetition at work in the trilogy, of which epanorthosis is the rhetorical manifestation, can be referred more broadly to what Deleuze characterizes as a "disjunctive synthesis." Deleuze's term describes a relation that effects a divorce or disjunction between its terms while simultaneously maintaining and affirming their difference. That is, it holds them together *as* disjunct, referring their difference to no other ground than its own differentiating operation, whereas a dialectical or reflective operation would subordinate this difference to a given identity (such as the identity of an "I"). Simultaneously a synthesis and a splitting, the disjunctive synthesis is an essentially "schizophrenic" articulation that gives rise to two or more heterogeneous orders, and that Deleuze characterizes with the formula "either . . . or . . . or" (Deleuze and Guattari, *Anti-Oedipus* 12).[23]

In Beckett's trilogy, a disjunctive articulation likewise precedes the recuperation of elements into a narrative continuity. Consider again Molloy's writerly advice: "Not to want to say, not to know what you want to say, not to be able to say what you think you want to say, and never to stop saying, or hardly ever, that is the thing to keep in mind, even in the heat of composition" (*Three Novels* 28; original French 43). Rather than read this as a claim about the doomed enterprise of self-expression, we might pause over an iteration of clauses that, while formally repetitive, depict distinct and mutually exclusive states or ideas. The first four clauses describe, for example, not wanting, wanting but not knowing, wanting and knowing but not being able, and finally, doing. A relentless parataxis juxtaposes these distinct logical possibilities. With "never to stop saying" and "hardly ever," we encounter the absurd pairing of an absolute with its qualification, a peculiar form of epanorthosis that might be called a figure of *paradoxical exception*.[24] It is tempting to reduce this figure to an expression of psychological motive, so that we would read it in terms of Molloy's need to adjust or soften his claims. But in the contradictory passage from "never" to "hardly ever," might these lines not also reveal the impossibility of all the relations they purport to accomplish—here the relation of the absolute and the relative, or the infinite and the finite—by any means other than sheer juxtaposition? If so, it would be in keeping with the formal parataxis that characterizes this passage. The joke, however, lies in Molloy's triumphant conclusion: "That is the thing to keep in mind [*voilà ce qu'il importe de ne pas perdre de vue*]." In other words, the joke of this passage is the ironic claim of the pronoun "that" (*ce que*) to totalize the series that precedes it. Just *what*, exactly, are we expected to keep in mind?

Ultimately, the lesson of this passage may be one of non-relation and non-totalization. Yet I do not wish to advocate for something like the impossibility of reading Beckett—far from it. The importance of identifying the figure of epanorthosis is that it reveals the mechanism by which apparently incompatible assertions are articulated and organized, the ways they are linguistically related, imbued with meaning and pathos, and mobilized under the guise of necessity. That is, this particular figure transports us from the iterative and disjunctive aspects of Beckett's prose to our ability to make meaning out of it, and it does so by leaning heavily on the pathos that is implied by the act of self-correction. Molloy and other heroes in the trilogy frequently interrupt themselves to comment disparagingly on the nature of linguistic invention, for instance. "Saying is inventing," Molloy proposes, then continues doubtfully, "Wrong, very rightly wrong. You invent nothing, you think you are inventing, you think you are escaping, and all you do is stammer out your lesson, the remnants of a pensum one day got by heart and long forgotten" (*Three Novels* 32). Molloy measures speaking against creation, then relegates it to some other status, the failed recitation of a child's lesson. Referring to a "pensum," or schoolwork imposed as punishment, he evokes the image of the chastised pupil (Has the pupil been punished, paradoxically, for confusing his lesson with his pensum?),[25] surreptitiously drawing on the humility and shame that such an image brings with it. Molloy's conflicting assertions can conceivably be organized into two disparate discourses, so that one appears to be fictional, the other metafictional, but the very disparity between these discourses is covered over by means of distressingly familiar emotions, which invite the reader to participate in the emotions of the text. As I suggested earlier, we can take stock of the production of these emotions when we shift from the question "What does the text mean?" to "How does it work?"

The disjunction between discourses in the trilogy, in sum, not only foregrounds the act of writing but works to imbue it with pathos. Emotions, as Rei Terada suggests, function as interpretative acts insofar as they tend to "mitigate epistemological uncertainties": on one level they work rhetorically in the same way metaphors do, organizing exchanges between two distinct properties or states of being; on a second level, they function as synthetic forces that displace and disguise the discrepancies that emerge in such exchanges, filling an absence of identity with their presence (29). Following this understanding, I would venture that the disjunction of discourses in Beckett's work gives rise to two emotions: first of all, shame, which organizes the differential relation between the discourses as one of the inadequacy or failure of the first in the face of the projected standards of the second; and second, guilt, which works to synthesize the experience of inadequacy by making it into a kind of a priori truth or existential condition. Franz Kafka has perhaps gone further than any modern author in diagnosing the nature of this existential guilt; in Beckett this takes the form of the one who is born "headforemost mewling in the charnel-house" (*Three Novels* 225), given "birth to into death" (283). The collapsed temporality of a death coincident with life is the figure of originary guilt, a failure that has become the ground of existence. Finally, we might call pathos, in the classical sense, any language that provokes an identificatory exchange between the reader and the imagined figure of the author through the shared emotion generated by the work.

Whereas Deleuze draws on a Kantian terminology to speak of a logical synthesis (even if this is the logic of schizophrenia), my own interest lies in the ability of a rhetorical terminology to bring to light the synthesizing function of Beckett's figures and the way those figures organize our reading by coloring the terms they articulate with meaning and emotion. Where Deleuze identifies a "disjunctive synthesis" that gives rise to two or more heterogeneous orders, we can put this notion to work for literary criticism, identifying a rhetorical operation that gives rise to the heterogeneous discourses of Beckett's novels: a discourse of assertion on the one hand, and of censure, correction, and depreciation on the other. Both, it should be emphasized, are equally constitutive of the language of the text. Epanorthosis constructs a complex of assertions whose most adequate expression lies in the movement created between its two poles, or two discourses, a forward movement of which both of these poles are equally constitutive (Clément 423). The importance of such a rhetorical reading is that it takes both discourses together in their contradictory, differentiating, and essentially productive movement. Consider the often quoted terminal lines of the trilogy: "You must go on, I can't go on, I'll go on" (*Three Novels* 414). Does the narrative thread, in fact, not pass through a series of different assertions: the first in the form of an unquestioning obligation, the second addressing the first with an attitude of revisionary complaint, and the third speaking in an attitude of stoic compromise, which in turn might become the primary assertion for a subsequent operation? No self-reflection here, but self-differentiation in repetition. No self-effacement, but the endless generation and displacement of an obligation coded as "originary." If we were to examine the role of the assertion of obligation more closely, together with the ways it is figured in the text, we might discover an aesthetics of necessity in Beckett's work—and by aesthetics I mean the image that makes the text cohere, its formal cause or principle—rather than an aesthetics of failure.

Despite appearances to the contrary, then, Beckett's work is not governed by a straining toward silence, or a critique of the subject, or an undoing of the traditional integrity of the novel. Despite the deliberate impoverishment of its content and the self-deprecation of the narrative voice, it is as artfully crafted, and perhaps as dedicated to values of truth and expressivity, as any masterwork of the past. But the question it thrusts before us, if we let it, is above all a question of reading. The limits of self-reflection in the trilogy bring into question the specular structure of reading itself, and the metaphysics of identification that make what we call reading possible. These do not necessarily correspond to the mechanism that makes the text work: this is the fissure internal to the text, the source of a generative movement of division and differentiation.

# CHAPTER 6

# Hyperbole in Proust's
## *A la recherche du temps perdu*

C'est pourquoi la meilleure part de notre mémoire est hors de nous, dans un souffle pluvieux, dans l'odeur de renfermé d'une chambre ou dans l'odeur d'une première flambée.

MARCEL PROUST, A la recherche du temps perdu

Il ne faut pas avoir peur d'aller trop loin, car la vérité est au-delà.

MARCEL PROUST, letter to E. R. Curtius

In this chapter, I take up another figure of productive differentiation, one that should give us some purchase on the consistency of the work of art according to the vision of Marcel Proust.[1] While attention to figures of difference—indeed, to rhetorical figures in general—may be associated with American-style deconstruction, my own interest lies in bringing to light the generative, rather than aporetic, aspects of these figures. Drawing on a mode of reading indebted to deconstruction, but taking my distance from the essential negativity that links some deconstructive practices to romanticism, I look instead to the role rhetorical figures play in generating systems of narrative, in organizing signs and affects, and—in this chapter especially—in constructing subjects.

My focus is on the role played in Proust's *A la recherche du temps perdu* by the figure of hyperbole. Hyperbole, though generally understood as a synonym for exaggeration, has a significant function in Proust's text, I will argue, connecting figures of identity with figures of contradiction, yet without being reducible to either. In particular, in articulating and organizing differences in language, hyperbole presents us with a model for the way the Proustian self is organized, especially the way it incorporates its sense impressions and transforms these impressions into a verbal work of art.

*A la recherche du temps perdu* abounds in hyperbole, to the extent that hyperbole seems to be the rule of linguistic production rather than the exception. Whether Proust's narrator is comparing an episode from his childhood to a world-historical event, or is transported by emotions that seem to exceed their provocations and led to employ a superabundant number of images or quantity of discourse, the generative principle of the narrative seems to be one of excess in one form or another. From the cup of tea that opens onto the whole of Combray, to the uneven paving stones that provoke in the narrator an indifference to death, even involuntary memory takes the form of a projection and a traversal of boundaries; perhaps it even takes the form of an exaggerated claim.

Hyperbole, from *hyper,* "over," and *bollein,* "to throw," is defined by the *Rhetorica ad Herennium* as "a manner of speech exaggerating the truth, whether for the sake of magnifying or minifying something" (Cicero 341).[2] The Dutch philosopher Desiderius Erasmus gives prominent place to this figure in his manual *Copia: Foundations of the Abundant Style* (1512), which instructed students in a variety of means of amplifying their writing, and which suggests that there might be a connection between figures of exaggeration and verbal abundance in general.[3] If we were to investigate the meaning and purpose of hyperbole in Proust's work, we would have to confront the difficult task of selecting a few exemplary passages from an ocean of narrative—from a novel that, as Malcolm Bowie puts it, is "famous for being long" (216)—and moreover, of generalizing on the basis of these passages. No doubt this gesture would itself be hyperbolic, as claims made on behalf of examples frequently are.[4] Nevertheless, if reading Proust is the best instruction in reading Proust, I propose we examine two key passages from the earlier volumes of the *Recherche* for the way that exaggerated claims are produced and developed in them, in the hope that they will elucidate other patterns of meaning in the novel.

## AN ALLEGORY OF HYPERBOLE

The young narrator's description of the steeples of Martinville is not the first act of writing represented in the novel—this would be his note to his mother, begging her to come upstairs to his bedroom in Combray[5]—but it is the first and only representation of his attempt at literary writing. I turn to this passage in part because of the exemplary status the narrative grants it, both as a pivotal moment in the narrator's discovery of his vocation to write, and as a key stage in the reader's own instruction in the Proustian aesthetic, as it presents a fragment of writing for what seems, at least at first, to be its literary merits. Yet as Joshua Landy aptly puts it, in this passage "the ratio between notoriety and justification reaches its zenith; which is to say, almost all readers of Proust know that they are supposed to take it seriously, yet very few are quite sure why" (52). Thus, I turn to this passage wondering whether its exemplary status might be overstated, and, if so, to what end. At the very least, the passage has a certain excessive quality for the simple reason that the description of the steeples is essentially produced for the reader not once, but twice.[6]

Like many episodes in the novel, the events described here emerge against a backdrop of habitual action, here the narrator's unhappy reflections on his future failure in a literary career, "the poetic future on which my lack of talent precluded me from counting" (1: 194/147).[7] Suddenly, a sense impression would interrupt these habitual thoughts, sunlight on a stone or the smell of a garden path "quite outside of all these literary preoccupations" (translation modified), an impression that seemed to conceal something else yet, something "beyond what my eyes could see . . . beyond the thing seen or smelt" (1: 195/147).[8] The importance of these impressions, the narrator tells us, is that their real significance lay elsewhere than in the scene in which they manifest themselves, in an "outside" or a "beyond," which he underscores with "bien en dehors de" and a repetition of "au-delà." They offer the narrator "an unreasoning pleasure [*un plaisir irraisonnée*]"—an irrational pleasure, but perhaps also an unwarranted one, in the sense of a pleasure without reason (1: 196/148). On this particular occasion, the narrator is once again struck by "an impression of this kind," an impression that leads him to "that special pleasure which was unlike any other" (1: 197/148, translation modified).[9] "Unlike any other" is, of course, an overstatement if these impressions are numerous enough to belong to a "genre," and if these pleasures are repeated often enough to merit the use of the grammatical imperfect in this passage, along with the exclamation that opens it: "How often . . . in the course of my walks . . . " (1: 194/147).[10]

On this particular occasion, the narrator's walk being "prolonged . . . beyond its ordinary limits,"[11] which means that it is later in the day than usual and he and his parents have to accept a carriage ride home to hasten their return, the narrator is struck by the sight of church steeples against the sky, and by the apparent movement of the steeples as he speeds toward and then away from them in the carriage (1: 196/148). Not just the language but also the content of what the narrator sees has an element of superfluity to it, as the sight of the twin steeples of Martinville-le-Sec is enhanced by that of a third steeple, Vieuxvicq, "which, although separated from them by a hill and a valley, and rising from rather higher ground in the distance, appeared none the less to be standing by their side" (1: 196/148).[12] The distance as well as the elevation of Vieuxvicq heightens the thrill of the illusion that draws the steeples together. Interestingly enough, in the fragment of writing the narrator produces, this illusory proximity is rewritten as an identity, so that the three towers end up merging completely, becoming, at a great distance, "no more than a single dusky shape" (1: 198/150).[13] (See appendix for the full text of the fragment.)

If the narrator's claims about the importance of his experience or the worth of his writing are hyperbolic, then we might say that, in this scene, form imitates content: his exaggerated speech imitates the distance between a sense impression and its supposed significance, and works to convey the emotion of traversing this distance. Furthermore, a case can be made for reading the narrator's vision as a sort of allegory of hyperbole. The drama of his perception derives from the tension between the distant third steeple and the trick of perception that would bring it near the other two. This is not unlike the drama of a hyperbolic claim, which unfolds in the distance between what it says and what it is supposed to represent, a distance it both preserves in exaggerating, and feigns at covering over in its claim to authentic representation.

The narrator is initially struck, moreover, by the vertical projection of the steeples, "rising from the level of the plain, and seemingly lost in that expanse of open country" (1: 198/149),[14] not unlike the way one is struck by a figure of speech that stands out from ordinary language, or draws attention to itself over and above what it communicates. In *The Arte of English Poesie* (1589), which contains the Renaissance's most detailed definition of hyperbole, George Puttenham calls hyperbole not only a "false semblant," along with metaphor and allegory, but a "lowd lyer," underscoring the fact that hyperbole is an untruth whose aim is not so much to deceive as to draw attention to itself.[15] Puttenham is writing in an Elizabethan, courtly milieu, a context removed from Proust's own, but what he says can give us an initial framework for considering the relationship between hyperbole and truth. He writes, "Now when I speake that which neither I my

selfe thinke to be true, nor would haue any other body beleeue, . . . I
meane nothing lesse then that I speake" (138). If, as Puttenham suggests, hyperbole means nothing less than the fact that I speak, that
is, if, beyond the object that it represents, hyperbole is above all concerned with itself as a heightened or self-conscious mode of language,
then we might consider it to be a rhetorical figure whose real referent
is figurative language itself. In other words, we might consider hyperbole to be a sort of figure of figures.

There have been other candidates for this "figure of figures," if
for no other reason than that the verbal attempt to describe figurality—that is, the attempt to use language to describe a linguistic
effect—unavoidably raises the question of the proper representation of representation. In "The Turns of Metaphor," Jonathan Culler
cites a long-standing tendency among critics to ascribe to metaphor
an exemplary status over other figures. Diagnosing this tendency, he
argues that treating metaphor as the "figure of figures" ends up fore-
grounding tropological language's referential aspect, since the claim
that metaphor makes is the claim to represent something authenti-
cally. Metaphors, in this view, claim to set up referential relationships
between concepts and imaginative images (189–91). By contrast, in
"Prosopopeia," Michael Riffaterre suggests that prosopopeia, not
metaphor, may be a figure of figurative language precisely insofar as
prosopopeia can *never* be referential.[16] Lending a face to a faceless
object, prosopopeia, he argues, is the very index of fiction and thus
of literariness in general (110). If we were to follow Riffaterre's reasoning, we could assert the same of hyperbole: that in intentionally
departing from its object of reference to assert an exaggerated truth,
hyperbole is nothing less than the index of figurality as such. Perhaps
we should also consider the possibility that the difference between
truth and fiction, or literal and figurative language, can be stated only
in hyperbolic terms.[17]

The ecstatic page of writing produced by Proust's narrator—
ecstatic both in its tone and, following the etymology of "ecstatic," in
its standing out from the rest of the narrative—is set off from the text
with quotation marks, presented to us wholesale, we are told, with
"only a slight revision here and there" (1: 197/149).[18] We are left to
wonder what the exact nature and magnitude of these changes might
have been: whether nothing has been altered, in fact, and "slight revision" is an exaggeration, or whether the page has actually been substantially rewritten, and the author downplays his labor, whether out

of pride or for other reasons. The difference between the two texts—
the page as we read it and the fictional page that we will never read,
but of whose existence we are assured by the narrative—might be
infinitely small or infinitely large, but it is ultimately undecidable. It
mirrors, of course, the difference between the text of *A la recherche
du temps perdu* and the great work the narrator claims to be ready
to write by the end of the novel. A number of critics have referred to
what appears to be the circular structure of Proust's novel, in which
the work the narrator dreams of writing will turn out to be the very
work we have been reading all along.[19] But as Landy has convincingly
demonstrated, there is sufficient evidence in the narrative, in fact, to
preclude the identity of these two texts (36–49).[20] Even if there were
not a shred of evidence to disrupt the supposition of a seamless identity between the two texts, however, we still could not disregard the
fact that the existence of the future work rests exclusively on what
remains a fictional claim. That is, the minimal difference between the
texts remains the difference of fiction.

 After unloading his impressions onto the page, the narrator begins
to sing "at the top of [his] voice," happy as "a hen [who] had just laid
an egg" (1: 199/150).[21] At the same time, he claims, hyperbolically,
"I never thought again of this page" (1: 198/150).[22] "Never" ends up
being much shorter than we might expect, for we subsequently discover that the narrator shows what he calls a "prose poem" to his
father's colleague M. de Norpois, a page he claims to have composed
"years before at Combray on coming home from a walk," and "in
a state of exaltation" that sounds suspiciously like the rapture with
which the Martinville page was written (1: 491/365).[23] Years later,
in *Le côté de Guermantes*, the narrator lets slip in a parenthetical
remark that his description of the steeples has been cleaned up for
publication, a piece of writing "which, as it happened, I had recently
unearthed, altered and sent in vain to the *Figaro*" (2 : 412/1053).[24]
*La prisonnière* opens with the narrator regularly checking the paper
each morning, eager to see himself in print (3: 4–5/1612); he continues to check the paper (3: 114/1692), though it is not until the next
volume, *Albertine disparue*, that the article finally appears. The narrator invites us to share in his surprise and delight by dramatizing his
ignorance just prior to opening the paper: "No doubt there was some
article by a writer whom I admired, which, as he wrote seldom, would
be a surprise for me," he writes with implausible ingenuousness (and
plausible narcissism; 3: 579/2032).[25] The meaning of the episode, as

he finally makes clear in *Le temps retrouvé*, is its contribution to his discovery of his vocation to write, the "invisible vocation" of which the present narrative is but the history. He writes, "Whether I was concerned with impressions like the one which I had received from the sight of the steeples of Martinville or with reminiscences . . . the task was to interpret the sensations as signs of so many laws and ideas, by trying to think—that is to say, to draw forth from the shadow—what I had merely felt, by trying to convert it into its spiritual equivalent. And this method, which seemed to me the sole method, what was it but the creation of a work of art?" (3: 912/2271).[26] The destiny of the steeples, he claims in this passage, is their conversion into a "spiritual equivalent," and their reappearance in a work of art. I will have more to say on the nature of this work in a moment, and on this theory of the spiritual conversion of sensations. For the present, let me note that Proust's hyperbolic description of the narrator's first encounter with the steeples is matched by his narrative strategy of belated disclosure.

That is, the hyperbolic rhetoric in the narrator's first impressions of the steeples can be understood to echo the position of the episode with respect to the rest of the narrative, and to dramatize the anticipation of the discovery of its significance. In this way, hyperbole proves to be more than a figure of style and to serve equally as a principle of narrative structure. Like a great many other events in the novel, the significance of the Martinville steeples is belatedly and progressively revealed; and in this case, a series of relays is established, so that each time the narrator recalls the page of writing, he points toward a future moment in which its meaning will be manifest, or at least in which his prose will be manifest in print. At the time of the episode, however, the narrator claims not yet to admit to himself what was hidden "behind" the sight of the steeples, though he suggests what it was: "What lay hidden behind the steeples of Martinville must be something analogous to a pretty phrase, since it was in the form of words which gave me pleasure that it had appeared to me" (1: 197/149).[27]

How, then, are we to read the fragment of writing the narrator produces? In it the steeples are soldiers lost in battle; they are birds perched on a plain; they are golden pivots, painted flowers, and girls huddled together at dusk. I must admit I find this to be one of the most difficult passages to read in the whole *Recherche*, if only because I am unable to penetrate the emotional relationship the narrator seems to have with his own writing.[28] However attractive I find the individual images to be, in combination they seem gratuitous, and the description is at once excessive and yet too meager to produce the exultation the narrator describes. All of the metaphors, we might note, are products of the optical effects of light and movement. As the narrator makes clear, he is principally struck by the form, line, and surface of the steeples: "the shape of their spires, their shifting lines, their sunlit surfaces" (1: 196/148, translation modified).[29] Even the comparison of the steeples to painted rather than real flowers underscores the two-dimensionality of the perception. It seems to be the superficial nature of his impressions that the narrator delights in, and that draws our attention to a superficiality of the passage's meaning. At the same time, this very superficiality compels the narrator to believe that something else must lie below the surface. He insists, "I felt that I was not penetrating to the core of my impression, that something more lay behind that mobility, that luminosity, something which they seemed at once to contain and to conceal" ( 1: 196/148).[30] This description and treatment of sense impressions is extremely close to, perhaps even indistinguishable from, an account of a listener in the presence of figurative speech, who senses that something more is being said: in this figurative speech in which tenor relates to vehicle just as this unknown "something" relates to the sense impressions enveloping it, "the mystery that lay hidden in a shape or a perfume . . . protected by its visible covering" (1: 195/148).[31] Indeed, the passage continues to read as an allegory of figurative language. But before we proceed any further with an analysis of this passage, let us develop a working understanding of figurality in Proust's novel, and of hyperbole in particular, by leaping ahead to a second passage.

## HYPERBOLIC SUBJECTS

Hyperbole often contains a metaphorical aspect, and rhetoricians have usually classified the two figures together.[32] Aristotle, for example, wrote that "successful hyperboles are also metaphors" (*Rhetoric* III.11). Yet hyperbole also departs from metaphor, as I consider in the following passage, and especially in the way the figurative language of this passage is developed by the narrative that surrounds it. On the verge of his departure from Paris for a vacation in Balbec, after having longed for years to make the trip, the narrator offers the rather unexpected comparison of a trip by train to the crucifixion of Christ. What gives him license to do this? At first, nothing seems less probable; but Proust has ways of convincing us. Consider the passage in its entirety, beginning with the narrator's striking description of the Saint-Lazare train station:

> Unhappily those marvelous places, railway stations, from which one sets out for a remote destination, are tragic places also, for if in them the miracle is accomplished whereby scenes which hitherto have had no existence save in our minds are about to become the scenes among which we shall be living, for that very reason we must, as we emerge from the waiting room, abandon any thought of presently finding ourselves once more in the familiar room which but a moment ago still housed us. We must lay aside all hope of going home to sleep in our own bed, once we have decided to penetrate into the pestiferous cavern through which we gain access to the mystery, into one of those vast, glass-roofed sheds, like that of Saint-Lazare into which I went to find the train for Balbec, and which extended over the eviscerated city one of those bleak and boundless skies, heavy with an accumulation of dramatic menace, like certain skies painted with an almost Parisian modernity by Mantegna or Veronese, beneath which only some terrible and solemn act could be in process such as a departure by train or the erection of the Cross. (1: 694/513, translation modified)[33]

Taken out of context, the language of this passage is fairly inexplicable; the physical appearance of the Saint-Lazare station alone does not seem to warrant this description. But we know that the passage is also motivated by the narrator's delight in the wonder of train travel, and his agony over his impending separation from his mother. The characterization of the station as "marvelous" and the trip as a "miracle," even the use of the word *grâce* in the French establish an important continuity with the previous page, echoing the narrator's description of train trips as "miraculous" and "mysterious" journeys that, because of their speed as well as the unrelenting nature of their course, do not lessen but intensify the contrast between one's place of origin and that of one's arrival (1: 693/512–13). With its Christian connotations, this language also clearly helps prepare the way for the crucifixion that terminates the passage. The "pestiferous cavern through which we gain access to the mystery," too, is a more appropriate description of the empty tomb of Jesus than of the glass-roofed station; and even the station's namesake, Lazarus, evokes the miraculous resurrection. Was it only the name of the station that triggered this chain of associations in the narrator in the first place? Names, as we know, have a special evocative power for Proust's narrator: "Words present to us a little picture of things, clear and familiar. . . . But names present to us—of persons, and of towns which they accustom us to regard as individual, as unique, like persons—a confused picture, which draws from them, from the brightness or darkness of their tone, the colour in which it is uniformly painted" (1: 420/312).[34]

Yet a theory of names is not enough to account for Proust's poetics, for the theory belongs to the fictional world of the narrator; and while it might explain that character's associations, it does not account for the presence of the name in the text in the first place. The image of crucifixion at the end of the passage, moreover, remains outlandish and excessively violent, as does the description of the sky, seen through the vaulted glass-and-iron ceiling of the Saint-Lazare station, as "heavy with dramatic menace" and the city itself as "eviscerated."[35] In the paragraph that follows, we learn that the narrator's anxiety stems from his having to stay in an unfamiliar room at the Balbec Hotel, and from the fact that he just learned the previous evening that his mother will not be making the trip with him (1: 694/513). He admits to being unhappy. Yet it is not until we glimpse the reflection of his unhappiness in his mother's and grandmother's behavior that we begin to understand the real depths of his emotion. His mother, having invented a pretext for leaving the station early so as to spare her son the pain of saying goodbye at the last possible moment, knows her son well, for he subsequently reveals to the reader that he is panicked by the thought of separation, imagining that his mother is about to begin a new life without him, and that she has chosen to do so because of the series of disappointments he has caused her. "For the first time," he laments, "I began to feel that it was possible that my mother might live . . . without me, otherwise than for me" (1: 697/515).[36]

At this point, the crucifixion metaphor that earlier seemed only tangentially or poorly motivated by the name Saint-Lazare can be understood as an instance of hyperbole employed for the sake of emotional insight. And so, though hyperbole may be a "lowd lyer" and "false semblant," we can see how an exaggerated or seemingly inappropriate image may succeed, not in stretching or disguising the truth of a situation, but in aiming more precisely at its psychological content. That is, it may reveal another kind of truth.[37] When Aristotle treats hyperbole as a kind of metaphor, he goes on to state that hyperboles should be used by "young men" and "angry people," because "they show vehemence of character" (*Rhetoric* III.11). This seems to suggest that hyperboles reveal less about the objects they refer to than the character of the person who uses them. In the Saint-Lazare passage, Proust's narrator can be understood to be writing from the pit

of his distress to demonstrate that he will experience the pain of separation from his mother like an evisceration, and ultimately like a
death on the cross. Hyperbole, in this case, communicates a subjective truth.

Let us push ahead even further, for there is more precision to
Proust's language than the expression of extreme emotion. When the
narrator finally arrives at his hotel room in Balbec after a long and
tiring journey, he describes, in a well-known passage, his anxiety at
having to sleep in a strange room. He claims to be as uncomfort-
able as a man in a cage, crowded by the unfamiliar things around
him. After finding temporary relief in his grandmother, who tucks
him into bed and then retreats to her own room next door, his dread
returns, and he ruminates on its meaning. He finds a unique kind of
resistance in his surroundings: "Perhaps this fear that I had—and that
is shared by so many others—of sleeping in a strange room, perhaps
this fear is only the most humble, obscure, organic, almost unconscious form of that great and desperate resistance put up by the things
that constitute the better part of our present life towards our mentally
acknowledging the possibility of a future in which they are to have no
part" (1: 720/532).[38] Perhaps it is the bedroom in Paris that, persisting
in the narrator's memory, protests against being replaced in his consciousness by the new bedroom in Balbec. Or perhaps it his grandmother—"the better part of our present life"—who, in her absence
that evening, protests against the inevitability of her being irrevoca-
bly forgotten. After all, we will discover that this scene foreshadows
the narrator's subsequent grief over his grandmother's death years
later, a grief he is able to experience only upon returning to the Balbec hotel. On this second trip, he hardly notices his bedroom at all,
except to mention that he has been inadvertently assigned to the same
room as before. The bedroom will have become unremarkable, com-
fortable, and forgettable, just as his grandmother's absence—the narrator will discover with fresh horror—has become familiar to him.
Finally grieving a year after the fact, he will realize: "On finding her
at last . . . I had lost her forever" (2: 785/1328).[39]

Thus it may be that the resistance described in the earlier passage
belongs not only to those bedroom things in Paris, which resist being
supplanted by new surroundings, but also to those of the Balbec room
itself, which resist being forgotten in some future time. In this case,
the brutal presence of unfamiliar things is nearly indistinguishable
from a future in which they will have been irretrievably lost. The

narrator's anxiety suggests that the unease of a first encounter resembles and projects the image of a future loss, encounter and loss perhaps being like symmetrical bookends to a brief-lived presence, and bounded by oblivion on either side.

But *what* oblivion, exactly, is at stake here? The narrator continues: "[This] resistance . . . was also at the root of the difficulty that I found in imagining my own death, or a survival such as Bergotte used to promise to mankind in his books, a survival in which I should not be allowed to take with me my memories, my frailties, my character, which did not easily resign themselves to the idea of ceasing to be, and desired for me neither extinction nor an eternity in which they would have no part" (1: 721/532).[40] In a swift reversal, it seems no longer to be a question of the resistance of objects to a future time in which they will be forgotten, but of the *persistence* of objects in a future time from which the narrator himself, his memories and feelings, will be absent. Just as he imagines a life apart from these low bookcases and high ceiling of the Balbec hotel room, so he recoils from the idea of these phenomenal objects continuing their existence, not only apart from him, but after his death. Particularly upsetting is the indifference of these objects in the face of his death, the kind of wounding indifference of which only nonsentient beings are capable.

Indeed, it is nothing less than the death of the self that the narrator describes in these passages. His ruminations turn to the probability of his surviving the loss of his parents and friends, and in a motif he often repeats later, he describes his horror, even more than at the thought of their loss, at what will be his inevitable indifference to this loss: "And our dread of a future in which we must forgo the sight of faces and the sound of voices which we love . . . this dread, far from being dissipated, is intensified, if to the pain of such a privation we feel that there will be added what seems to us now in anticipation more painful still: not to feel it as a pain at all—to remain indifferent . . . that would be in a real sense the death of the self, a death followed, it is true, by resurrection, but in a different self" (1: 722/533).[41] Indifference to loss is experienced by the narrator as a genuine death: a death of the self. A change in feeling is indeed a kind of death, we are made to understand, for a self that is constituted by its affections.

My point here is that the claim that the self dies when it changes its affections would be a hyperbolic claim, were it not perfectly continuous with the narrator's stated theory of the self. When he first arrives in his alien room in Balbec, he refuses to lie down, arguing that there is in fact "no place" for him there:

> I should have liked at least to lie down for a little while on the bed, but to what purpose, since I should not have been able to procure any rest for that mass of sensations which is for each of us his conscious if not his physical body, and since the unfamiliar objects which encircled that body, forcing it to place its perceptions on the permanent footing of a vigilant defensive, would have kept my sight, my hearing, all my senses in a position as cramped and uncomfortable . . . as that of Cardinal La Balue in the cage in which he could neither stand and sit? (1: 716/529)[42]

What is crowding him is not so much the objects in the room, as I first suggested, but more precisely the sensations these objects inflict on his "corporeal consciousness," and the demands they make of his perceptual apparatus. Because these encounters "force" his perceptions, another self finds itself excluded, the self born from and protected by habit. "It is our noticing them that puts things in a room," he writes, "and habit which takes them away again and clears a space for us" (1: 717/529, translation modified).[43] Presumably, the self that has no place in the room is an immaterial and intellectual self, one in which sensations have been properly absorbed and integrated into a spiritual consciousness.[44] Yet it is the self of the "conscious body," the self of the sense encounter, that the narrator laments as condemned to die, and to die in fragments: "It is they [the elements of the old self that are condemned to die]—even the meanest of them, such as our obscure attachments to the dimensions, to the atmosphere of a bedroom—that take fright and refuse, in acts of rebellion which we must recognise to be a secret, partial, tangible and true aspect of our resistance to death, of the long, desperate, daily resistance to the fragmentary and continuous death that insinuates itself throughout the whole course of our life, detaching from us at each moment a shred of our self" (1: 722/533).[45]

If we accept the internal logic of this episode in the hotel room, then we can see that when Proust's narrator suggests only pages earlier that his journey to Balbec will be like a crucifixion, he says exactly no more and no less than what he means. Death was indeed at stake in the Saint-Lazare station, and a resurrection was anticipated, like new cell growth where old parts of the self have died, as the narrator later writes (1: 722/533). The metaphor of crucifixion implicates this structure of sacrifice and rebirth very precisely, and suggests that a corporeal self will be sacrificed to a spiritual one, or that some sort of transubstantiation will occur. Moreover, we can see how the narrator's fascination with the speed and automation of train travel participates in this logic, for he focuses on the train's capacity of "making the difference between departure and arrival not as imperceptible but as intense as possible"[46]; and he further qualifies the difference between here and there as the difference, not between two physical places, but between the destination as it affects the senses and "as it existed in us when our imagination bore us from the place in which we were living right to the very heart of a place we longed to see" (1: 693/512).[47] Effecting this transubstantiation of imagination and desire, train travel indeed accomplishes a "miraculous leap" (1: 693/512, translation modified).[48]

In short, what first appeared to be hyperbolic rhetoric in the description of Saint-Lazare—language that was ill-fitting for the situation and exaggerated with respect to its meaning—turns out to be far more precise than we could have known. What we thought was emotionally exaggerated language turns out to be quite apt, only according to a logic that is developed for us after the fact. This structure of belated revelation is typical of Proust's novel; and the movement from surface to depth, impression to understanding, is, moreover, explicitly and repeatedly thematized. Earlier, I claimed that the rhetoric of hyperbole affords us insight into Proust's hyperbolic narrative structure. Now let us consider what this narrative structure can reveal, conversely, about the rhetoric of hyperbole, and about hyperbole's relation to other figures.

The narrator's story about the fragmentary and successive deaths of the sensual self, the sacrifice and conversion of these affections into a spiritual self, mirrors, in fact, the structural position of hyperbole with respect to metaphor. While metaphor can be understood to effect a kind of complete "transubstantiation,"[49] setting up a reciprocal exchange between a sensual image and a conceptual content, hyperbole is recognized as such only insofar as the exchange it claims to set up is necessarily partial, ill-fitting, unconvincing, or unsuccessful—in other words, exaggerated. This is not to say that hyperbole is an unsuccessful figure of speech, but rather that its very success lies in its being recognized as different from metaphor, and in at least part of its meaning lying beyond the supposed reciprocity of metaphorical exchange. In exaggerating, hyperbole has the additional purpose of communicating an attitude toward the objects it treats (perhaps conveying what Aristotle called "vehemence"). Doing so, hyperbole carves out a space for a speaking subject among the objects depicted—or rather, it projects a subject, much as the magic lantern projects the figures of Golo and Geneviève de Brabant on the narrator's bedroom wall. In fact, I think it would not be wrong to characterize hyperbole as a subject-forming figure. In this respect, hyperbole bears an important affinity to irony.

Irony is the figure of self-consciousness par excellence, in which, as Paul de Man points out, the subject of an ironic utterance is split into a knowing, ironic self and a displaced, inauthentic self, the object of the irony ("Rhetoric of Temporality" 214), just as self-consciousness divides into a subject and object of consciousness. In both hyperbole and irony, "the relationship between sign and meaning is discontinuous," and in both figures, moreover, this relationship relies on "an extraneous principle that determines the point and the manner at and in which the relationship is articulated" (209). That is, both figures depend on the projection of an intentional speaker "beyond" the utterance to account for the disjunction between language and meaning, or between language and context. But hyperbole lacks the totalizing specularity of irony: the subject and object of hyperbole do not coincide, as they do in irony (unless one is being hyperbolic and ironic at the same time, in which case hyperbole is usually put in the service of irony, and irony remains the determining factor). In this way, hyperbole seems to be situated somewhere between metaphor and irony, a figure of self-differentiation in excess of metaphor but lacking with respect to self-conscious irony.[50]

In sum, if the image of crucifixion in the description of the Saint-Lazare station is later revealed to be more appropriate than it first appeared, if the meaning of the image is explicated in the passages that follow it, then the image also possesses a hyperbolic status with respect to the narrative itself, much as we saw earlier with the impressions of the Martinville steeples. Moreover, in the movement from ill-fitting to fitting, exaggeration to representation, we experienced the transformation of our own understanding of the figure from hyperbole to metaphor (or at least to something approaching metaphor). But such a transformation can take place only through the construction of this other hyperbole at the level of narrative structure, a diachronic hyperbole in which the isolated passage points beyond itself toward a future revelation. In so doing, the diachronic hyperbole also projects a new subject to account for this temporal disjunction. If hyperbole is a subject-forming figure, in other words—if hyperbole as a rhetorical figure projects a speaking subject—then hyperbole as a narrative figure likewise projects a subject, but a subject of a different kind. This new subject of Proust's narrative is, of course, still the narrator; but it is the narrator no longer grasped as an affective self synchronous with a single scene, but as a diachronic consciousness comprising multiple states that undergo progressive transformation and synthesis. This second hyperbolic subject exists to ensure narrative continuity. Hyperbole resembles irony in this respect, too, as it is capable of being expanded into an allegory of revelation and self-transformation.

## THE SUBSTANCE OF ART

Returning to the episode of the narrator's encounter with the Martinville steeples, we might ask whether the fragment of writing he produces has an ironic status with respect to the rest of the text. Perhaps this fragment is not presented to us as an example of especially fine writing, as we are initially encouraged to believe, but as the narrator's novice and ultimately failed attempt to convert a sense impression into prose that is worthy of it, the representation of a technique and a philosophy of writing that the narrator no longer subscribes to by the end of the novel. In other words, perhaps the page is indicative of a naïve position that will be displaced by a greater self-consciousness, and by a more developed style of writing indicative of this self-consciousness.[51]

In the explicitly superficial nature of its images, which I noted earlier, the writing that Proust's hero produces lacks any real development or continuity beyond that of the continuous and continually shifting vantage point of the narrator. An abundance of metaphors, similes, and personifications are pressed into the service of capturing these sense impressions; but unlike the crucifixion metaphor in the Saint-Lazare passage, this language seems to have no significance other than its sensory content, which is perhaps what makes it so difficult to read. That is, unlike the narrator's poetic descriptions of his jealous loves, or of his experiences of high society, or of almost any other event in the novel, the lyrical and densely figurative writing in this fragment seems to reveal no higher truth, nor idea, nor meaningful law, nor insight into character psychology or human behavior. The choice of images here does not even draw very deeply on elements from the surrounding landscape, as Proust's treatments of steeples elsewhere tend to do.[52] The steeples' significance, we are told, is a personal one for the narrator, the aspiring writer whose ultimate task will be to translate the hieroglyphics of his own impressions, that "inner book of unknown symbols" (3: 913/2272), into a universally intelligible work of art.

Critics have long observed the discrepancy between the classical conception of metaphor and what goes by the name of metaphor in Proust, in which claims of resemblance are bolstered or even replaced by relations of spatiotemporal or linguistic contiguity. In his foundational study "Métonymie chez Proust," Gérard Genette, following Stephen Ullmann's observations in *Language and Style*, notes that "examples of supposedly 'natural' metaphors in *Le temps retrouvé* are in fact, typically, synecdochical substitutions" (58, translation mine).[53] So often that it appears to be the rule rather than the exception in Proust, "metaphor finds its support and its motivation in a metonymy" (45).[54] Even the operation of involuntary memory, which is supposed to deliver what Proust's hero calls the "essence" of the past, draws its real power from metonymic, and not metaphoric, association. That is, what the madeleine of involuntary memory ultimately reveals is not a similar madeleine dunked in tea once before, but what Proust calls "the vast structure of recollection": "all the flowers in our garden and in M. Swann's park, and the water-lilies on the Vivonne and the good folk of the village and their little dwellings and the parish church and the whole of Combray and its surroundings, taking shape and solidity . . . town and gardens alike, from my cup of tea" (1: 51/47).[55]

The philosophical problem with Proust's assertions, as both de Man in "Reading (Proust)" and Culler in "The Turns of Metaphor" make clear, is that what the narrative explicitly claims to be an essential relationship, the "'necessary link' of a resemblance (and potential identity) rooted in a shared property" (de Man 66), is repeatedly revealed to be contingent and accidental. In Genette's terms, claims about resemblances are revealed to rely on relations of merely spatiotemporal proximity. Yet I would argue that any discrepancy between Proust's claims and the actual construction of his figures, between what he calls the essence of the past and what he demonstrates to be the metonymic structure of involuntary memory, appears as such only if we look for meaning on the side of the objects described rather than on the side of the describing subject.

That is, if we take the narrator at his word when, recounting the phenomenon of involuntary memory and the "precious essence" delivered by his mouthful of tea and cake, he exclaims, "This essence was not in me, it *was* me" (1: 48/45),[56] we might understand the relationship of metonymy to metaphor quite differently. Samuel Weber observes that the spatiotemporal unity that guarantees the sense of Proustian metonymy is not an objective one, in fact, but a subjective one: "Their [the metonymies'] place is never simply homogeneous space but the site of the subject. . . . It is not contiguity as such but *contiguity with the subject* that determines the Proustian metonymy" (929). Thus the narrator recalls a series of sensations and images of Venice, not because of the proximity of space and time in which they were first experienced, but because of his own bodily participation in the scene, which has conferred a unity on them: "It was Venice . . . which the sensation which I had once experienced as I stood upon two uneven stones in the baptistery of St Mark's had, recurring a moment ago, restored to me complete with all the other sensations linked on that day to that particular sensation," he writes, making clear the metonymic concatenation of sensation (3: 900/2263).[57] Just as we saw hyperbole relying on an extraneous principle—an intentional subject—to account for the disjunction between sign and meaning, so, too, does Proustian metonymy continually and quite explicitly appeal to a metaphoric operation of appropriation and identity formation, the formation of a uniquely subjective vision.[58] Perhaps metonymy and metaphor are not opposed in Proust so much as they represent the two opposite poles of a movement of subjective appropriation, a movement I would characterize as hyperbolic, as it traces hyperbole's constitutively incomplete passage from disjunction to recognition (that is, from the disjunction of sign and meaning to the recognition of the one in the other). I do not wish to claim that hyperbole effectively mediates the passage from metonymy to metaphor, or from contingency to necessity; rather I suggest that, such a passage being constitutively impossible, hyperbole may be the only way to represent this passage or even claim that it is possible in the first place.

In *Le temps retrouvé*, Proust's narrator gives us a clear, if idiosyncratic, definition of what he means by metaphor, and indicates its role in the book he will undertake: "Truth will be attained by him only when he takes two different objects, states the connexion between them—a connexion analogous in the world of art to the unique connexion which in the world of science is provided by the law of causality. . . . Truth—and life too—can be attained by us only when, by comparing a quality common to two sensations, we succeed in extracting their common essence and in reuniting them to each other . . . within a metaphor" (3: 924–25/2280).[59] A writer will discover truth not in the relation between two similar objects, but between two dissimilar ones. The "essence" he extracts cannot logically belong to either one of them, but indicates a kind of third term in the equation, this strange point at which an unmotivated comparison is converted into a relationship as necessary as a law of physics. This third term can only be understood as the narrator's own self, a self constituted by so many corporeal sensations and perceived relations.

In his reading of the steeples of Martinville passage, Joshua Landy similarly argues that "the aim of a metaphor can be—and in Marcel's description quite explicitly is—to convey not an objective but a subjective connection between two impressions or ideas, and that this subjective connection can possess a type of local inescapability" (73). Following this, and returning to the steeples of Martinville episode, we can understand the variegated images proposed by the narrator's page of writing to reveal the "local" necessity of a subjective vision, insofar as the metonymic stutter of images becomes nothing more than the very locus *of* the narrator's subjectivity, the knit-together surface on which it is projected.

Landy goes on to interpret the significance of the narrator's writing in two ways. First, he argues, the images ultimately represent the "unique aspect of his perspective, the part he shares with nobody else"—this being, Landy claims, the narrator's predilection for flowers and girls (59). Second, he proposes that "the set of impressions considered as a whole . . . communicates a universal, objective truth, namely that every human being has a unique perspective" (77). Thus he concludes that "the images do not, in the end, teach us anything about the steeples themselves" (67). Unfortunately, this conclusion seems to me to be doubly unconvincing. While it is clear that girls and flowers are significant throughout the *Recherche*—given Marcel's predilection for hawthorns and Swann's for cattleyas, not to mention the extended botanical metaphor that opens *Sodome et Gomorrhe*—their appearance in the Martinville passage is not so unique or idiosyncratic to be deeply revealing of a perspective shared "with nobody else." Flowers and girls, considered in general as Landy proposes, are rather pedestrian symbols, and they are isolated enough from other flowers and girls in the novel to suggest that they are called upon here as culturally available clichés. On the other hand, the idea that this passage can be meaningfully summarized by the proposition "Every human being has a unique perspective" is equally unsatisfying, as it disregards any particularity whatsoever in the narrator's perception. What *is* unique, *pace* Landy, is simply the articulation of these particular metaphors themselves, the irreducibility of these images to a general preference for flowers and girls, as well as their stubborn insistence on *still* teaching us something about the steeples—that is, their refusal to give up their referential function, even as they indicate an intentional or subjective one.

What the narrator claims lay "behind" the steeples, or hidden "inside" them—"as if they had been a sort of rind, peeled away," he writes—is rather his own prose: "something analogous to a pretty phrase" (1: 197/149),[60] as we have seen. Proust's metaphors of depth are turned inside out when he suggests that a page of writing may be the true "meaning" of these three-dimensional objects. But what, then, can possibly be "behind" the page of writing?

There is such a thoroughgoing immanence of the self to its impressions in the *Recherche*, and of impressions to the objective world, that a hyperbolic movement is required to appropriate and synthesize these elements into a meaningful whole. Earlier, we saw that the narrator's corporeal self was made up of a successive concatenation of sensations, like so many fragments or "slices" (*lambeaux*). We should note that the "whole of Combray" or the whole of Venice is not available to this self contemporaneous with its sense experiences, but only to a temporal self, one transcendent to the experience in question, in keeping, of course, with Proust's discourses on the anesthetizing effects of habit. Yet this temporal self is available, in turn, only to an extratemporal subject, the "ecstatic" subject of involuntary memory. Just as the writer places two dissimilar objects side by side to reveal their "common essence," this atemporal subject grasps two isolated moments in time to reveal their necessary connection, "something that, common both to the past and to the present, is much more essential than either of them" (3: 905/2266).[61] Thus with the madeleine as well as with the paving stones, the narrator discovers a joyous indifference to death, and truly becomes "a man freed from the order of time" (3: 906/2267).[62] However, because these impressions appeal hyperbolically to a subject who stands outside them and appropriates their meaning, they cannot help but testify to the possibility of a reversal or a remainder, thus raising the specter of a persistent noncoincidence between this subject, the experiencing self, and the sensory world. They offer intimations of a self that persists as mere sensation, and of sensation that threatens to dissolve in turn into the many scattered, inanimate phenomena that first gave rise to it.[63]

What the extratemporal subject ultimately discovers is the destiny of the experience of his life to become the material for a book, a destiny that can only be represented as a vocation. Perhaps this book will be the site of a new subject, the transcendent subject of art: the text will be "the very locus of his thought" (Genette, "Proust et le language indirect" 22, translation mine),[64] the site of a superior self-consciousness and a revealed truth, "life at last laid bare and illuminated—the only life in consequence which can be said to be really lived" (Proust 3: 931/2284).[65] Or perhaps his book will be like a tomb, a lifeless monument to people, places, and things that have been covered over and forgotten. "A book is a huge cemetery," the narrator writes a few pages later, "in which on the majority of the tombs the names are effaced and can no longer be read" (3: 940/2291).[66] When Proust's narrator describes the process of uniting two different objects in a metaphor, he goes on to say that a writer must "link forever in his phrase the two sets of phenomena . . . enclose them in the necessary links of a well-wrought style" (3: 925/2280),[67] revealing that his theory of essences is, thus, also a theory of style. At the same time two objects are supposed to be lifted outside of themselves and converted into their "common essence," we witness their committal to prose, or to a prosaic style whose chain-like "links" (*anneaux*) recall the very metonymic concatenation that was supposed to be superseded by metaphor.

If there is a spiritualization in Proust, a conversion of impressions into truths, there is a concomitant substantialization of truth into art, which we witness in discussions of an artist's or writer's style, described as "a new and distinct material" (3: 904/2265),[68] where, as Proust writes in *Contre Sainte-Beuve*, "all the elements of reality are rendered down into one . . . unanimous substance" (*On Art and Literature* 170; *Contre Sainte-Beuve* 201).[69] It remains unclear whether this substance belongs to the higher life of literature, or to the lifeless materiality of the letter.[70] What is so revealing about the figure of hyperbole in the case of Proust is not only the disjunction it initiates between what it says and what it means, or between what it claims and what it knows—a disjunction also present in irony (and certainly the *Recherche* is rich in irony)—but also and more precisely the disjunction it *perpetuates* in never fully departing from reference, and never quite coming together as a full-fledged guarantee of self-consciousness. Hyperbole is constitutionally bound to what it overcomes; it does not surrender its objective aspect even as it gains a subjective one. With one foot in the phenomenal world, and the other beyond it, this figure helps expose the precariousness and genuine reversibility of Proustian claims about the transcendence of art.

And yet, if we refuse to adopt the standpoint of this transcendence, if we do not install ourselves in the perspective of the end of the novel and expect the novel's development to reflect this end as it unfolds—if instead we take the narrator's claims about the redemptive function of art as themselves to some degree hyperbolic, this reversibility takes on quite a different meaning. The precariousness of the narrator's theory of art, which makes up such a large part of *Le temps retrouvé*, resides in the fact that it does not correspond wholly and without remainder to what Proust's novel actually *does*. It exceeds it; it "marks the point of the book's own overflow," in Rebecca Comay's words (90). We would seem to face two choices: either to take the theory with a grain of salt, reading it (as I think it should be read) as the concoction of Proust's fictional narrator rather than as Proust's own statement, or else to approach the rest of the novel with critical insight where we assume Proust was blind, drawing out those moments that fail to correspond fully to the novel's own aesthetic theory.

The logic of hyperbole presents us with a third option. Hyperbole does not exist to be debunked, but to persuade; it works not by effacing, but by drawing out a difference between what is said and what is meant. Just as hyperbole in speech works by introducing a difference between sign and meaning, so does hyperbole as literary form introduce a difference between what the text says and what it actually does. And just as hyperbole in speech projects the image of an intentional subject to account for this difference, so that I was able to describe the figure as subject-forming, so does hyperbole as literary form project the space of a work in which this difference unfolds, a work in which this difference can be recognized and made meaningful *as* a difference. In Proust's novel, the totality of the work assumes the form of a difference. The chain-like "links" of the style Proust envisioned, then, perhaps describe neither a spiritual necessity nor a mortal coil, but the inextricability of the one from the other, a relation forged from the noncoincidence and incompleteness that yet more completely characterizes this novel than anything else.

# CHAPTER 7

# "How Anything Can Be Different from What It Is"

*Tautology in Stein's* The Making of Americans

The question of systematicity, and specifically the compatibility of systematicity with novelty, has been at the heart of this book from the beginning. In chapter 1 we saw that system and freedom were pitted against one another in a theory of the fragment in German romanticism. Subsequently, we found totalizing treatments of literary form to rely on idealist conceptions of self-reflection and organic development. In chapters 5 and 6, by contrast, we saw how Beckett's trilogy and Proust's novel each pose distinct challenges to the romantic view of the work as a self-reflecting system: each stages a certain noncoincidence with itself, problematizing those readings that would approach them as providing their own lucid self-commentary. In this chapter, I argue that Gertrude Stein's epic novel *The Making of Americans: Being a History of a Family's Progress* (1925) develops a unique approach to the question of what a system is, and by extension what the integrity of a text is. In this work as well as related literary-critical texts, Stein deploys a number of oppositions that, on the surface, may appear to be familiarly romantic ones—mind and nature, theory and practice, part and whole—but she does so to uniquely modern ends. Through a series of meditations on repetition, habit, and "wholeness," Stein engages in a practice of composition that opens onto a theory of the creative powers of the cognitive faculties. Ultimately, the way she locates this creative cognition within the domain of experience has radical implications for our understanding of the relationship between philosophy and art.

Of all the features of Stein's prose style, the most commented on, most parodied, and most recognizable is surely her use of repetition.

And repetition is usually cited as what makes Stein difficult. Words, grammatical structures, whole chunks of syntax repeated—such repetition can be vexing because it doesn't seem to *go* anywhere. Like her famous phrase "Rose is a rose is a rose is a rose," which she had printed in a small ring on the 1933 cover of *The Autobiography of Alice B. Toklas*, repetition seems to bring us back to where we started, frustrating the demand that sentences or paragraphs progress by presenting new information. What is the relationship, then, between Stein's repetition, her experimentalism, and her novelty? What is Stein's own attitude toward novelty?

Stein's engagements with repetition and system building converge—if not reach their breaking point—in her mammoth, experimental novel *The Making of Americans*. At once a twist on the nineteenth-century genre of family chronicle and a self-conscious theory of repetition, *The Making of Americans* examines the way people repeat behaviors, the way character types emerge in families and across groups of individuals, and the way such repetition is processed and interpreted by others. What it means to build a system—or what Stein calls a *composition*—in this work and perhaps for the remainder of Stein's career, is simultaneously an epistemological question and an aesthetic one. The double nature of the question, however, has not yet been adequately recognized. While recent critical work has enriched our understanding of Stein's intellectual formation by tracing her concerns to the psychological and philosophical models of mind of her time, detailing her engagements with Darwin and Bergson, William James and Otto Weininger, the wider importance of the relationship between Stein's more "scientific" concerns and her aesthetic ones still needs to be elaborated. To tackle this relationship head-on as it plays out in *The Making of Americans*—this relationship between knowledge and art, or between what can be known and what can be made—we need to examine the distinctive formal features of the text and connect them to the epistemological problems that inform them.

TAUTOLOGIES

Stein worked on *The Making of Americans* intermittently from 1903 to 1911,[1] though the novel did not find a publisher until 1925, when it was brought out in Paris by Robert McAlmon's Contact Editions. The novel is disproportionate in every sense. At 925 pages, its girth is matched only by the scope of its ambitions. Its subtitle announces it will be a family history, but the aim of the book soon expands to include "histories of every one [the family] ever came to know in their living" (284). A diffuse and idiosyncratic character typology edges out most of the narrative action, a typology in which the narrator attempts to identify and classify people's "bottom natures" with the newly readjusted purpose of describing "every kind of men and every kind of women who ever were or are or will be living" (220).[2] While Edmund Wilson's definitive *Axel's Castle* (1931), which devoted an entire chapter to Stein, suggested that the novel may be impossible to read (239), Stein's own estimation placed *The Making of Americans* alongside *Ulysses* and *A la recherche du temps perdu* as one of the three truly "important things written in this generation" (*"Portraits and Repetition"* 184).

Recent critics take the work more seriously than Wilson, usually noting its destructive or deconstructive effects. Stein's *Making of Americans* "amounts to a slow murder of the Victorian novel," writes Lisa Ruddick; even more fundamentally, it "has the effect of unsettling key categories of Victorian thinking: objective history; science as 'truth'; and character, or the integrated subject" (125). "The primary strategies of Stein's *Making of Americans*," writes another critic, "self-reflexively dismantle their own and, by inference, other texts' narrative and rhetorical conventions" (Taylor 27); and another: "The frustration caused by endless disruptions forces readers to confront their own longing for . . . narrative conventions" (Wald 239). Though the novel certainly engages in a critical and disruptive project, such views risk disseminating the idea that Stein's endeavor amounts to an essentially negative exercise. A different picture emerges when we consider the positive or constructive aspects of the novel, even if these involve the construction of certain tensions.

We could do worse than begin with the passage that gave Wilson so much trouble:

> Some are needing themselves being a young one, an older one, a middle aged one, an older one, an old one to be ones realizing what any one telling about different ways of feeling anything, of thinking about anything, of doing anything is meaning by what that one is telling. Some are needing themselves being a young one, an older one, a middle aged one, an older one, an old one to be one being certain that it is a different thing inside in one being a young one, from being an older one, from being a middle aged one, from being an older one, from being an old one. (Stein, *Making* 817)

What can be said about this style? It is rhythmic, generalizing, monotonous, surprising, childish, serious, funny, grandiose, and banal all at once. It is distinctly pleasurable and undeniably tedious to read, and often pleasurable *because* it is tedious. Formally, it proceeds with a serial enumeration—"a young one, an older one, a middle aged one"— and a conspicuous reliance on the present progressive. The first half of the first sentence is repeated in the second sentence, phrases of which are echoed again in a weak repetition at the end of the passage. Out of the 110 words that make up the passage, only 37 are unique, yielding a type-token ratio (number of different words divided by total number of words) of less than 34 percent (40 to 50 percent is considered low; Pound 32). A paraphrase of the content, meanwhile, is decidedly brief and admittedly commonplace, running something like the following: Some people need to experience themselves at various ages in life in order to understand other people's points of view, as well as their own, as it differs from age to age. Enumeration and repetition overwhelm a content that is self-evident enough that it might be said in fewer words, or even go without saying at all. In general, repetition is the most pronounced formal oddity of this novel, with this passage being far from the worst of it. The final chapter, for example, rehearses for some nineteen pages variations of only seventeen sentences (Clement 443).

What does it mean to make use of repetition as an intentional element of style? If we look to the rhetorical tradition, we find that the question is a peculiar one. Rhetoricians have almost exclusively classified repetition as a vice, a linguistic flaw that the very development of style was intended to correct. Quintilian designated "the repetition of a word or phrase" with the term *tautologia* (from the Greek ταὐτό, "the same" + λογος, "saying"), and characterized such repetition as an oversight that risks obscuring the meaning of a discourse (Quintilian 239). Erasmus, who drew on Quintilian and whose popular sixteenth-century manual *Copia: Foundations of the Abundant Style* was meant to root out repetition by instructing students in how to lend variety to their language, condemned tautology as "an ugly and offensive fault": "It often happens that we have to say the same thing several times. If in these circumstances we find ourselves destitute of verbal riches and hesitate, or keep singing out the same old phrase like a cuckoo, and are unable to clothe our thought in other colours or other forms, we shall look ridiculous when we show ourselves to be so tongue-tied, and we shall also bore our wretched audience to death"

(302). In philosophy, the term *tautology* has been used to describe a logical fallacy, as, for example, when Kant characterized tautologous propositions as "empty of consequences" because they repeat in the predicate what has already been stated in the proposition's subject (*Lectures on Logic* §37). Here the term designates not only repeated words but repeated ideas, so that the same idea may be restated in different words, implying a redundancy of language with respect to meaning. From this treatment probably derives the common-sense use of the term to refer to any statement of the obvious or self-evident.

Tautology, in short, has been used to mark both an aesthetic failing—a lack of novelty—and an epistemological failing—an empty claim. Yet the term gives us some purchase on the stylistic effects of Stein's repetition. In *The Making of Americans*, rather than providing emphasis or generating intensity (as in, for example, Keats's "happy, happy boughs"), repetition seems to render Stein's point more diffuse; it rehearses what we already know or what should go without saying; it draws equivalences and accumulates without necessarily amounting to anything. Identifying *tautologia* as a major figure of speech in this novel not only helps us put our finger on the repetition that structures Stein's prose and gives it its distinctive rhythm; it also captures the feeling of narrative stasis that comes from a scarcity of new information, a feeling of inertia that, I think, lies at the heart of why this novel is difficult to read.

*Not* coming to the point, however, may be part of Stein's point. The gesture *tautologia* makes is one of refusing organizing statements or conceptual headings. Humbly remaining just what it is, *tautologia* eschews transcendence, poeticization, abstraction, hierarchy, and—seemingly—progress. Its grammatical expression is parataxis, a purely lateral linking without the complexity of subordinate clauses. In the next section, I look at the particular kinds of stasis tautology sets up before examining Stein's way of making tautology productive.

## HISTORY AND KINDS

The syntax of tautology refuses subordination. Thematically, the refusal of subordination, or at least the struggle to refuse it, is introduced at the outset of *The Making of Americans* in a familial mini-drama that some critics have referred to as "oedipal" (Watten, Ruddick). In fact, the opening lines introduce a number of tensions that run through the entire work. The novel begins, "Once an angry man dragged his father along the ground through his own orchard. 'Stop!' cried the groaning old man at last, 'Stop! I did not drag my father beyond this tree.'" The anecdote reads like a joke with an obscure punch line, describing what seems to be an act of rebellion and an act of compliance at one and the same time, both a show of passion and the acculturation of that passion. Stein borrows the anecdote from Montaigne (Meyer, introduction xxxiv), who repeats the story from book 7 of Aristotle's *Nicomachean Ethics*. In Montaigne, the story illustrates the idea that custom may "infringe on the rules of nature" to such a degree that we confuse it with nature itself (122–30), while in Aristotle, conversely, the anecdote conveys the idea that if a temperament is customary enough, it must be natural.

Offering her own, somewhat murky interpretation, Stein's narrator remarks, "It is hard living down the tempers we are born with" (*Making* 3). Beyond the opposition of nature and culture, these words draw attention to the struggle between the givenness of one's temper and the open-ended activity of "living it down," or perhaps simply living it. They also hint at the particular form of progress (or lack thereof) at stake in the novel, less the forward march of generations than the genealogical research of pattern recognition. Indeed, when Stein writes, "There is nothing we are more intolerant of than our own sins writ large in others" (3), she suggests that the specular structure of recognition is part of what is at stake in what she calls "history."

Stein's novel will wrestle with all of these concerns, as well as with their immediate complication: it charts static, psychological types— "the tempers we are born with"—at the same time as it attempts to chronicle a dynamic family history and a history of individual expression; moreover, it poses the question of where each one begins and the other ends. Jennifer Ashton notes that the relationship between "history" and "kind"—or between progressive development and static typology—remains undefined throughout the novel (36). And it is true Stein does not offer neat definitions of these terms. Nonetheless, the tension between "history" and "kind," or between progress and stasis, marks the poles of a problem worked out over the course of the entire novel.

We might characterize the tension between "history" and "kind" as one of diachronic versus synchronic knowledge, or of knowledge from temporal experience versus knowledge from static concepts. In the opening of *The Making of Americans*, Stein introduces her chronicle of the Dehning family with an observation about the way we tend to experience personal identity in time, our own identity as well as that of others:

> We, living now, are always to ourselves young men and women.
> When we, living always in such feeling, think back to them who make
> for us a beginning, it is always as grown and old men and women
> or as little children that we feel them, these whose lives we have just
> been thinking. . . . Yes it is easy to think ourselves and our friends,
> all our lives as young grown men and women, indeed it is hard for
> us to feel even when we talk it long, that we are old like old men and
> women or little as a baby or as children. Such parts of our living are
> never really there to us as present, to our feeling. (4–5)

While to us other people may be babies or old people, and while these are the positions they occupy in our family narratives, we only really experience ourselves as young adults, or "grown and young." Even as children, Stein writes, we experience ourselves as young adults, and even when we age, we continue to experience ourselves as young adults, because "no one can be old . . . to himself in his feeling" (5). Stein's observations implicate a more general distinction between different temporal perspectives: between formed identities or completed events on the one hand, and the still mutable, living present on the other, a present one experiences and within which one feels capable of action, direction, and self-determination. In grammatical terms, this distinction might be described as one of aspect, where the imperfect is distinguished from the perfect, and which in English is marked by the use of progressive verbs (or -ing forms) such as *living, feeling, thinking*. One form indicates a completed action, viewed from outside, while the other shows us the inside of the action, stretching it into what Stein will later call a "prolonged" or "continuous present" ("Composition" 31).

The refusal of top-down categories, the even-keeled quality of Stein's repetitive, tautological statements gives her prose a sort of democratic and "unemphatic" character (Katz 92). Such a character reflects the subject matter of *The Making of Americans*, whose interest lies not in extraordinary events, but in "daily living," and not in heroes, but in "decent ordinary people": "in ordinary middle class existence, in simple firm ordinary middle class traditions, in sordid material unaspiring visions, in a repeating, common, decent enough kind of living with no fine kind of fancy ways inside us, no excitements to surprise us" (34).

Narratologically, Stein prefers the flat geometry of situations over the peaks and valleys of events. From her first novella, titled *Q.E.D.*, onward, she envisions the action of her stories as expressions of her characters' fixed natures, often with tragic consequences. In *The Making of Americans*, she defuses drama by eliminating narrative suspense almost entirely, often sketching far-reaching events of a character's life with a single statement, as, for example, in this description of Fanny Hissen (who will become Fanny Hersland):

> The mother who was to bear the three children, she perhaps would come to an important feeling, she did not have it as a natural thing to have really an important feeling. With her it must come from a, to her, not natural way of living, and it first had its beginning with her friendship with the Shilling women. Then it came to be stronger with the living in Gossols in the ten acre place in the part of Gossols where no other rich people were living, where she was cut off from the rich living which was for her the natural way of being. (77)

This passage begins with the temporally condensed perspective of the future anterior, and it presents several major phases of Fanny Hersland's life that will later unfold over the course of hundreds of pages. By taking suspense out of the narrative, Stein creates a kind of temporally "flattened" perspective.

Temporal flattening is one effect of Stein's use of tautology, and it is coupled with a spatial flattening. The latter is the object of some theorizing in later lectures and interviews. In a well-known interview given in the last year of her life, for example, Stein commented on the inspiration she drew early on from the visual arts. Cézanne's paintings, above all, impressed upon her "a new feeling about composition": "Up to that time," she claimed, "composition had consisted of a central idea to which everything else was an accompaniment and separate but was not an end in itself, and Cézanne conceived the idea that in composition one thing was as important as another thing. Each part is as important as the whole and that impressed me enormously" ("Transatlantic Interview" 98). This equality among parts and whole, which contributed to what art critics have called a "flatness" in Cézanne's paintings,[3] Stein termed "evenness"; she suggests that her early experimental narrative, and in particular her turn from *Three Lives* to the much more radical, final versions of *The Making of Americans*, was motivated by "a need for evenness." (99). "Evenness" was bound up with experiments in a new kind of realism: "It was not solely the realism of the characters," she explained, "but the realism of the composition which was the important thing" (98). This was a realism in which "every possible variety of human type" was to "have the same value"—as in a landscape painting, Stein explains, where "a blade of grass has the same value as a tree" (98).

Tautology, in short, gives us not only a feeling of temporal stasis, but also an evenness of relations between things as they are, not as they would be governed by a central idea. "Act so that there is no use in a center," as *Tender Buttons* advises (498). The problem tautology sets up for narrative, however, is that it appears to have no forward momentum. In this "history of a family's progress," in other words, it can be difficult to tell what counts as "progress." It doesn't help when Stein repeatedly returns to spatial concepts to describe her narrative work (calling her verbal descriptions of Matisse and Picasso "portraits," for example, or referring to her plays from the 1930s as "landscapes"). What is the relationship between tautological repetition and narrative progression? Between repetition and production as such? Stein's answers are bound up with her understanding of the relationship between the parts and the whole of an aesthetic composition.

## PARTS AND WHOLES

*Tautologia* draws equivalences and refuses hierarchies, but Stein also uses it to cultivate an evenness between parts and wholes. In other words, even as she repeats the same details again and again, she does not relinquish her interest in the whole. The latter remains immanent to its repeating parts (or its "pieces," as she calls them in her later work). This immanence of parts and wholes governs Stein's approach to character in *The Making of Americans*, and it also gives us insight into how her "history" and "kinds" are not only opposing forces in this novel, but thought as mutually constitutive.

Stein's approach to character seems to take its cue from the visual arts, so that, like repeated brush strokes gradually giving rise to a painted image, tautological statements accumulate to form general, psychological portraits. Analysis takes precedence over action, and individuals are considered not in terms of narrative development but always generally, in relation to repeated behaviors and statements, and schematically, in relation to others of similar or different kinds. Every one is "a kind of men and women." "Everybody is a real one to me," Stein's narrator says; "everybody is like some one else too to me" (*Making* 333). Individual being is sketched in relation to type, and minute variations in repeating are recorded for what they reveal about a person's total identity or "bottom nature."

The mutual dependence Stein sets up between parts and wholes, individuals and types, repetition and character, might be taken as another way that she circumvents dynamism or temporal progression altogether. A whole equal to its parts, after all, does not seem to have room for anything new in its ambit, so it is not clear how anything new can be produced from it. Yet Stein's approach turns out to give us a model for thinking production as immanent to repetition, particularly as she thematizes the production of both character and type out of habit.

Repeating phrases in Stein's prose, first of all, echo the repeating statements and gestures of characters themselves. According to the novel's theory of character, a person's nature expresses itself in repetition: "The nature in every one is always coming out of them from their beginning to their ending by the repeating always in them, by the repeating always coming out from each one. . . . The whole of every one is always coming out in repeating" (*Making* 186). This may sound like a claim about the unidirectional nature of repetition, whereby repetitions radiate from a person's essential nature. But "coming out" might conversely describe the production, and not just the expression, of a person's nature. In this way, following the ethos of compositional "evenness," repetitions appear not as the result of a given and fixed nature but as creative of that nature, as the many habits that make up a person's "daily living" (181).[4]

Characters are accordingly distinguished by activities such as washing, eating, or giving advice. Take David Hersland (senior), who has gone out west to make his fortune: "In David Hersland the father of the three children whose lives we are now soon to be watching, to David Hersland beginning was all of living to him. For him there was in his living ways of eating, ways of doctoring, ways of educating his children, ways of making his great fortune here in Gossols where he was to make his important beginning" (*Making* 120). When we consider repetition as habit, and habit as productive of character, we see that such repetition cannot be cumulative in any simple way, indifferently aggregating into a quantitative whole; rather it hangs together to produce a meaningful or qualitative whole, yielding what Stein will later call the "complete rhythm of a personality" ("Gradual Making" 249; Meyer, *Irresistible Dictation* 183).[5] Stein equates "the history of someone," not with a bare record of his repeating, but with a reading of it, with a living interpretation that bears within it "the meaning of all the repeating" (*Making* 316).[6]

In her considerations on habit, Stein likely draws on William James, especially his *Psychology: The Briefer Course*, an abridgment of *Principles of Psychology* and assigned reading for Stein's introductory philosophy course at Radcliffe (Bridgman 20). James was a valued mentor of Stein's, "the important person in [her] Radcliffe life," as she declared (*Autobiography* 73); she worked with him for several years at the Harvard Psychological Laboratory and later followed his advice in enrolling in medical school at Johns Hopkins (Meyer, *Irresistible Dictation* 3, 75). James, for his part, notoriously considered the young Stein to be one of his most brilliant pupils (Wilson 237).[7]

What might Stein have learned from James on habit? Habit, as James describes it, marks a phase of "relative stability" in action and reaction; as such it has its corollary in the plasticity of human nature, where plasticity refers to "a structure weak enough to yield to an influence, but strong enough not to yield all at once" (2). Habit is character-forming, while character, in turn, is a malleable structure, one that yields "in proportion to the uninterrupted frequency with which the [repeated] actions actually occur, and the brain 'grows' to their use" (14). Furthermore, as James sees it, habit lends shape not only to individuals but to social structures, being "the enormous fly-wheel of society, its precious conservative agent" (10). In this way, habit marks the peculiar give-and-take of nature and culture, individual and group.

For Stein, focusing on habits in daily living allows her to shuttle back and forth between individuals and "kinds," for the repetitions she observes characterize the behavior of individuals as well as groups. Habit is both microscope and telescope, revealing human being to be repetition and variation all the way down and all the way up. David Hersland, for example, is introduced in remarks that individuate him from a general kind of men: "As I have been saying there are many kinds of men and there are many millions made of each kind of them. David Hersland who had come to Gossols to make for himself a great fortune was of one kind of all the world around them. He was of the kind of them that feel themselves to be as big as all the world around them" (*Making* 118). The habits peculiar to David Hersland, moreover—his ways of beginning, eating, doctoring, and educating—are considered general "kinds" of behavior: "There are many ways of beginning, there are some things in living that have in them always more of beginning than other things in living, education is such a part of living, eating and doctoring, all have it in them to be always in a beginning" (118).

As the novel progresses, Stein's focus on kinds increases, and she begins grouping all men and women into two opposing, general types of people: "resisters" and "attackers," or those with "dependent independent" natures and others with "independent dependent" natures. "Resisters" are slow to respond, have a "resisting earthy slow" nature, and generally "let things sink into them" (*Making* 343, 154), while attackers have "poignant and quick reaction" and tend to strike first in a conflict (343). The unique mixture of these kinds within each person is what accounts for that person's character, while the interplay among various degrees of these kinds is what produces action in the novel. In fact, the kinds are mixed in each person to such an extent that, as Ruddick argues, they are less suggestive of distinct character types than of the "warring principles that exist *in every mind*" (20). We might thus read them as descriptive of the two poles of character formation: what might be termed the "attacking" activity of repeated behaviors, on the one hand, and the "resisting" reception of the plasticity of character, on the other.

What is more, we might read the two poles of "attacking" and "resisting" as descriptive of the mental activity of characterizing *other* people and things—that is, as descriptive of the activity of concept formation. The production of character through the repetition of habits, in other words, ends up modeling the production of concepts through the repetition of perceptual data. In making this argument, I am relying on the resonance Ruddick draws out between Stein's categories and James's treatment of perception, where perception is divided between apprehension and retention, and thus is organized much like James's treatment of character. Ruddick argues that *The Making of Americans* "dramatizes as affective play *between people* the play of faculties James attributed to the individual mind" (70).[8] She cites the *Briefer Course* on the mutability of concepts with respect to new perceptions: "There is an everlasting struggle in every mind," James writes, "between the tendency to keep unchanged, and the tendency to renovate, its ideas. Our education is a ceaseless compromise between the conservative and the progressive factors. Every new experience must be disposed of under some old head" (James 194, qtd. in Ruddick 20). *The Making of Americans* labors under these very same tensions—between the old and the new, repetition and conceptual heading, experience and generalization—at the same time as it dramatizes this conflict with its typologies of human kinds, "resisters" and "attackers," and all of the possible variations of mixtures of these kinds. Its system-building character is on display in the negotiations it sets up between its own conservative and progressive factors, its attempt to capture the living history of what is "endlessly the same and endlessly different" (Stein, "Gradual" 243).

Making conservative and progressive factors communicate in this way, *The Making of Americans* reveals its epistemological aims. The problem it lays out, and indeed "the preoccupation that had governed [Stein's] intellectual life almost from its beginning," as Leon Katz puts it, is that of capturing "'the last touch' of human being" (iii). But this "last touch" turns out to have nothing to do with the most intimate or unique thing about an individual person. Characterization is never personal in this book but general, relational, and differential. Characters are related and distinguished by habits, as we have seen, and every one belongs to a general type: "Every one is one inside them, every one reminds some one of some other one" (*Making* 333). Everywhere, Stein seeks to typologize and categorize, classify and subdivide, so that what passes for individual being is only thought in relation to a whole, and slight variations in repeating are recorded for what they reveal about a person's bottom nature. There is no interest in detail for its own sake, but only for the sake of a system of knowledge in which the "whole" of a person and the "complete description of everyone" might be possible (549).

I emphasize this point—that Stein relates the individual to the whole for the sake of a system of knowledge—because there is still work being done on Stein claiming that her experimental writing speaks a private idiolect, one that attempts to communicate a purely subjective experience. Robert Chodat, for example, takes issue with recent descriptions of Stein's work as "scientific" (Meyer's *Irresistible Dictation* is his extended target), arguing instead that Stein privileges a first-person perspective to the neglect of any intersubjective considerations or any of the normative distinctions that belong to ordinary language (Chodat 596–97). Versions of this claim have been around since the 1930s and tend to appear whenever critics want to emphasize Stein's obscurity at the expense of her meaning-making.[9] But such assessments cannot begin to explain Stein's interest in the problem of histories and kinds in *The Making of Americans*; really, they cannot account for any of the subject matter of this book beyond the fact that it is idiosyncratic.

If Stein set out to record the private events of her inner life, why does she choose the framework of a family chronicle? Why make so many appeals to common attitudes? Why the nearly constant push to generalize? Or the heavy use of impersonal pronouns? To be fair, Chodat focuses his attention on the more radical text "If I Told Him," not the *Making of Americans*, even if the former is meant to stand in for Stein's work as a whole. Yet it is instructive to push against his claims in thinking about *The Making of Americans*. The idiosyncratic and the personal are key values in this novel, as Chodat would have it, but only insofar as they are bound to the general. This, I would venture, is the work's systematic character: the network it creates between parts and wholes, subjects and objects, repetitions and "bottom natures," human mind and human nature, knowing and living. And this is what makes *The Making of Americans* a "scientific" project—scientific in the etymological sense of *scientia*, as pertaining to knowledge as opposed to belief or opinion—the novel is invested in building a system of shared knowledge as well as in exposing the inner workings of this system.

The question of how we know what we know, of how we turn the data of experience into relatively stable conceptual categories turns out to be just as much at stake in this novel as the question of character formation. For there is no objective repetition in this book that is not paired with the subjective question of how we learn to recognize or "listen" to repeating. If we return to the narrator's theory of character, for example, we can see how much weight is given to the position of a witness; repetitions are never simply given but must be remembered or forgotten, stored or discarded, by an observer—and a potentially flawed observer, at that:

> The nature in every one is always coming out of them from their beginning to their ending by the repeating always in them. . . . Sometimes, often, one looking at some one forgets about that one many things one knows in that one, always soon then such a one brings it back to remember it about that one the things one is not then thinking by the repeating that is always in each one. Always then everybody is always repeating the whole nature of them and to any one who looks always at each one always the whole of that one one is then seeing keeps coming out of such a one. So any one can know about any one the nature of that one from the repeating that is the whole of each one. (*Making* 186)

In passages such as these, Stein's narrator appears as a kind of experimental scientist who, seeking to observe and chart her observations, and occasionally remarking on her failure to do so, reminds us that her character typologies are not equivalent to objective reality but always relative to her knowing. Though sometimes easy to overlook, the question of knowing is present throughout the course of the novel: nearly every time the narrator offers a statement on being, she follows it with remarks about learning, listening, and knowing. From the moment the subject matter of the book is announced—"The old people in the new world, the new people made out of the old, that is the story that I mean to tell, for that is what really is and what I really know" (3)—what "really is" is linked to what is "really know[n]." The project of the novel may be to chart "every possible variety" of human nature, but we are repeatedly urged, along the way, to tune in to the relativity of this project: "Always one must remember each one has their own way of feeling other people's natures" (210).

All of this underscores the degree to which Stein's aesthetic project and her epistemological project are bound together. Later, she will make the connection to the aesthetic even more explicit, suggesting that learning to listen to repetition is a form of heeding beauty. "I am describing what is to me a beautiful thing," the narrator explains, "learning being in women and in men. Every little bit, every single bit of learning being in women and men is to me a beautiful thing" (*Making* 646). Most of all, from the intrusion of the narrative voice into the story we gain an enlarged sense of what counts as the "completeness" of a composition, for when Stein's narrator writes, "They are all of them repeating and I hear it. I love it and I tell it. I love it and now I will write it. This is now a history of my love of it" (291), we learn that the novel's stated goal of gathering "a complete history of every one" is meant to include the history of the one lovingly compiling such a history. The system Stein puts to work, in short, is not two-dimensional, shuttling back and forth between repetition and identity, part and whole, but prismatic, kaleidoscopic, refracted through the immanent synthesis of observers who produce—and are produced by—different readings of repetition, and different ways of taking pleasure in it.

A SCIENCE OF THE SENSIBLE

In examining *how* our most familiar concepts are constructed, Stein returns the data of sense experience to the open wild, reconsidering how we build basic notions of subjects and objects, time and space, personhood, identity, and what counts as experience. The question raised in *The Making of Americans* is not so much whether a static grid of categories might be overlaid on experience, but rather how such grids are constructed out of experience's immanent variations. In other words, Stein's interest lies not in categorization as such but in the genesis of categories and concepts. Ways of living and forms of knowing are produced creatively in space and time, and in a way that has radical implications for our understanding of the relationship between philosophy and art. These implications involve a rearticulation of what Deleuze calls the two senses of the term *aesthetic*. They also return us to the most general concerns of my argument: the question of system.

Traditional aesthetics, Deleuze argues, "suffers from a wrenching duality": "On one hand, it designates the theory of sensibility as the form of possible experience; on the other hand, it designates the theory of art as the reflection of real experience. For these two meanings to be tied together, the conditions of experience in general must become conditions of real experience" (*Logic of Sense* 260). In *Difference and Repetition*, Deleuze's critique is even sharper. When the aesthetic is divided into two domains, he argues, the real slips through our conceptual nets. On the one hand, "the theory of the sensible . . . retains from the real only what conforms to possible experience," while on the other hand, "the theory of the beautiful . . . deals with the reality of the real only insofar as it is reflected" (67, translation modified).[10] In both of these remarks, Deleuze draws on a major thread in *Difference and Repetition*, one that returns us to the critique of the concept of possibility that I undertook in chapter 3.

In chapter 3, recall, I took issue with any theory of art that would rely on the notion of the possibility of a work preceding its actual existence. With reference to Bergson's *The Creative Mind*, I argued that the very concept of possibility relies on a retrograde movement of thought—a reflection of the real projected backward in time in the form of "what will have been possible"—and that, in privileging images of the already-made, such a theory of art will fail to apprehend the genuinely new. For what is new cannot be articulated in advance of its creation.

To think the new is *the task of any contemporary philosophy of art*. Existence—real, sensual existence—and not possibility, is the domain of art; thus to think the being of a work of art requires granting creative powers to existence itself. But when we pose the question of the new in terms of what has been reflected in advance as possible, "we are forced to conceive of existence as a brute eruption," as Deleuze argues, or as a mere shadow that adds nothing to the concept. In this impoverished view, "existence is *the same* as but outside the concept. Existence is therefore supposed to occur in space and time, but these are understood as indifferent milieu" (*DR* 211).

In his comments on the separation of the two senses of the aesthetic, Deleuze condemns the Kantian view of sensibility for "retain[ing] from the real only what conforms to possible experience": this means that the real is limited by a priori forms (space and time, as well as the categories that depend on them), which are granted primacy over sense experience, determining in advance the texture and consistency experience will have, and assuring its conformity to a transcendental subject envisioned as purely receptive. A "more profound aesthetic," on the other hand, as Deleuze terms it in passing, would accord a creative priority to experience itself, granting it the power to compose characteristic and local forms "step by step"—that is, *gradually* (to borrow a term from Stein)—at the same time as it would construct an experiencing subject (*DR* 98).

We discover, in short, that art and concept formation have a common vocation: both seek to respond to and sustain the creativity of the real. When the two senses of the aesthetic are brought back together—when the theory of sense experience rejoins the theory of art—each takes on qualities of the other, so that thinking becomes creative, and art becomes "scientific."

To say that thought becomes creative entails revising our very notion of what concepts are and how they are made. *The Making of Americans* is a knowledge project insofar as every empirical variation in it is related to a concept, but it can be described as such only if concepts themselves are grasped as the products of creative activity. The problem with conceptual determination as it has been thought by the philosophical tradition is that concepts absorb the singular—they absorb the truly *new*—into a preexisting system of representation, mobilizing a logic of identity and recognition in order to determine, distribute, and judge the data of experience according to given categories and hierarchies (cf. Deleuze, *DR* 29). The particular is supposed to reflect the general, and any idiosyncrasies or discrepancies that intrude in this reflection appear to be merely epiphenomenal, mediate, and negative. This is what Deleuze calls the "long error" of the philosophical tradition: the subordination of difference to the requirements of conceptual representation (301), or the failure of thought to connect to the transformations of the real. Conversely, thought becomes genuinely creative when it can construct a path from a singular thing to a concept made to the measure of that thing. This is not to give up on concepts and advocate for a world of mute and swarming differences, but rather to insist on concepts as the objects of constructive activity.[11]

Again, concept formation becomes creative when the two senses of the aesthetic are brought together. Art, on the other hand, becomes "scientific." In Deleuze's words, "It leaves the domain of representation in order to become 'experience' [and 'experiment'], a transcendental empiricism or science of the sensible" (*DR* 56). *The Making of Americans* partakes in a project of science, not because it reflects knowledge about the world gleaned elsewhere, but because it joins forces with what I identified in chapter 4 as the problem-solution complex: it does not reflect but constructs solutions that remain relative to the local transformations in the problems it identifies. *The Making of Americans* is an "experiment" because it will be evaluated by the real problem to which it remains attached; it is an "experience" because its formal construction will become the object of a new sense encounter, or new experience of reading. To remain relative to the transformations of the real means to defer to its vitality and note the dangers of abstraction, even as the latter remains necessary.

In this vein, much of Stein's work has circulated around the threat that reflection and conceptual recognition pose to art. In *The Geographical History of America, or, The Relation of Human Nature to the Human Mind* (1935), Stein raises what she terms "the question of identity" (99). "I am I because my little dog knows me," she quips, paraphrasing a nursery rhyme and repeating the line frequently in the second half of the essay, which became the basis of her marionette puppet play, *Identity a Poem*, performed in 1936. This line suggests that identity is constructed in recognition, or more precisely that the specular nature of self-relation is supported by the recognition of an other.[12] "Identity is recognition," Stein asserts, "you know who you are because you and others remember anything about yourself" ("What Are Masterpieces" 84). "What Are Masterpieces and Why Are There So Few of Them," a lecture written on the heels of *The Geographical History*, condenses and clarifies her thoughts on this point: "What are master-pieces and why after all are there so few of them. . . . All this summer I meditated and wrote about this subject and it finally came to be a discussion of the relation of human nature and the human mind and identity. The thing one gradually comes to find out is that one has no identity that is when one is in the act of doing anything" (84). While identity is constructed when "you and others remember anything about yourself," real creation is without identity, because it takes place in the absence of recollection or telos. Most importantly, creation is aligned with activity, with "the act of doing anything." Stein continues: "Creatively speaking the little dog knowing that you are you and your recognising that he knows, that is what destroys creation" (84). The ability to create oneself without being beholden to the past is in part at stake here, a concern no doubt very present for Stein in 1936, as she came to terms with her new-found fame: "At any moment when you are you you are without the memory of yourself because if you remember yourself while you are you you are not for purposes of creating you" (85–86).[13]

Above all, the question of identity bears on artistic creation. In the domain of art, "recognition" threatens to intervene in the relation of the writer to his audience—"One of the things I discovered in lecturing," Stein says, "was that gradually one ceased to hear what one said one heard what the audience hears one say, that is the reason that oratory is practically never a master-piece"—as well as in the relation of "the act of creation to the subject the creator uses to create that thing" ("What Are Masterpieces" 86, 85). In what sounds like a typically high-modernist rejection of realism,[14] Stein discusses the ostensible "subject" of art: "There is always the same subject there are the things you see and there are human beings and animal beings and everybody you might say since the beginning of time knows . . . everything about these things. After all any woman in any village or men either if you like or even children know as much of human psychology as any writer that ever lived . . . and it is not this knowledge that makes master-pieces" (85). It is not the subject matter that makes a master-piece, but the composition—the arrangement of this repeating subject matter in a unique and immanent whole.

Recollection, meanwhile, kills creation: "Any of you when you write you try to remember what you are about to write and you will see immediately how lifeless the writing becomes" ("What Are Masterpieces" 89). Recollection must not intervene in the act of composition, which is conceived as an immanent process of creation and discovery. Immanence is key, for a masterpiece must be "a thing made by being made," not "a thing prepared" ("Composition" 27).[15]

In an interview conducted on the last day of her American lecture tour, Stein explains to a fellow writer, "You will write . . . if you will write without thinking of the result in terms of a result, but think of the writing in terms of discovery, which is to say that creation must take place between the pen and the paper, not before in thought or afterwards in a recasting. Yes, before in a thought, but not in careful thinking. It will come if it is there and if you will let it come, and if you have anything you will get a sudden *creative recognition*" (Preston 154, italics mine) With this passage, we come full circle. On the one hand, Stein wants to divorce masterpieces from what she calls "the business of living" ("What Are Masterpieces" 88) so as to situate them outside of the time of lived experience, and beyond the received ways of looking, thinking, and talking characterized as what "everybody knows" and "everybody says" (*Geographical History* 190–91). Writing inaugurates its own time (it is without "beginning and ending"), its own arrangement ("flatness"), and its own intentions (it is without a "motive" except for what can be reconstructed from the crime scene of the text).[16] A masterpiece thus exists in a certain "continuous present": it cannot be anticipated, and the question remains whether it can ever really be apprehended by an audience, or if it only risks being reconstituted in misrecognition. "After the audience begins," Stein laments, "naturally they create something that is they create you" ("What Are Masterpieces" 95). On the other hand, in the passage above, Stein refers to a "sudden creative recognition" that a writer experiences with respect to her own work in progress, a kind of immanent recognition that presumably does not impede but fosters creation. Here again, the values of activity associated with lived experience do not seem to be rejected so much as reconstituted within the continuous present of the artwork.

"But what can a master-piece be about[?]" Stein asks. "Mostly it is about identity and all it does and in being so it must not have any" ("What Are Masterpieces" 91). Moments like these, where Stein complicates the relation between art and knowledge, prove to be more revealing than those where she draws stricter divisions. Here she contends that masterpieces have a more nebulous relation to the common-sense categories we develop in lived experience than simple refusal. "It is not extremely difficult not to have identity," she writes, "but it is extremely difficult the knowing not having identity. . . . That it is not impossible is proved by the existence of master-pieces which are just that" (90). The image of a different form of knowledge emerges in these lines, one that refuses the rigidity of categories dictated by common sense ("identity"), but that at the same time aspires to a knowledge of this refusal, and attempts to use "pieces" of lived experience in the construction of this new knowledge. I would not suggest that Stein advocates for a heightened self-consciousness of art, but rather the opposite. She continues by offering an illustration: "I was just thinking about anything and in thinking about anything I saw something. In seeing that thing shall we see it without it turning into identity, the moment is not a moment and the sight is not the thing seen and yet it is" (91). It is as if Stein would suspend the process of concept formation, that operation of what she calls "human mind," while holding on to its constituent elements, retaining the integrity of the process as a creative and living activity, but distributing its elements across the static landscape of an aesthetic composition. What is composed is the site of a new meditation, where "each part is as important as the whole" ("Transatlantic Interview" 98) because the meditation's conclusions are not given in advance, and the relation of experience to knowledge is not determined but complicated and displayed for the sake of a new aesthetic.

Gertrude Stein's *Making of Americans*, in sum, may not have single-handedly transformed the history of art in the twentieth century, and the aesthetic experience it offers is not necessarily one that has been shared widely, but Stein's own assessment of the book—that it be counted alongside *A la recherche du temps perdu* and *Ulysses* as one of the truly "important things written in [that] generation"— seems appropriate. What *The Making of Americans* reveals is the degree to which knowledge and art, or what can be known and what can be made, are intimately bound up with one another. The system Stein develops and puts into practice attempts to envision the creative production of concepts outside of a structure of reflection and recognition, a structure that, from its first articulation in romanticism, has dictated the terms of the relationship between literature and philosophy, or literature and criticism, ever since. Stein's experimental writing gives us a glimpse of a different trajectory for the novel, and for a non-romantic reimagining of the relationship between knowledge and art.

# Conclusion

"The spirit of the times is not blowing in the direction of formalist and intrinsic criticism" (de Man, "Semiology" 27). This seems even more true of today than of 1973, when de Man made this remark at the opening of "Semiology and Rhetoric." A conspicuous longing for the extratextual real, for the more immediately political, for the concreteness of objects or affects over abstract questions of language and form marks a number of recent critical trends, from "surface reading" and "affect theory" to "thing theory," "object-oriented ontology," and an assortment of "new materialisms." Coupled with a longing for the real is a manifest antihumanism—or at least an "anti-correlationism," to borrow a term from Quentin Meillassoux's *After Finitude*, an essay challenging the Kantian legacy by marking the limitations of any philosophy that would be hemmed in by the "correlation" between consciousness and world. These philosophical and critical developments together reveal a common yearning for *le grand dehors*, or at least for a means of removing the blinders of an all too human point of view. Yet it is far from obvious that such a mistrust of critical reflection can be reconciled with actual critical practices.[1]

In literary studies, these developments testify to a widely shared desire for what might be called a "postcritical" approach to texts, one in which human consciousness would no longer be at the center of interpretation. This distrust of consciousness is like a muscle we strengthened in the heyday of structuralist and poststructuralist criticism; postcritical critics continue to flex it even as they cast aside structuralism's formal insights. They end up challenging those humanistic values of depth, interiority, subjectivity, and self-reflection that can be traced back to the romantic period. Yet by overlooking the genealogy of the concepts they seek to criticize—that is, by overlooking the way a romantic metaphysics has been transmitted through mid-century theory to present-day criticism—these trends risks rehashing the same critical maneuvers of previous generations. Specifically, when they mount a critique at the level of what is represented in literary texts, as is the case with "thing theory," they leave intact old methodologies of reading. Conversely, when they target practices of reading, as is the case with "surface reading," they leave untouched the metaphysics of form that underlies these practices. These critics ignore questions of form at their own peril, for the subjectivity they seek to flee is reinstated in old habits of reading, and the closure of self-identity they would disrupt is merely bracketed when questions of metaphysics are bracketed. In seeking to overcome the limitations of the romantic subject, they succeed only in expanding its scope.

In this book, I've taken aim at some familiar targets: those presumptions of unity, closure, and self-reflection that govern reading practices no less than they determine conceptions of literary form. But I have done so by approaching the literary work as an object worthy of an ontological question: What is the being of a work? While refusing to elevate literature "beyond" philosophy by investing it with a superior access to truth or being—the romantic move par excellence—I have nevertheless treated the literary work as a site where a different articulation of being is possible. Drawing on extraliterary resources, I have addressed the question of the ontology of the work—have said the being of the work—in many ways: as novelty, as problematic genesis, and as differential relation. In each case, the literary work is grasped as essentially self-differing. Or rather *difference itself is conceived as form*. This difference is borne out as an experimentation immanent to real experience.

I have tried to show how this experimentation works on the ground, so to speak, through readings of the novelistic experiments of Beckett, Proust, and Stein; and I have tried to show how these texts not only depart from the forms of the nineteenth century, but also put to work a poetics of difference that ends up generating new and distinctly modern forms, organizing affective or narrative systems, and constructing forms of subjectivity. If I have focused on rhetoric—treating rhetorical figures as particular kinds of differential relations—it is because these figures serve as a site where a thesis about the nature of the literary object meets with a practice of reading, a practice equal to the difference in the work.

Art belongs to existence; its domain is not the idea but concrete forms of experience, just as the domain of the new is not the possible but the real in all its spatiotemporal richness and inventiveness. The foil of this book has been an idealism or a romanticism that would suppose otherwise: one that would locate the reality of a literary work in a possibility that would prefigure it, in an intention that would animate it, or in a truth that would exceed it. In all of these cases, the actual work is conceived along the lines of a reflection of ideas located elsewhere, or else as a faded version of these ideas, the shadow or fragment of a truth that has a wider import than itself. We lose, in other words, the specificity of a genuine literary thinking. It is this thinking I have tried to bring into focus—and think along with—in the preceding pages. Embedded, dynamic, and transformative, this literary thinking cannot be given shape or form in advance. Nor can we measure its reach unless we are first willing to grasp it—like Molloy at the bottom of his ditch—there where it happens to be.

Seuls, s'élevant du niveau de la plaine et comme perdus en rase campagne, montaient vers le ciel les deux clochers de Martinville. Bientôt nous en vîmes trois: venant se placer en face d'eux par une volte hardie, un clocher retardataire, celui de Vieuxvicq, les avait rejoints. Les minutes passaient, nous allions vite et pourtant les trois clochers étaient toujours au loin devant nous, comme trois oiseaux posés sur la plaine, immobiles et qu'on distingue au soleil. Puis le clocher de Vieuxvicq s'écarta, prit ses distances, et les clochers de Martinville restèrent seuls, éclairés par la lumière du couchant que même à cette distance, sur leurs pentes, je voyais jouer et sourire. Nous avions été si longs à nous rapprocher d'eux, que je pensais au temps qu'il faudrait encore pour les atteindre quand, tout d'un coup, la voiture ayant tourné, elle nous déposa à leurs pieds; et ils s'étaient jetés si rudement au-devant d'elle, qu'on n'eut que le temps d'arrêter pour ne pas se heurter au porche. Nous poursuivîmes notre route; nous avions déjà quitté Martinville depuis un peu de temps et le village après nous avoir accompagnés quelques secondes avait disparu, que restés seuls à l'horizon à nous regarder fuir, ses clochers et celui de Vieuxvicq agitaient encore en signe d'adieu leurs cimes ensoleillées. Parfois l'un s'effaçait pour que les deux autres pussent nous apercevoir un instant encore; mais la route changea de direction, ils virèrent dans la lumière comme trois pivots d'or et disparurent à mes yeux. Mais, un peu plus tard, comme nous étions déjà près de Combray, le soleil étant maintenant couché, je les aperçus une dernière fois de très loin qui n'étaient plus que comme trois fleurs peintes sur le ciel au-dessus de la ligne basse des champs. Ils me faisaient penser aussi aux trois jeunes filles d'une légende, abandonnées dans une solitude où tombait déjà l'obscurité; et tandis que nous nous éloignions au galop, je les vis

timidement chercher leur chemin et après quelques gauches trébuche-
ments de leurs nobles silhouettes, se serrer les uns contre les autres,
glisser l'un derrière l'autre, ne plus faire sur le ciel encore rose qu'une
seule forme noire, charmante et résignée, et s'effacer dans la nuit.
(Proust, *A la recherche du temps perdu* 150).

# NOTES

## INTRODUCTION

1. My understanding of this paradox is drawn especially from Derrida's "Psyche: Inventions of the Other," in the collection by the same name.

2. See Schaeffer 91.

3. Franco Moretti makes this point in "History of the Novel, Theory of the Novel": "Prose is not a gift; it's work: 'productivity of the spirit,' Lukács called it in *Theory of the Novel*, and it's the right expression: hypotaxis is not only laborious—it requires foresight, memory, adequation of means to ends—but truly productive: the outcome is usually more than the sum of its parts because subordination establishes a hierarchy among clauses, meaning becomes articulated, aspects emerge that didn't exist before. That's how complexity comes into being" (2).

4. See Macherey, *A Theory of Literary Production* 122.

5. See Deleuze and Guattari, *Anti-Oedipus* 108.

## 1. FORM AND FRAGMENTATION: ROMANTIC LEGACIES

1. Jacques Rancière was thus in good company when he opened *La parole muette* (1998) with the remark "There are some questions we no longer dare pose" (*Mute Speech* 29).

2. See Heidegger's critique of representation in "The Age of the World Picture," especially 66–67.

3. For an early example in the French context, René Wellek cites François Granet's series *Réflexions sur les ouvrages de littérature* (1736–40). In the English context, he cites Adam Ferguson's chapter "Of the History of Literature" in Ferguson's *Essay on the History of Civil Society* (1767) and Robert Chambers's *A History of English Language and Literature* (1836) ("Literature and Its Cognates" 82).

4. Wellek also notes that Voltaire speaks of "les genres de littérature" in *Le Siècle de Louis XIV* (1751) and mentions L'Abbé Sabatier de Castres's *Les Siècles de littérature française* (1772) and Tiraboschi's *Storia della letteratura italiana* (also 1772). See Wellek, "Literature and Its Cognates"; Escarpit.

5. Cf. Lacoue-Labarthe and Nancy 82.

6. See also T. C. Pollock's *The Nature of Literature* (1942): "It is interesting to note that the term literature even in its broad modern sense did not appear until the term science had been specialized to its modern meaning; and that literature did not receive its restricted modern meaning until the assumptions of inductive science were widely understood" (qtd. in Escarpit 50).

7. Heidegger's "Question Concerning Technology" and Derrida's "Economimesis" are especially helpful on this point.

8. See, for example, Kant's *Critique of the Power of Judgment* §§44, 16.

9. Morse Peckham is also noteworthy in this context, for in *The Triumph of Romanticism* not only does he attempt to "reconcile Wellek and Lovejoy" (as well as "Lovejoy with himself"), but the content he claims for romanticism involves opposing tensions (a "positive romanticism" and a "negative romanticism"), which are ultimately resolved in a global conception of romanticism as a break with Enlightenment reason (8).

10. Consider also Friedrich's Schlegel's remark in a letter to his brother August: "I can hardly send you my explication of the word Romantic because it would take—125 pages" (qtd. in Lacoue-Labarthe and Nancy 6).

11. Outside of Friedrich's writings, significant use of the term *romantic* appears in August Schlegel's *Lectures on Dramatic Art and Literature* (1809–11). Jean Paul Friedrich Richter's *School for Aesthetics* (1804) was another important source, while Mme de Staël's *De l'Allemagne* (1814) was largely responsible for its dissemination.

12. Roughly, they used the term *romantic* to characterize a new poetry in a way that meant to oppose it to both classical and neoclassical works, while *romanticism*, by contrast, became the retrospective designation of a literary movement that, at least in Germany as well as England, did not describe itself as "romantic." See Wellek's "The Concept of Romanticism" for a semantic history of the terms *romantic* and *romanticism*.

13. See *On the Study of Greek Poetry* (1797; completed in 1795), especially 111n18. Schlegel replaces the phrase "romantic poetry" with "poetry of the Middle Ages" in an 1822 edition, revealing that he once thought of these two phrases as synonyms.

14. Lovejoy's "On the Meaning of 'Romantic' in Early German Romanticism" is key to understanding the trajectory of this term's development. In particular, Lovejoy argues that *romantic* cannot be understood merely as a genre term synonymous with *novelistic*. Frederick Beiser's chapter "The Meaning of 'Romantic Poetry'" in *The Romantic Imperative* is also helpful in pointing out the way Schlegel mixes a normative and a historical assessment in this term.

15. The number in citations to the *Athenaeum Fragments* refers to the fragment, not the page number. I give Schlegel's name in reference to the volume in which they are collected even if a particular fragment was not written by him.

16. See Beiser's *The Fate of Reason* and Paul Franks's *All or Nothing* for an account of the intellectual climate in Germany following the publication of Kant's *Critique of Pure Reason*. Both are helpful in explaining the rage for system building in this period.

17. There are only three Ideas of reason: the postulates of God, freedom, and the immortality of the soul. Ideas refer to the "absolute totality of all possible experience," which is itself not an object of experience (Kant, *Prolegomena* §40).

18. See Beiser, *The Romantic Imperative*; Frank; Millán-Zaibert.

19. See, for example, Beiser, *The Romantic Imperative*, chapter 1, n7.

20. Translated into German in 1797 and reviewed favorably by August Schlegel (Firchow 14).

21. Gasché likewise observes a schism between the concept of the fragment and the literary devices on which the fragments rely ("Ideality in Fragmentation" x).

22. In German, consult *Athenäum: Eine Zeitschrift* (Dortmund: Harenberg Edition, 1989). In English, the most complete set of Schlegel's fragments can be found in *Philosophical Fragments*, while *Grains of Pollen* can be found in Bernstein, *Classic and Romantic German Aesthetics*.

23. Following Frank, Millán-Zaibert argues compellingly for the romantics as antifoundationalist thinkers and signals the importance of the concept of *Wechselerweis*, or mutual confirmation, in Schlegel's thought (see 18–23, chapters 6 and 7). Beiser, meanwhile, stresses the Platonic underpinnings of early romanticism (see Chapter 4 of *The Romantic Imperative*, especially 68–70).

24. These terms might recall those of Abrams's classic *The Mirror and the Lamp*. While Abrams identifies a change in the dominant metaphors of critical discourse from neoclassicism to romanticism, I mean instead to draw attention to the particular host of figures used by Schlegel and his group. This group did not conceive of fragments solely in terms of projection (fragments as "lamps," to use Abrams's term), but saw them participating in, and indeed lending form to, a complex productive and specular economy. Metaphors of "seeds" and "embryos" abound.

25. For a more detailed discussion of the role of reflection in romanticism, and its relation to literary form and to the structure of self-consciousness, see chapter 5.

## 2. THE BOOK OF THE WORLD: FORM AND INTENT IN NEW CRITICISM, REVISITED

1. I have in mind de Man's well-known arguments in "The Rhetoric of Temporality."

2. Of course these comments can be read as equivalent insofar as Marxist critique aims precisely at notions supposed to be metaphysical in order to expose them as mystifications. Nevertheless, I think it is important to hold on to the double edge of Eagleton's critique: that New Criticism makes the political error of removing the poem from the processes of history, and the metaphysical error of substantializing a process of meaning.

3. Articles in the "Life" and "Style" sections of the London *Telegraph* and the *Guardian* reveal to this American author that pebbledash walls are standard on semidetached houses in most suburbs in Britain, having become

popular in the postwar years as a means of covering up shoddy workmanship in new buildings (*Guardian*). Now, apparently, pebbledash has the same cultural resonance as woodchip wallpaper or shag carpets (*Telegraph*). In addition to his explicit criticism, Eagleton seems to be accusing New Criticism of a certain vulgarity of taste. Adam Edwards, "Pebbledash: Time to Cut a Dash," *Telegraph*, May 21, 2010, http://www.telegraph.co.uk/property/7736907/Pebbledash-time-to-cut-a-dash.html; Laura Barnett, "Grey, Lumpy, Impossible to Remove—but Pebbledash Isn't All Bad," *Guardian*, April 21, 2010, http://www.guardian.co.uk/lifeandstyle/2010/apr/21/pebbledash-homes-nick-clegg.

4. In his 1975 essay "The Poetics of Surrender," Richard Strier argues similarly that the New Critics are both drawn to, and struggle with, the notion of a necessary sequence of metaphors as constituting the unity of a poem (176–77). What these critics champion as a necessary "logic of metaphor," Strier argues, turns out to be merely a *metaphor of logic* (189). Strier's point could not be more relevant to my analysis. This metaphor of logic is a direct consequence of Kantian philosophy, for when Kant broke with rationalism to set limits on what we could know, he disrupted the rationalist continuum between mind and nature. As we saw in chapter 1, in Kant's third *Critique*, the productive order of man is no longer conceived as continuous with the order of nature, but as analogous to it. Reflection is made the fulcrum between these two orders of production, and the form of the beautiful, or the work of art, takes on the role of reflecting—without being continuous with—the necessity of nature. In this way, literature is made beholden to a project of reason, which it must reflect as a metaphor or a dream would reflect it, without actually being able to participate in it.

5. He writes in the *Biographia Literaria*, for example, "It has been before observed that images, however beautiful, though faithfully copied from nature, and as accurately represented in words, do not of themselves characterize the poet. They become proofs of an original genius only as far as they are modified by a predominant passion" (2: 16).

6. The metaphor of nature as hieroglyphic poem is a major theme in August Schlegel's *Lectures on Art and Fine Literature* (Lacoue-Labarthe and Nancy 93), and is in turn borrowed from Kant's third *Critique*, which refers to "the cipher by means of which nature figuratively speaks to us in its beautiful forms" (§ 42).

7. Delivered in Vienna in 1808 and published in 1809–11. The lines in question are "Organical form, again, is innate; it unfolds itself from within, and acquires its determination contemporaneously with the perfect development of the germ" (A. Schlegel 241).

3. TYRANNY OF THE POSSIBLE: BLANCHOT

1. For a lucid treatment of Blanchot's relation to Heidegger, see Clark's *Derrida, Heidegger, Blanchot.*

2. See Bataille on negativity in "Hegel, Death and Sacrifice."

3. See, for example, Blanchot, "The Crude Word and the Essential Word," in *The Space of Literature* (38).

4. The title of this section is from Novalis, "Monologue," qtd. in Schmidt, *Lyrical and Ethical Subjects*, 191.

5. "L'art et la littérature ne semblent avoir rien d'autre à faire qu'à se manifester, c'est à dire à s'indiquer, selon le mode obscur qui leur est propre: se manifester, s'annoncer, en un mot se communiquer" (Blanchot, *L'entretien infini* 521).

6. Moreover, when Derrida refers to literature as "interesting," he might be alluding to its ethical dimension, specifically to the solicitation of our interest and concern that comes from what is completely other.

7. See Sartre's *L'imaginaire*.

8. Translation mine. This paragraph appears to have been excised from the English translation.

9. For a treatment of this paradox in Derrida's work, see especially "Psyche: Inventions of the Other."

10. Though Deleuze draws on Blanchot's work and cites him favorably in a number of texts (especially *Difference and Repetition*, *Cinema* 2, and *Foucault*), I would emphasize that his answers to fundamental metaphysical questions remain incompatible with Blanchot's.

11. Deleuze addresses this question with Félix Guattari in *What Is Philosophy?* and more indirectly in his readings of individual literary works, but he does not privilege it over broader questions of being and difference as such.

## 4. A GENESIS OF THE NEW: DELEUZE

1. "Poetry is the universal art of the spirit which has become free in itself and which is not tied down for its realization to external sensuous material; instead, it launches out exclusively in the inner space and the inner time of ideas and feelings. Yet, precisely, at this highest stage, art now transcends itself, in that it forsakes the element of a reconciled embodiment of the spirit in sensuous form and passes over from the poetry of the imagination to the prose of thought" (Hegel, *Hegel's Aesthetics* 89).

2. See Blanchot's "The Future and the Question of Art" in *The Space of Literature*.

3. Jean-Marie Schaeffer's analysis in *Art of the Modern Age* goes straight to the heart of this matter. Schaeffer argues that the speculative theory of art—his term for the romantic paradigm and its philosophical inheritance—necessarily yields a specific determination of the content of art while simultaneously dictating the place art must occupy within a general ontology. Art reveals Being, and at the same time must be situated within the Being it reveals. This is the logic of the romantic fragment par excellence. Thus "we no longer encounter artistic works but only manifestations of Art . . . so many empirical realizations of the same ideal essence" (70–71).

4. For a recent survey of approaches to this topic, see the collection *Deleuze, Guattari and the Production of the New* edited by Simon O'Sullivan and Stephen Zepke.

5. A long footnote in *Difference and Repetition* is one of Deleuze's most explicit statements on Heidegger, one that serves to mark affinities between these two thinkers' projects (64–69).

6. On the importance of Bergson to a positive conception of problems in twentieth-century French thought, see Elie During's "'A History of Problems.'" Although I won't be discussing all of Deleuze's sources here, it should be noted that Deleuze also draws on the philosopher of mathematics Albert Lautman for his conception of problems (see especially "The Method of Dramatization," in *Desert Islands and Other Texts* 107; Deleuze and Guattari, *What Is Philosophy?* 163–64, 178–79, 324n9), and more broadly on a formalization of the activity of thinking that Deleuze develops from Spinoza's rationalism. For more on Deleuze's Spinozism, see Knox Peden's *Spinoza contra Phenomenology*, chapters 6–7, and my essay "Deleuze's Expressionism." For a consideration of Plato, Kant, Bergson, and Nietzsche as other philosophical sources of Deleuze's treatment of problems, see my essay "How Do We Recognise Problems?"

7. See Lévi-Strauss's *Structural Anthropology* (1963). Strauss's interpretation of the Oedipus myth, for example, is that its many versions arise in response to "the inability, for a culture which holds the belief that mankind is autochthonous . . . to find a satisfactory transition between this theory and the knowledge that human beings are actually born from the union of man and woman. . . . The Oedipus myth provides a kind of logical tool which relates the original problem—born from one or born from two?—to the derivative problem: born from different or born from same?" (216). Ultimately, "the purpose of myth is to provide a logical model capable of overcoming a contradiction (an impossible achievement if, as it happens, the contradiction is real)" (229).

8. A note on the term *genesis*: Kant's transcendental project went beyond causal explanation by locating cause-effect relations in the understanding, seeking categories of the understanding that would define the conditions of possible experience. Yet by characterizing the relation of the categories to experience as one of possibility, Kant, Deleuze argues, engages in an illegitimate act of "tracing" the transcendental from the empirical (*DR* 143). That is, Kant relies on a sort of preformism of the conditioned in the condition. He invents the notion of the transcendental, but his version of the transcendental merely reproduces the structure of experience without getting behind it to discover its source. Sharing in a dissatisfaction with Kant's system first articulated by post-Kantians such as Fichte and Salomon Maimon, Deleuze seeks to develop a more robust transcendental field, one that can articulate its own coming-to-be in the real. It is meant to account not just for the conditions of possible experience, but for the conditions of real experience, of concepts as well as material objects. These conditions should be intrinsic, not extrinsic; they fit so tightly to the real that the very notion of "conditioning" is transformed into one of causation or "genesis." For more on transcendental conditioning versus real genesis, see Daniel W. Smith, "The Conditions of the New," in *Essays on Deleuze*, 237–41.

9. Toscano's *The Theatre of Production* (2006), as well as recent issues of *Parrhesia* 7 (2009) and *Pli* 24 (2012), are notable exceptions. In its own right, Simondon's work has experienced a recent surge of interest. In 2012, *SubStance* and *INFLeXions* devoted special issues to Simondon's work, and

Edinburgh University Press published *Gilbert Simondon: Being and Technology*, the first book-length treatment of Simondon's work in English. English translations of Pascal Chabot's *La philosophie de Simondon* (2003) and Muriel Combes's *Simondon, Individu et collectivité* (1999) were published in 2013. Edinburgh University Press has also published *Gilbert Simondon's Psychic and Collective Individuation: A Critical Introduction and Guide* (2014), though an English translation of Simondon's work on individuation has still not been published. For more on Simondon's contemporary significance, see Joe Hughes, "The Intimacy of the Common."

10. Simondon's thesis was originally published by Presses Universitaires de France in partial form in two separate works: *L'individu et sa genèse physicobiologique* (1964) and *L'individuation psychique et collective* (1989). Deleuze reviewed the former work in 1966 for the *Revue philosophique de la France et de l'étranger*, in a piece now reprinted in *Desert Islands*.

11. "Pour rendre compte de la genèse de l'individu avec ses caractères définitifs, il faut supposer l'existence d'un terme premier, le principe, qui porte en lui ce qui expliquera que l'individu soit individu et rendra compte de son eccéité. Mais il resterait précisément à montrer que l'ontogenèse peut avoir comme condition première un terme premier: un terme est déjà un individu ou tout au moins quelque chose d'individualisable."

12. "La notion de *principe d'individuation* sort dans une certaine mesure d'une genèse à rebours, d'une ontogénèse *renversée*. . . . Dans cette notion même de principe, il y a un certain caractère qui préfigure l'individualité constituée, avec les propriétés qu'elle aura quand elle sera constituée."

13. "Car l'individuation n'épuise pas d'un seul coup les potentiels de la réalité préindividuelle."

14. Deleuze describes these dynamic structures as "spatio-temporal dynamisms," genetic elements of the space and time in which an individual will appear (or be "actualized"). Unlike the process of realization, which is supposed to *take place in* space and time, individuation *creates* a local space and time concomitant with its individuals.

15. Interestingly, the notion of *milieu* has a rich history in nineteenth- and twentieth-century French thought; it is not unique to Simondon. For a synoptic study of the development of the concept—from Newton and Lamarck to Comte, Balzac, and Taine—see the chapter by Georges Canguilhem (who was Simondon's doctoral thesis advisor), "Le vivant et son milieu," in *La connaissance de la vie* (1952).

16. "Ce que l'individuation fait apparaître n'est pas seulement l'individu mais le couple individu-milieu."

17. "Il lui est associé, il est son milieu associé."

18. "Ce qui est vraiment et essentiellement l'individu est la relation active, l'échange entre l'extrinsèque et l'intrinsèque. . . . L'intrinsèque, l'intériorité de l'individu n'existerait pas sans l'opération relationnelle permanente qui est individuation permanente."

19. "Le théâtre et l'agent d'une relation."

20. A heterogenetic system entails a differential production, and is itself productive of difference. In Smith's words, "It must have as its aim the

genesis of the heterogeneous, the production of difference, the creation of the *new*" (xiii). See also Deleuze's "Letter Preface": "I believe in philosophy as system. For me, the system must not only be in perpetual heterogeneity, it must be a *heterogenesis*—something which, it seems to me, has never been attempted" (8).

21. In other words, what counts as an "individual" with respect to a milieu is not fixed, but is constituted by an act of reading. Similarly, the distinction Deleuze draws between the "virtual" and the "actual" is often mistakenly believed to be a rigid one, when it is better understood as corresponding to a certain reading or point of view. The virtual-actual relation is a differential one. Deleuze conveys this thesis best in his work on the cinema, as, for example, in these lines from *Cinema 2*: "In fact, there is no virtual which does not become actual in relation to the actual, the latter becoming virtual through the same relation: it is a front side and an obverse which are totally reversible" (69, translation modified). "En effet, il n'y a pas de virtuel qui ne devienne actuel par rapport à l'actuel, celui-ci devenant virtuel sous ce même rapport: c'est un envers et un endroit parfaitement réversibles" (*L'image-temps* 94).

22. See Aristotle's *Nicomachean Ethics* IV, 4.

23. We can read here the echo of Althusser's assertion that to practice philosophy is to a take up a position, within philosophical discourse as well as within the wider historical, material conjuncture. See, most notably, *Philosophie et philosophie spontanée des savants*.

24. My description of criticism as an activity that produces its objects draws on Macherey's *A Theory of Literary Production*, especially chapter 2, as well as on Althusser's conception of philosophy as a practice that likewise produces its objects rather than reflects on empirically given reality. See *Philosophie et philosophie spontanée des savants*, and for a different formulation of this idea, *Reading Capital*, part 2: "The Object of *Capital*."

25. In *A Thousand Plateaus*, Deleuze and Guattari do not abandon the concepts of individual and milieu, but rearticulate them in increasingly complex ways. They retain the category of milieu, for example, but qualify certain milieus as "territories" when, beyond indicating neutral blocks of space and time, they become expressive and qualitative for an individual. See "1837: Of the Refrain," especially 314.

26. My understanding of the assemblage owes much to a presentation given by Gillaume Sibertin-Blanc, "L'analyse des agencements et le groupe de lutte comme expérimentateur collectif."

## 5. FROM FIGURE TO FISSURE: SELF-CORRECTION IN BECKETT'S *MOLLOY*, *MALONE DIES*, AND *THE UNNAMABLE*

1. The first epigraph: "Our own image comes back to us from the mirror of the literary absolute. And the massive truth flung back at us is that we have not left the era of the Subject" (Lacoue-Labarthe and Nancy, *The Literary Absolute* 33). The second epigraph: "No need to try, it goes on by itself" (Beckett, *Three Novels* 402). Quotations from *Molloy*, *Malone Dies*, and

*The Unnamable* are from the English Grove edition, *Three Novels* (1958). In those instances where it is helpful to examine the French alongside the English, I supply the French text from the original editions.

2. I am following the convention among critics in referring to the three postwar novels as a trilogy, though it might be observed that Beckett himself disliked the term, requesting that the "3-in-1" editions published in Britain and the United States (Calder and Grove Press, respectively) appear without this term (see Gontarski, introduction to *Nohow On*, xi–xii). Both presses originally entitled the collection *Three Novels*, though the current Calder edition has the word *trilogy* printed sideways on the book's cover. The three novels were originally, and continue to be, published as separate volumes in French by Éditions de minuit.

3. See Fowler, "The Future of Genre Theory" 294.

4. As I had the opportunity of confirming in an exposition of Beckett's work at the Centre Pompidou in Paris, 2007.

5. The novel's principal plots—the quest narrative, the marriage plot, the Bildungsroman, the Künstlerroman—all revolve around the growth and eventual fulfillment of the individual. On the convergence of the birth of the novel with the concept of the individual, see, for example, foundational studies by Ian Watt, *The Rise of the Novel* and Nancy Armstrong, *Desire and Domestic Fiction*. Famously, Watt links the form of the novel to an individualism that emerged from historical changes wrought by industrial capitalism and the spread of Protestantism (60), and he draws parallels between the novel and the primacy of the individual in Cartesian philosophy (15). Hugh Kenner also acknowledges this connection between the birth of the novel and Descartes's emphasis on the individual in *Samuel Beckett* (17).

6. Consider Mme de Lafayette's *La Princesse de Clèves* (1678) and especially Samuel Richardson's *Pamela* (1741), which differs from the more episodic narrative of Defoe's *Moll Flanders* (1722), for example, by the real and sustained coherency it gains from the psychological integrity of its narrator (cf. Watt, *The Rise of the Novel* 32,164–65, 297; Armstrong, *Desire and Domestic Fiction* 108–34). Georg Lukács makes one of the earliest and strongest arguments for the convergence of interiority with the novel form in *Theory of the Novel*.

7. Compare Bakhtin: "Of all the major genres, only the novel is younger than writing and the book: it alone is organically receptive to new forms of mute perception, that its, to reading" (3).

8. I say "more or less" because, as Steven Connor points out, *Malone Dies* is more precisely named not after its principal character but after an event that is actually absent from the text (Malone's death), which structures the first-person narrative but cannot be included in it (70). In fact, Beckett originally titled this story "L'Absent." See Admussen, *The Samuel Beckett Manuscripts* 66.

9. At the origin of this trend are Richard Coe's *Samuel Beckett* (1964) and Michael Robinson's *The Long Sonata of the Dead* (1969); other major statements include Adorno, "Trying to Understand Endgame"; Pilling, *Samuel Beckett*; Alan Jenkins, "A Lifelong Fidelity to Failure," *Times Literary*

*Supplement*, November 14, 1986; Trezise, *Into the Breach*; Toyama, *Beckett's Game*; Bersani, *Arts of Impoverishment*; Critchley, *Very Little . . . Almost Nothing*; Jaurretche, *Beckett, Joyce and the Art of the Negative*. For an indispensable survey of Beckett criticism in three languages through the mid-1990s, see Murphy, *Critique of Beckett Criticism*. By 1989, Ruby Cohn had already commented on the excessive use of the *Dialogues* in her foreword to Beckett's *Disjecta*.

10. See Pedretti's "Late Modern Rigmarole" for a convincing argument on the connection between Beckett's aesthetics and his self-positioning as late modernist.

11. In 1989, Beckett repeats this sentiment in an interview with biographer James Knowlson: "I realized that James Joyce had gone as far as one could in the direction of knowing more, [of being] in control of one's material. . . . I realized that my own way was in impoverishment, in lack of knowledge and in taking away, in subtracting rather than in adding" (Knowlson 319).

12. See, for example, Toyama: "Beckett proposes to fail to express. . . . Despite this effort, he will fail to fail to express" (15).

13. See, for example, Gendron, "A Cogito for the Dissolved Self."

14. I am following de Man in using the term *metaphor* more generally to describe any figure, including synecdoche, that functions on the basis of a presumed resemblance between its terms. See "Reading (Proust)" 63.

15. Benjamin, for example, writes that "mere thinking" becomes "matter" for reflective thinking (127).

16. Following Cicero and Quintilian, I mean *allegory* here in the general sense of "extended metaphor."

17. Blanchot first introduces the term *désoeuvrement* in *The Space of Literature*.

18. Cf. Deleuze's remarks on Proust: "The modern work of art has no problem of meaning, it has only a problem of use" (*Proust and Signs* 129).

19. "De proposer à la fois une fiction et un discours sur cette fiction, ou plutôt d'imposer subrepticement l'idée qu'elle contient, l'une dépendant de l'autre, ces deux instances."

20. This is one of the major theses of Clément's book (see 72–73, 90).

21. Clément may run into trouble, however, when he goes so far as to argue that Beckett only gives the appearance of undermining classical elements of the story, or of the traditional novel, or of notions of genre, while in fact, in figuring their absence, he succeeds in consecrating them absolutely (see 90, 108–9). By this logic, both the most conventional and the most unconventional novel could be read as upholding convention equally. It would be impossible for Beckett's work—or any other, for that matter—to challenge literary convention in the least if every attempt at experimentation were understood merely to be upholding, albeit inversely, the very conventions they purport to challenge. The problem lies once again with a tendency to read Beckett's work according to a schema of reflection: one risks treating experimentation merely as a negative reflection of convention.

22. Matei Calinescu similarly describes the rhetoric of retraction in Beckett as a form of "palinode" (from the Greek, implying a "taking back what

one has said in an 'ode' or song of praise"), arguing that palinode is a strat-egy Beckett shares with a number of postmodern texts (309).

23. This formula refers to what is probably the best-known discussion of the concept of the "disjunctive synthesis" in relation to other syntheses, in chapter 1 of Deleuze and Guattari, *Anti-Oedipus*. Other notable discussions of the concept can be found in Deleuze, *Logic of Sense* (203, 337–44) and in Deleuze's own readings of Beckett in "The Exhausted" (57–61) and "He Stuttered" (110–11). See also my article "A Relentless Spinozism," 126–28.

24. While this peculiar figure of paradoxical exception recurs through-out Beckett's work, perhaps the most definitive example of it can be found in Wordsworth's "She Dwelt among the Untrodden Ways." The figure appears in the poem's third stanza: "She lived unknown, and few could know / When Lucy ceased to be." Here, as in Beckett's work, the contradictory juxtapo-sition of an absolute claim ("she lived unknown") with a relative one ("few could know"), or the exception taken to a term admitting no exception, char-acterizes this figure. Although these lines from Wordsworth's third stanza echo the movement from "none" to "few" that occurs in the first stanza—"A maid whom there were none to praise / and very few to love"—the essential irreversibility that determines this figure and gives it its paradoxical qual-ity appears with the stricter coupling of "unknown"/"known." See Words-worth, *Selected Poetry* 147.

25. As *The Unnamble*'s narrator admits, "I confused pensum with lesson" (*Three Novels* 310).

## 6. HYPERBOLE IN PROUST'S *A LA RECHERCHE DU TEMPS PERDU*

1. First epigraph: "That is why the better part of our memories exists outside us, in a blatter of rain, in the smell of an unaired room or of the first crackling brushwood fire in a cold grate" (1: 692/511). Throughout, the first set of page numbers refers to the English translation, the second to the French. Second epigraph: "One should never be afraid of going too far, for the truth lies beyond" (*Selected Letters* 4: 444).

2. My understanding of hyperbole is indebted to Christopher Johnson's *Hyperboles* as well as to Goran Stanivukovic's "Mounting above the Truth."

3. Quintilian finds another way to connect figures of excess with literal abundance when he defines hyperbole with the following example from Cicero: "As he vomited, he filled his lap and the whole platform with gobbets of food" (Cicero 8.6.76).

4. In *Copia*, Erasmus lists hyperbole among the means by which examples are included in a discourse: "Any illustrative example you choose may be var-iously incorporated by means of a simile, contrary, comparison, hyperbole, epithet, likeness, metaphor, or allegory" (550).

5. See Samuel Weber's "The Madrepore," for an analysis of this scene of writing.

6. In fact, Proust's description of the steeples appears for a reading public no less than four times: first in the November 19, 1907, issue of *Le Figaro* in the form of an article entitled "Impressions de route en automobile," which

Yves Tadié celebrates as "an embryo of his future work," then in *Du côté de chez Swann*, where it is doubled, as I suggested, by the narrative, and finally in *Pastiches et mélanges* (1919), a collection of occasional pieces (Tadié 498, qtd. in Danius 101).

7. "Un avenir poétique sur lequel mon manque de talent m'interdisait de compter."

8. "Bien en dehors de toutes ces préoccupations"; "Au-delà de ce que je voyais . . . au-delà de l'image ou de l'odeur."

9. "Une impression de ce genre"; "Ce plaisir spécial qui ne ressemblait à aucun autre."

10. "Combien depuis ce jour, dans mes promenades."

11. "Prolongée fort au-delà de sa durée habituelle."

12. "Qui, séparée d'eux par une colline et une vallée, et situé sur un plateau plus élevé dans le lointain, semblait pourtant tout voisin d'eux."

13. "Qu'une seule forme noire."

14. "S'élevant du niveau de la plaine et comme perdus en rase campagne."

15. Pierre Fontanier, by contrast, whose *Figures du discours* (1827) has been definitive for subsequent French-language studies of rhetoric (see pieces by Gans, Genette, and Derrida cited here), argues that hyperbole has no intention to deceive. Its success is bound up with its honest appeal to the judgment of its listener, and above all to its conspicuousness as figure: "Hyperbole . . . should exhibit the character of good faith and frankness, and on the part of the speaker, seem no more than the language of persuasion itself [Hyperbole . . . doit porter le caractère de la bonne foi et de la franchise, et ne paraître, de la part de celui qui parle, que le langage même de la persuasion]" (123–24, translation mine).

16. Riffaterre is in turn echoing de Man's claim that prosopopeia is the "master trope of poetic discourse" ("Hypogram and Inscription" 48).

17. Derrida makes a similar argument in "La mythologie blanche": that any attempt to describe the difference between metaphorical and literal language ends up relying on metaphorical terms to do so (301). My point here is that, if the distinction between literal and figurative language cannot be stated in terms that are themselves exempt from such a distinction, then the certainty of such pronouncements will have to be, to some extent, rhetorical—that is, exaggerated.

18. "Peu de changements."

19. Howard Moss, for example, describes the end of the novel: "We have just read, of course, the very work Marcel is about to undertake. Like *Finnegans Wake*, *Remembrance of Things Past* is its own self-sealing device. Circular in structure, its end leads us back to its beginning" (109, qtd. in Landy 178n). Similarly, Roger Shattuck claims, "Marcel and the Narrator move slowly toward one another, until they finally meet in the closing pages. That reunited *I* . . . produces a whole which is the book itself" (38, qtd. in Landy 37).

20. Landy largely points to passages in *Le temps retrouvé* where the narrator makes it clear that he has already drafted much of his memoirs, which he frequently calls his "récit," but that he has yet to begin his novel, to which

he refers in the future tense as "mon oeuvre" or "mon livre" (Proust 3: 1088–100/2389–97/). Landy's claim also includes a carefully worked-out chronology of the narrator's writing life (39). Likewise, Roland Barthes writes that the *Recherche* tells the story of "the birth of a book which we shall not know, but whose harbinger is Proust's own book" (55). Even if we imagine that the narrator will transform the very same material of his memoirs into his new novel, and thus we take him at his word when he says, "the function and the task of a writer are those of a translator [le devoir et la tâche d'un écrivain sont ceux d'un traducteur]" (3: 926/2280–81), the difference between these two texts remains infinitely unknowable. That is, we will never know the magnitude of the revisions that will take place, which might be infinitely large, infinitely small, or somewhere in between.

21. "Comme si j'avais été moi-même une poule et si je venais de pondre un œuf, je me mis à chanter à tue-tête."

22. "Je ne repensai jamais à cette page."

23. "Autrefois à Combray en revenant d'une promenade . . . avec une exaltation."

24. "Précisément retrouvée il y avait peu de temps, arrangée, et vainement envoyée au *Figaro*."

25. "Sans doute y avait-il quelque article d'un écrivain que j'aimais et qui écrivant rarement serait pour moi une surprise."

26. "Qu'il s'agit d'impressions comme celle que m'avait donnée la vue des clochers de Martinville, ou de réminiscences . . . il fallait tâcher d'interpréter les sensations comme les signes d'autant de lois et d'idées, en essayant de penser, c'est-à-dire de faire sortir de la pénombre ce que j'avais senti, de le convertir en un équivalent spirituel. Or, ce moyen qui me paraissait le seul, qu'était-ce autre chose que faire une oeuvre d'art?"

27. "Ce qui était caché derrière les clochers de Martinville devait être quelque chose d'analogue à une jolie phrase, puisque c'était sous la forme de mots qui me faisaient plaisir, que cela m'était apparu."

28. Interestingly, the French rhetorical tradition has tended to emphasize the central importance of the listener or reader in constituting the meaning of hyperbole. Dumarsais, in *Des tropes* (1730), for example, argues that the true meaning of a hyperbolic expression resides with the listener: "Those who understand us take from our expression what they are supposed to take from it; they form in their minds an idea more conforming to the one we meant to incite than if we had spoken literally [Ceux qui nous entendent rabattent de notre expression ce qu'il en faut rabattre, il se forme dans leur esprit une idée plus conforme à celle que nous voulons y exciter, que si nous nous étions servis de mots propres]" (1.147, translation mine). Fontanier echoes this sentiment when he categorizes hyperbole as a figure of "reflection," one whose meaning is decided only once the listener or reader "reflects" on what is said. Eric Gans, a contemporary reader of Fontanier, likewise argues that "the right meaning [la juste valeur]" of a hyperbolic statement depends on the extraverbal, shared community of speaker and listener, "le contexte référentiel du bon sens communautaire" (489–90). Gans goes on to argue that the shared context between an author and a reader may be constituted by the

totality of a literary work. With respect to Proust's work, this line of think-ing would suggest that Proust intentionally alienates his readers at certain moments in his narrative in order to appeal to a more refined sense of judg-ment that will be constructed over the course of his work. I will return to this idea later in the chapter.

29. "La forme de leur flèche, le déplacement de leurs lignes, l'ensoleillement de leur surface."

30. "Je sentais que je n'allais pas au bout de mon impression, que quelque chose était derrière ce mouvement, derrière cette clarté, quelque chose qu'ils semblaient contenir et dérober à la fois."

31. "Cette chose inconnue qui s'enveloppait d'une forme ou d'un par-fum . . . protégée par le revêtement d'images."

32. See Lausberg §579.

33. "Malheureusement ces lieux merveilleux que sont les gares, d'où l'on part pour une destination éloignée, sont aussi des lieux tragique, car si le miracle s'y accomplit grâce auquel les pays qui n'avaient encore d'existence que dans notre pensée vont être ceux au milieu desquels nous vivrons, pour cette raison même il faut renoncer, au sortir de la salle d'attente, à retrouver tout à l'heure la chambre familière où l'on était il y a un instant encore. Il faut laisser toute espérance de rentrer coucher chez soi, une fois qu'on s'est décidé à pénétrer dans l'antre empesté par où l'on accède au mystère, dans un de ces grands ateliers vitrés, comme celui de Saint-Lazare où j'allai chercher le train de Balbec, et qui déployait au-dessus de la ville éventrée un de ces immenses ciels crus et gros de menaces amoncelées de drame, pareils à certains ciels, d'une modernité presque parisienne, de Mantegna ou de Véronèse, et sous lequel ne pouvait s'accomplir que quelque acte terrible et solennel comme un départ en chemin de fer ou l'érection de la Croix."

34. "Les mots nous présente des choses une petite image claire et usuelle. . . . Mais les noms présentent des personnes—et des villes qu'ils nous habituent à croire individuelles, uniques comme des personnes—une image confuse qui tire d'eux, de leur sonorité éclatante ou sombre, la couleur dont elle est peinte." See Barthes's "Proust and Names" for a seminal reading of the function of names in the *Recherche*, albeit one that does not successfully maintain the distinction between Marcel's theory and Proust's poetics.

35. Proust mentions the Renaissance artists Mantegna and Véronèse, but the unnamed referent of his description of this "eviscerated" sky, and what allows him to make the less than apparent connection to the somber skies of these Italian painters, is likely Claude Monet's *Gare Sainte-Lazare* (1877; Liu 221). Proust was a great admirer of Monet, as we know from *Contre Sainte-Beuve*. His description of the station certainly makes more sense in light of Monet's painting, though the painting in itself cannot account for Proust's motivation in drawing on the image at this particular moment in the narrative.

36. "Pour la première fois je sentais qu'il était possible que ma mère vécût sans moi, autrement que pour moi."

37. Consider Fontanier on hyperbole and truth: "Hyperbole augments or diminishes things with excess, and presents them well above or well

below what they are, with the aim, not of deceiving, but of drawing nearer to the truth [L'Hyperbole augmente ou diminue les choses avec excès, et les présente bien au-dessus ou bien au-dessous de ce qu'elle sont, dans la vue, non de tromper, mais d'amener à la vérité même]" (123, translation mine).

38. "Peut-être cet effroi que j'avais—qu'ont tant d'autres—de coucher dans une chambre inconnue, peut-être cet effroi n'est-il que la forme la plus humble, obscure, organique, presque inconsciente, de ce grand refus désespéré qu'opposent les choses qui constituent le meilleur de notre vie présente à ce que nous revêtions mentalement de notre acceptation la formule d'un avenir où elles ne figurent pas."

39. "En la retrouvant enfin . . . je l'avais perdue pour toujours."

40. "[Ce] refus . . . était encore au fond de la difficulté que j'avais à penser à ma propre mort ou à une survie comme celle que Bergotte promettait aux hommes dans ses livres, dans laquelle je ne pourrais emporter mes souvenirs, mes défauts, mon caractère qui ne se résignaient pas à l'idée de ne plus être et ne voulaient pour moi ni du néant, ni d'une éternité où ils ne seraient plus."

41. "Et la crainte d'un avenir où nous seront enlevés la vue et l'entretien de ceux que nous aimons . . . cette crainte, loin de se dissiper, s'accroît, si à la douleur d'une telle privation nous pensons que s'ajoutera ce qui pour nous semble actuellement plus cruel encore: ne pas la ressentir comme une douleur, y rester indifférent . . . ce serait donc une vraie mort de nous-mêmes, mort suivie . . . de résurrection, mais en un moi différent."

42. "J'aurais voulu au moins m'étendre un instant sur le lit, mais à quoi bon puisque je n'aurais pu y faire trouver de repos à cet ensemble de sensations qui est pour chacun de nous son corps conscient, sinon son corps matériel, et puisque les objets inconnus qui l'encerclaient, en le forçant à mettre ses perceptions sur le pied permanent d'une défensive vigilante, auraient maintenu mes regards, mon ouïe, tous mes sens, dans une position aussi réduite et incommode . . . que celle du cardinal La Balue dans la cage où il ne pouvait ni se tenir debout ni s'asseoir."

43. "C'est notre attention qui met des objets dans une chambre . . . et l'habitude qui les en retire et nous y fait de la place."

44. The opposition of the intellect to the sensuous self in Proust is well known, as is the role it plays in the distinction between voluntary and involuntary memory. Proust opens *Contre Sainte-Beuve* with a statement on this opposition: "Every day I set less store on intellect. Every day I see more clearly that if the writer is to repossess himself of some part of his impressions, get to something personal, and to the only material of art, he must put it aside. What intellect restores to us under the name of the past, is not the past. In reality, as soon as each hour of one's life has died it embodies itself in some material object, as do the souls of the dead in certain folk-stories, and hides there" (*On Art and Literature* 19). "Chaque jour j'attache moins de prix à l'intelligence. Chaque jour je me rends mieux compte que ce n'est qu'en dehors d'elle que l'écrivain peut ressaisir quelque chose de nos impressions, c'est à dire atteindre quelque chose de lui-même et la seule matière de l'art. Ce que l'intelligence nous rend sous le nom de passée n'est pas lui. En réalité, comme il arrive pour les âmes des trépassés dans certaines légendes

populaires, chaque heure de notre vie, aussitôt morte, s'incarne et se cache en quelque objet matériel" (*Contre Sainte-Beuve* 43).

45. "Ce sont elles [les parties de l'ancien moi condamnées à mourir]—mêmes les plus chétives, comme les obscurs attachements aux dimensions, l'atmosphère d'une chambre—qui s'effarent et refusent, en des rébellions où il faut voir un mode secret, partiel, tangible et vrai de la résistance à la mort, de la longue résistance désespérée et quotidienne à la mort fragmentaire et successive telle qu'elle s'insère dans toute la durée de notre vie, détachant de nous à chaque moment des lambeaux de nous-mêmes."

46. "De rendre la différence entre le départ et l'arrivée non pas aussi insensible, mais aussi profonde qu'[il] peut."

47. "Telle qu'elle était dans notre pensée quand notre imagination nous portait du lieu où nous vivions jusqu'au coeur d'un lieu désiré."

48. "Un bond miraculeux."

49. Indeed, Proust uses this very term to describe the conversion of life into language. In a letter to Léon Daudet from November 27, 1913, he envisions a kind of writing that would be "the supreme miracle . . . the transubstantiation of the irrational qualities of matter and life into human words [le miracle suprême, la transsubstantiation des qualités irrationnelles de la matière et de la vie dans des mots humains]" (*Selected Letters* 3: 213; *Choix de lettres* 195). See citations of this letter by Julia Kristeva in *Le temps sensible* (264) and Genette in "Proust palimpseste" (4). *Transubstantiation* is indeed the word Proust intends, for in his view the matter of life is not insubstantiated by language but converted into a new substance, what he calls the writer's "style." In *Contre Sainte-Beuve*, he writes, "In Flaubert's style, now, all the elements of reality are rendered down into one unanimous substance. . . . Everything is shown there, but only in reflection, and without affecting its uniform substance [Dans le style de Flaubert, par exemple, toutes les parties de la réalité sont converties en une même substance. . . . Toutes les choses s'y peignent, mais par reflet, sans en altérer la substance homogène]" (*On Art and Literature* 170; *Contre Sainte-Beuve* 201). Deleuze likewise points to Proust's substantialization of style by referring to it as "this luminous substance . . . this refracting medium [cette matière lumineuse . . . ce milieu réfractant]" (*Proust and Signs* 47; *Proust et les signes* 61).

50. Rhetoricians have long considered the plausibility of a logical order of figures of speech. In *The New Science* (1725, 1740), Giambattista Vico identified four basic tropes to which all others could be reduced—metaphor, metonymy, synecdoche, and irony—which, he argued, represented successive stages of consciousness as well as the ages of history (White, *Metahistory* 32). In *Metahistory*, as well as in "Narrative, Description, and Tropology in Proust," Hayden White makes use of the same tropological sequence. Harold Bloom, in *A Map of Misreading*, argues instead for a sequence of six major tropes to describe the process of poetic influence, and he specifies their particular order: irony, synecdoche, metonymy, hyperbole, metaphor, and metalepsis (70).

51. That is, what appears to be hyperbolic at one moment in the text is ironic from a later point of view. I use the term *hyperbole* here to describe the reader's deferred understanding, and *irony* to describe the negation of a previously held position. Gans makes a similar argument: that both hyperbole and

irony may be used to describe the movement of the interpretation of a literary text in its entirety. Hyperbole, for Gans, corresponds to the temporal delay in the construction of a text's meaning, while irony appears wherever the text reveals its fictional status in a gesture of self-reflection. For my purposes, de Man makes the latter point most clearly: irony is a figure of negation and self-reflection (see "The Rhetoric of Temporality," especially 208–28).

52. Genette's analysis in "Métonymie chez Proust" describes what the author terms "diegetic metaphors," and begins with two of Proust's descriptive passages in which objectively similar objects—the steeples of Saint-André-des-champs and the steeples of Saint-Mars-le-Vêtu—are treated with distinctly different language. One pair of steeples is likened to spears of wheat, while the other to scaly, pointy fish, because, Genette points out, of the distinctly different landscapes to which the steeples belong. This is typical enough of Proust's style: "Wheat-steeple (or wheatstack-church) in an open field, fish-steeple by the sea, purple-steeple overlooking a vineyard . . . in Proust there is obviously a sort of recurring, almost stereotypical, stylistic schema that we might call the topos of the *chameleon steeple* [Clocher-épi (ou église-meule) en plein champs, clocher-poisson à la mer, clocher-pourpre au-dessus des vignobles . . . il y a manifestement chez Proust une sorte de schème stylistique récurrent, presque stéréotypé, qu'on pourrait appeler le topos du *clocher-caméléon*]" (44, translation mine). While it is true the Martinville steeples are likened to birds on the plain, and at this moment Proust can be said to draw metonymically on an element of the surrounding landscape, this particular diegetic metaphor is not extended in any rigorous way. Instead we are presented with a kaleidoscope of different images like so many hasty, impressionistic sketches.

53. "Il faut observer que les exemples de métaphores 'naturelles' cités dans *Le temps retrouvé* sont en fait, typiquement, des substitutions synecdochiques."

54. "La métaphore trouve son appui et sa motivation dans une métonymie."

55. "L'édifice immense du souvenir . . . toutes les fleurs de notre jardin et celles du parc de M. Swann, et les nymphéas de la Vivonne, et les bonnes gens du village et leurs petits logis et l'église et tout Combray et ses environs, tout cela qui prend forme et solidité . . . sorti, ville et jardins, de ma tasse de thé."

56. "Cette essence n'était pas en moi, elle était moi."

57. "C'était Venise . . . que la sensation que j'avais ressentie jadis sur deux dalles inégales du baptistère de Saint-Marc m'avait rendue avec toutes les autres sensations jointes ce jour-là à cette sensation-là."

58. Cf. Kristeva 268.

59. "La vérité ne commencera qu'au moment où l'écrivain prendra deux objets différents, posera leur rapport, analogue dans le monde de l'art à celui qu'est le rapport unique de la loi causale dans le monde de la science. . . . Même, ainsi que la vie, quand en rapprochant une qualité commune à deux sensations, il dégagera leur essence commune en les réunissant l'une et l'autre . . . dans une métaphore."

60. "Comme si elles avaient été une sorte d'écorce"; "Quelque chose d'analogue à une jolie phrase."

61. "Quelque chose qui, commun à la fois au passé et au présent, est beaucoup plus essentiel qu'eux deux."

62. "[Un] homme affranchi de l'ordre du temps."

63. Leo Bersani is convincing on this point when he describes involuntary memory as a kind of death: "For if such memories revive the past as nothing more than the self that lived it . . . they also effect, belatedly and retroactively, a radical separation of the self from the world. If, for example, the madeleine resurrects a wholly internalized Combray, it also projects or throws forth from within that internalization a Combray of pure appearance, a Combray that persists phenomenally . . . from which Marcel himself [has] been evacuated" (*Culture of Redemption* 9).

64. "Le lieu même de sa pensée."

65. "La vie enfin découverte et éclaircie, la seule vie par conséquent pleinement vécu."

66. "Un livre est un grand cimetière où sur la plupart des tombes on ne peut plus lire les noms effacés."

67. "Enchaîner à jamais dans sa phrase les deux termes différents . . . les enfermera dans les anneaux nécessaires d'un beau style."

68. "Une matière distincte, nouvelle."

69. "Toutes les parties de la réalité sont converties en une même . . . substance homogène."

70. A similar ambiguity can be found in Mallarmé's "Prose pour des Esseintes." "Hyperbole! de ma mémoire / Triomphalement ne sais-tu/ Te lever," the poem begins; but it ends with the "sépulcre" and the "éternels parchemins" of the written word. I am grateful to an anonymous reader at *MLN* for drawing my attention to this poem.

### 7. "HOW ANYTHING CAN BE DIFFERENT FROM WHAT IT IS": TAUTOLOGY IN STEIN'S *THE MAKING OF AMERICANS*

1. Despite the claim of the title page of the first edition that the book was written in 1906–8, which Stein reiterates in *The Autobiography of Alice B. Toklas*, archival work reveals that the manuscript was begun in early 1903 (Katz 37). It was interrupted by Stein's work on *Three Lives* (1905–6). A full draft of the novel was produced between 1906 and 1908, and then substantially transformed from 1908 to 1911 (Katz 159, 265, 273).

2. In *The Autobiography of Alice B. Toklas*, Stein offers an efficient summary of the novel: "It had changed from being a history of a family to a history of everybody the family knew and then it became the history of every kind and of every individual human being. But in spite of all this there was a hero and he was to die" (94).

3. See, for example, Clement Greenberg's "Cézanne and the Unity of Modern Art."

4. For an excellent reading of habit as a character-shaping force in Stein, albeit one that focuses on *Three Lives*, see Omri Moses's "Gertrude Stein's Lively Habits."

5. Similarly, Deleuze distinguishes "qualitative multiplicities" from mere aggregates, describing them as wholes produced in such a way that they cannot be divided without changing in kind (*Bergsonism* 40).

6. Here I diverge from Jennifer Ashton's reading, which seeks to emphasize the successive nature of repetition over and against the instantaneity of knowledge. To be fair, Ashton observes Stein's claims about the immanence of the whole to the parts, but she seems to find them contradictory. She notes the tension in *The Making of Americans* between the temporal succession of repetition and the instantaneity of the whole, arguing that the novel runs up against "the discrepancy between experience as it accumulates and the knowledge that comes of it" (35). But she assumes that this discrepancy between experience and knowledge needs to be resolved. Likening it to the mathematical problem of the infinite, she asserts that in her later work Stein succeeds in figuring out how to separate the logical whole from an experience of progression, discerning the "formal conditions" of the whole (65) rather than deriving the whole from experience. I would point out that Ashton can make this argument only by denigrating experience itself, denying it any ability to form its own intrinsic categories or give rise to passive syntheses of knowledge.

7. For the definitive discussion of the importance of Stein's scientific training to her experimental writing, see Steven Meyer's *Irresistible Dictation*.

8. While Ruddick notes that "it is a commonplace of Stein criticism that her stylistic experimentation owes something to . . . James's idea of the 'stream of consciousness'" (13–14), her own approach differs—as does my own—by looking beyond just the prose style and turning to the content of *The Making of Americans* for an allegory of the mental faculties (18).

9. In the 1930s the critic Michael Gold declared that Stein's work represented "the most extreme subjectivism of the contemporary artist" (qtd. in Chodat 581). In 1970, in one of the first full-length studies of Stein's work, Richard Bridgman called *The Making of Americans* "a disaster" but at least worthy of interest as a record of Stein's psychological development (60–61).

10. "L'esthétique se scinde en deux domaines irréductibles, celui de la théorie du sensible qui ne retient du réel que sa conformité à l'expérience possible, et celui de la théorie du beau qui recueille la réalité du réel en tant qu'elle se réfléchit d'autre part" (Deleuze, *Différence et répétition* 94).

11. Interestingly enough, aesthetic judgment as Kant describes it comes very close to this kind of activity. Stimulated by a sense encounter, aesthetic judgment appeals to concept formation without actually attaining it, and it asks for universal assent without presuming it. Kant's "Analytic of the Beautiful" might be understood as a theory of what thought does, and what it might do, when confronted with a singular encounter. See Steven Shaviro's "Beauty Lies in the Eye."

12. The nursery rhyme was also quoted in an assigned text in one of Stein's philosophy classes at Radcliffe, Josiah Royce's *The Spirit of Modern Philosophy* (Bridgman 242n). Royce uses the rhyme to illustrate that "self-recognition . . . include[s] the binding of fact to fact in your experience," as part of his explanation of Kant's notion of the transcendental unity of apperception (Royce 128).

13. Stein describes confronting the effects of fame during her popular U.S. lecture tour of 1934–35: "We saw an electric sign moving around a building

and it said Gertrude Stein has come and that was upsetting . . . To suddenly see your name is always upsetting. Of course it has happened to me pretty often and I like it to happen just as often but always it does give me a little shock of recognition and non-recognition. It is one of the things most worrying in the subject of identity" (*Everybody's Autobiography* 175)

14. Admittedly, modernist experimentation was often carried out in the name not of a non-realism but of a superior realism, one meant to be adequate to the inner life of modern subjects. Yet this experimentation was often paired with critiques of nineteenth-century standards of objectivity, such as can be found in Virginia Woolf's essays on fiction, especially "Mr. Bennett and Mrs. Brown."

15. Compare William James: "We [may] find that the preparation we make for [a sense perception] always partly consists of the creation of an imaginary duplicate of the object in the mind" (99).

16. Stein made her fondness for detective fiction known in the 1930s, publishing "Why I Like Detective Stories" in *Harper's* in 1937, and trying her own hand at the genre with the novella *Blood on the Dining Room Floor* in 1933. In a lecture from the same period, she elaborates on the appeal of the genre, calling it "the only really modern novel form": "It is very curious but the detective story which is you might say the only really modern novel form that has come into existence gets rid of human nature. . . . The hero is dead to begin with and so you have so to speak got rid of the event before the book begins ("What Are Masterpieces" 87). Because it gets rid of the hero by killing him off and replacing him with "detection," crime fiction is intimately tied to the nature of composition as such. As Stein asserts elsewhere on writing in general, "What we write is really a crime story" (*Geographical History* 79).

CONCLUSION

1. For a fascinating discussion of "antihermeneutic" trends in recent criticism and a concomitant call for theorizing our hermeneutic practices differently, see Julie Orlemanski's "Scales of Reading."

Abrams, M. H. *The Mirror and the Lamp: Romantic Theory and the Critical Tradition.* New York: Oxford University Press, 1953.

Ackerley, Chris, and S. E Gontarski. *The Grove Companion to Samuel Beckett: A Reader's Guide to His Works, Life, and Thought.* New York: Grove Press, 2004.

Admussen, Richard L. *The Samuel Beckett Manuscripts: A Study.* Boston: G. K. Hall, 1979.

Adorno, Theodor W. "Trying to Understand Endgame." In *Notes to Literature.* Vol. 1. Ed. Rolf Tiedemann. Trans. Shierry Weber Nicholsen. New York: Columbia University Press, 1991.

Althusser, Louis. *Philosophie et philosophie spontanée des savants.* Paris: Maspero, 1967.

Althusser, Louis, and Etienne Balibar. *Reading Capital.* Trans. Ben Brewster. London: Verso, 1997.

Amiran, Eyal. *Wandering and Home: Beckett's Metaphysical Narrative.* University Park: Pennsylvania State University Press, 1993.

Aristotle. *Nicomachean Ethics.* Trans. Terence Irwin. Indianapolis: Hackett, 1999.

———. *Rhetoric.* Trans. W. Rhys Roberts. New York: Modern Library, 1954.

Armstrong, Nancy. *Desire and Domestic Fiction: A Political History of the Novel.* New York: Oxford University Press, 1987.

———. *How Novels Think: The Limits of British Individualism from 1719–1900.* New York: Columbia University Press, 2005.

Ashton, Jennifer. *From Modernism to Postmodernism: American Poetry and Theory in the Twentieth Century.* New York: Cambridge University Press, 2005.

Attridge, Derek. Introduction to *Acts of Literature* by Jacques Derrida. New York: Routledge, 1992.

Bair, Deidre. *Samuel Beckett: A Biography*. New York: Harcourt Brace Jovanovich, 1978.

Bakhtin, M. M. *Dialogic Imagination: Four Essays*. Ed. Michael Holquist. Trans. Caryl Emerson and Michael Holquist. Austin: University of Texas Press, 1981.

Banville, John. "The Last Word." *New York Review of Books*, August 13, 1992, 17–20.

Barthes, Roland. "Proust and Names." In *New Critical Essays*. Trans. Richard Howard. Evanston, IL: Northwestern University Press, 2009.

Bataille, Georges. "Hegel, Death and Sacrifice." Trans. Jonathan Strauss. *Yale French Studies* 78 (1990): 9–28.

———. "Molloy's Silence." Trans. John Pilling. In *On Beckett: Essays and Criticism*. New York: Grove Press, 1986.

Beckett, Samuel. *L'innommable*. Paris: Éditions de minuit, 1953.

———. *Molloy*. Paris: Éditions de minuit, 1951.

———. *Proust* and *Three Dialogues with George Duthuit*. London: John Calder, 1965.

———. *Three Novels: Molloy, Malone Dies,* and *The Unnamable*. New York: Grove Press, 1958.

Beiser, Frederick C. *The Fate of Reason: German Philosophy from Kant to Fichte*. Cambridge, MA: Harvard University Press, 1987.

———. *The Romantic Imperative: The Concept of Early German Romanticism*. Cambridge, MA: Harvard University Press, 2003.

Benjamin, Walter. "The Concept of Criticism in German Romanticism." In *Selected Writings*. Vol. 1. Ed. Marcus Bullock and Michael W. Jennings. Cambridge, MA: Harvard University Press, 1996.

Benziger, James. "Organic Unity: Leibniz to Coleridge." *PMLA* 66.2 (1951): 24–48.

Bergson, Henri. *Creative Evolution*. Trans. Arthur Mitchell. Mineola, NY: Dover, 1998.

———. *The Creative Mind*. Trans. Mabelle L. C. Andison. New York: Citadel Press, 2002.

Bernstein, Jay M., ed. *Classic and Romantic German Aesthetics*. Cambridge: Cambridge University Press, 2003.

Bersani, Leo. *Arts of Impoverishment: Beckett, Rothko, Resnais*. Cambridge, MA: Harvard University Press, 1993.

———. *Balzac to Beckett: Center and Circumference in French Fiction*. New York: Oxford University Press, 1970.

———. *The Culture of Redemption*. Cambridge, MA: Harvard University Press, 1990.

Blanchot, Maurice. *Faux pas.* Trans. Charlotte Mandell. Stanford: Stanford University Press, 2001.

———. *The Infinite Conversation.* Trans. Susan Hanson. Minneapolis: University of Minnesota Press, 1993. Originally published as *L'entretien infini* (Paris: Gallimard, 1969).

———. *The Space of Literature.* Trans. Ann Smock. Lincoln: University of Nebraska Press, 1982. Originally published as *L'espace littéraire* (Paris: Gallimard, 1955).

———. "The Two Versions of the Imaginary."

———. *The Work of Fire.* Trans. Charlotte Mandell. Stanford: Stanford University Press, 1995. Originally published as *La part du feu* (Paris: Gallimard, 1949).

———. "Where Now? Who Now?" In *The Book to Come.* Trans. Charlotte Mandell. Stanford: Stanford University Press, 2003.

Bloom, Harold. *A Map of Misreading.* New York: Oxford University Press, 1975.

Bowie, Malcolm. "Postlude: Proust and the Art of Brevity." In *Cambridge Companion to Proust.* New York: Cambridge University Press, 2001.

Breazeale, Dan. "Johann Gottlieb Fichte." In *The Stanford Encyclopedia of Philosophy,* ed. Edward N. Zalta. Winter 2006. Online.

Bridgman, Richard. *Gertrude Stein in Pieces.* New York: Oxford University Press, 1970.

Brooks, Cleanth. "The Heresy of Paraphrase." In *The Well Wrought Urn: Studies in the Structure of Poetry.* New York: Harcourt, Brace & World, 1947.

———. "Irony as a Principle of Structure." In *The Critical Tradition: Classic Texts and Contemporary Trends,* ed. David H. Richter. 2nd edition. Boston: Bedford Books, 1998.

———. "The Language of Paradox." In *The Well Wrought Urn: Studies in the Structure of Poetry.* New York: Harcourt, Brace & World, 1947.

Brooks, Cleanth, and Robert P. Warren. *Understanding Poetry.* New York: Holt, Rinehart and Winston, 1960.

Bruns, Gerald L. *Maurice Blanchot: The Refusal of Philosophy.* Baltimore: Johns Hopkins University Press, 1997.

Calinescu, Matei. *Five Faces of Modernity: Modernism, Avant-Garde, Decadence, Kitsch, Postmodernism.* Durham, NC: Duke University Press, 1987.

Canguilhem, Georges. *La connaissance de la vie.* Paris: Hachette, 1952.

Cassirer, Ernst. *Kant's Life and Thought.* Trans James Haden. New Haven, CT: Yale University Press, 1981.

Cavell, Stanley. "Ending the Waiting Game: A Reading of Beckett's *Endgame*." In *Must We Mean What We Say?* Cambridge: Cambridge University Press, 1969.

Chabot, Pascal. *La philosophie de Simondon*. Paris: J. Vrin, 2003.

Chodat, Robert. "Sense, Science, and the Interpretations of Gertrude Stein." *Modernism/modernity* 12.4 (2005): 581–605.

Cicero. *Ad C. Herennium de ratione dicendi (Rhetorica ad Herennium)*. Trans. Harry Caplan. Loeb Classical Library 403. Cambridge, MA: Harvard University Press, 1954.

Clark, Timothy. *Derrida, Heidegger, Blanchot: Sources of Derrida's Notion and Practice of Literature*. New York: Cambridge University Press, 1992.

Clemens, Justin. *The Romanticism of Contemporary Theory: Institutions, Aesthetics, Nihilism*. Burlington, VT: Ashgate, 2003.

Clément, Bruno. *L'oeuvre sans qualités: Rhétorique de Samuel Beckett*. Paris: Éditions du seuil, 1994.

Clement, Tanya. "The Story of One: Narrative and Composition in Gertrude Stein's *The Making of Americans*." *Texas Studies in Literature and Language* 54.3 (2012): 426–48.

Coe, Richard. *Samuel Beckett*. New York: Grove Press, 1964.

Cohn, Ruby. Foreword to *Disjecta: Miscellaneous Writings and a Dramatic Fragment* by Samuel Beckett. London: J. Calder, 1983.

Coleridge, Samuel Taylor. *Biographia Literaria*. Vols. 1 and 2. Ed. J. Shawcross. Oxford: Oxford University Press, 1954.

———. *Lay Sermons*. Ed. R. J. White. Vol. 6 of *The Collected Works*. London: Routledge & Kegan Paul, 1972.

———. "Shakespeare's Judgment Equal to His Genius." In *The Critical Tradition: Classic Texts and Contemporary Trends*, ed. David H. Richter. 2nd Edition. Boston: Bedford Books, 1998.

Comay, Rebecca. "Impressions: Proust, Photography, Trauma." *Discourse* 31.1–2 (2009): 86–105.

Connor, Steven. *Samuel Beckett: Repetition, Theory, and Text*. Oxford: Basil Blackwell, 1988.

Critchley, Simon. *Very Little . . . Almost Nothing: Death, Philosophy, Literature*. New York: Routledge, 2004.

Culler, Jonathan. "The Turns of Metaphor." In *The Pursuit of Signs: Semiotics, Literature, Deconstruction*. Ithaca, NY: Cornell University Press, 1981.

Cusset, François. *French Theory: How Foucault, Derrida, Deleuze, & Co. Transformed the Intellectual Life of the United States*. Trans. Jeff Fort with Josephine Berganza and Marlon Jones. Minneapolis: University of Minnesota Press, 2008.

Danius, Sara. "The Aesthetics of the Windshield: Proust and the Modernist Rhetoric of Speed." *Modernism/modernity* 8.1 (2001): 99–126.

Deleuze, Gilles. *Bergsonism.* Trans. Hugh Tomlinson and Barbara Habberjam. New York: Zone Books, 1988.

———. *Cinema 2: The Time Image.* Trans. Hugh Tomlinson and Robert Galeta. Minneapolis: University of Minnesota Press, 1989. Originally published as *L'image-temps* (Paris: Éditions de minuit, 1985).

———. *Desert Islands and Other Texts, 1953–1974.* Trans. Michael Taormina. Los Angeles: Semiotext(e), 2004.

———. *Difference and Repetition.* Trans. Paul Patton. New York: Columbia University Press 1994. Originally published as *Différence et répétition* (Paris: PUF, 1968). (cited as DR).

———. "The Exhausted." In *Essays Critical and Clinical.* Minneapolis: University of Minnesota Press, 1997.

———. *Foucault.* Trans. Séan Hand. Minneapolis: University of Minnesota Press, 1988.

———. "He Stuttered." In *Essays Critical and Clinical.* Minneapolis: University of Minnesota Press, 1997.

———. *Kant's Critical Philosophy: The Doctrine of the Faculties.* Trans. Hugh Tomlinson and Barbara Habberjam. Minneapolis: University of Minnesota Press, 1984.

———. "Letter Preface." In *Variations: The Philosophy of Gilles Deleuze* by Jean-Clet Martin. Trans. Constantin Boundas and Susan Dyrkton. Edinburgh: Edinburgh University Press, 2010.

———. *Logic of Sense.* Trans. Mark Lester with Charles Stivale. New York: Columbia University Press, 1990.

———. *Nietzsche and Philosophy.* Trans. Hugh Tomlinson. New York: Columbia University Press, 1983. Originally published as *Nietzsche et la philosophie* (Paris: PUF, 1962).

———. *Proust and Signs: The Complete Text.* Trans. Richard Howard. Minneapolis: University of Minnesota Press, 2000. Originally published as *Proust et les signes.* 3rd edition (Paris: PUF, 1998).

Deleuze, Gilles, and Félix Guattari. *Anti-Oedipus: Capitalism and Schizophrenia.* Trans. Robert Hurley, Mark Seem, and Helen R. Lane. Minneapolis: University of Minnesota Press, 1983.

Deleuze, Gilles, and Félix Guattari. *A Thousand Plateaus: Capitalism and Schizophrenia.* Trans. Brian Massumi. Minneapolis: University of Minnesota Press, 1987.

Deleuze, Gilles, and Félix Guattari. *What Is Philosophy?* Trans. Hugh Tomlinson and Graham Burchell. New York: Columbia University Press, 1994.

Deleuze, Gilles, and Claire Parnet. *Dialogues*. Trans. Hugh Tomlinson and Barbara Habberjam. New York: Columbia University Press, 1987.

de Man, Paul. "Form and Intent in the American New Criticism." In *Blindness and Insight: Essays in the Rhetoric of Contemporary Criticism*. Minneapolis: University of Minnesota Press, 1983.

————. "Hypogram and Inscription." In *The Resistance to Theory*. Minneapolis: University of Minnesota Press, 1986.

————. "Phenomenality and Materiality in Kant." In *Aesthetic Ideology*. Ed. Andrzej Warminski. Minneapolis: University of Minnesota Press, 1996.

————. "Reading (Proust)." In *Allegories of Reading: Figural Language in Rousseau, Nietzsche, Rilke, and Proust*. New Haven, CT: Yale University Press, 1979.

————. "Wordsworth and Hölderlin." In *The Rhetoric of Romanticism*. New York: Columbia University Press, 1984.

————. "The Rhetoric of Temporality." In *Blindness and Insight: Essays in the Rhetoric of Contemporary Criticism*. Minnesota: University of Minnesota Press, 1983.

————. "Semiology and Rhetoric." *diacritics* 3.3 (1973): 27–33.

Derrida, Jacques. *Acts of Literature*. Ed. Derek Attridge. New York: Routledge, 1992.

————. "Che cos'è la poesia?" In *A Derrida Reader: Between the Blinds*. Ed. Peggy Kamuf. New York: Columbia University Press, 1991.

————. *Demeure*. Ed. Elizabeth Rottenberg. Stanford: Stanford University Press, 2000.

————. "The Double Session." In *Dissemination*. Trans. Barbara Johnson. Chicago: University of Chicago Press, 1981. Originally published in *La dissémination* (Paris: Éditions du seuil, 1972).

————. "Economimesis." *diacritics* 11.2 (1981): 3–25.

————. "Force and Signification." In *Writing and Difference*. Trans. Alan Bass. Chicago: University of Chicago Press, 1978. Originally published as "Force et signification" in *L'écriture et la différence* (Paris: Éditions du seuil, 1967).

————. "The Law of Genre." Trans Avital Ronell. *Critical Inquiry* 7.1 (1980): 55–81.

————. "La mythologie blanche." In *Marges de la philosophie*. Paris: Éditions de minuit, 1972.

————. *Positions*. Ed. Alan Bass and Christopher Norris. London: Continuum, 2002.

————. "Psyche: Inventions of the Other." In *Psyche: Inventions of the Other*. Ed. Peggy Kamuf and Elizabeth Rottenberg. Stanford: Stanford University Press, 2007.

———. "Structure, Sign, and Play in the Discourse of the Human Sciences." In *Writing and Difference*. Trans. Alan Bass. Chicago: University of Chicago Press, 1978.

Descartes, René. *The Philosophical Writings*. Vol. 2. Trans. John Cottingham, Robert Stoothoff, and Dugald Murdoch. New York: Cambridge University Press, 1984.

Dumarsais, César Chesneau, and Pierre Fontanier. *Des tropes*. Genève: Slatkine Reprints, 1967.

During, Elie. "'A History of Problems': Bergson and the French Epistemological Tradition." *Journal of the British Society for Phenomenology* 35.1 (2004): 4–23.

Eagleton, Terry. *Literary Theory: An Introduction*. 2nd edition. Minneapolis: University of Minnesota Press, 1996.

———. "Political Beckett?" *New Left Review* 40 (2006): 67–74.

Eichner, Hans. Preface to *Literary Notebooks, 1797–1801* by Friedrich Schlegel. Toronto: University of Toronto Press, 1957.

Erasmus, Desiderius. *Copia: Foundations of the Abundant Style*. In *The Rhetorical Tradition: Readings from Classical Times to the Present*. Ed. Patricia Bizzell and Bruce Herzberg. Boston: Bedford/St. Martin's, 1990.

Escarpit, Robert. "Littérature." In *Dictionnaire international des termes littéraires*, ed. Robert Escarpit and Jean-Marie Grassin. The Hague: Mouton, 1973.

Fichte, Johann Gottlieb. *The Science of Knowledge*. Ed. and trans. Peter Heath and John Lachs. New York: Cambridge University Press, 1982.

Firchow, Peter. Introduction to *Lucinde and the Fragments* by Friedrich Schlegel. Minneapolis: University of Minnesota Press, 1971.

Fitch, Brian. *Beckett and Babel*. Toronto: University Toronto Press, 1988.

Fletcher, Angus. *Allegory, the Theory of a Symbolic Mode*. Ithaca, NY: Cornell University Press, 1964.

Fontanier, Pierre. *Les figures du discours*. Paris: Flammarion, 1968.

Fowler, Alastair. "The Future of Genre Theory: Functions and Constructional Types." In *The Future of Literary Theory*, ed. Ralph Cohen. New York: Routledge, 1989.

Frank, Manfred. *The Philosophical Foundations of Early German Romanticism*. Trans. Elizabeth Millán-Zaibert. Albany: State University of New York Press, 2004.

Franks, Paul. *All or Nothing: Systematicity, Transcendental Arguments, and Skepticism in German Idealism*. Cambridge, MA: Harvard University Press, 2005.

Gans, Eric. "Hyperbole et ironie." *Poétique* 24 (1975): 488–94.

Gasché, Rodolphe. "The Felicities of Paradox." In *Maurice Blanchot: The Demand of Writing*, ed. Carolyn Bailey Gill. New York: Routledge, 1996.

———. "Ideality in Fragmentation." In *Philosophical Fragments* by Friedrich Schlegel. Minneapolis: University of Minnesota Press, 1991.

———. *The Tain of the Mirror: Derrida and the Philosophy of Reflection*. Cambridge, MA: Harvard University Press, 1986.

Gass, William. Introduction to *The Geographical History of America* by Gertrude Stein. Baltimore: Johns Hopkins University Press, 1995.

Gendron, Sarah. "A Cogito for the Dissolved Self: Writing, Presence, and the Subject in the Work of Samuel Beckett, Jacques Derrida, and Gilles Deleuze." *Journal of Modern Literature* 28.1 (2004): 47–64.

Genette, Gérard. "Hyperboles." In *Figures I*. Paris: Éditions du Seuil, 1966.

———. "Métonymie chez Proust." In *Figures III*. Paris: Éditions du Seuil, 1972.

———. "Proust et le langage indirecte." In *Figures II*. Paris: Éditions du Seuil, 1969.

———. "Proust palimpseste." In *Figures I*. Paris: Éditions du Seuil, 1966.

Gontarski, S. E. Introduction to *Nohow On* by Samuel Beckett. New York: Grove Press, 1996.

Greenberg, Clement. "Cézanne and the Unity of Modern Art." In *The Collected Essays and Criticism*, Vol. 3: *Affirmations and Refusals: 1950–1956*. Ed. John O'Brian. Chicago: University of Chicago Press, 1995.

Hartman, Geoffrey. Preface to *The Gaze of Orpheus and Other Literary Essays* by Maurice Blanchot. Trans. Lydia Davis. Ed. P. Adams Sitney. Barrytown, NY: Station Hill, 1981.

Hegel, G. W. F. *The Difference between Fichte's and Schelling's System of Philosophy*. Trans. H. S. Harris and Walter Cerf. Albany: State University of New York Press, 1977.

———. *Hegel's Aesthetics: Lectures on Fine Art*. Trans. T. M. Knox. New York: Oxford University Press, 1975.

Heidegger, Martin. *Being and Time*. Trans. Joan Stambaugh. Albany: State University of New York Press, 1996.

———. "The Origin of the Work of Art." In *Basic Writings*. Ed. David Farrell Krell. Trans. Albert Hofstadter. New York: Harper Collins, 1993.

———. "The Question Concerning Technology." In *Basic Writings*. Ed. David Farrell Krell. Trans. Albert Hofstadter. New York: Harper Collins, 1993.

Hill, Leslie. *Blanchot, Extreme Contemporary*. London: Routledge, 1997.

Hughes, Joe. "The Intimacy of the Common: Gilbert Simondon Today." *Theory & Event* 17.2 (2014). Online.

James, William. *Psychology: The Briefer Course*. Mineola, NY: Dover, 2001.

Jaurretche, Colleen, ed. *Beckett, Joyce and the Art of the Negative*. Amsterdam: Rodopi, 2005.

Johnson, Christopher. *Hyperboles: The Rhetoric of Excess in Baroque Literature and Thought*. Cambridge, MA: Harvard University Press, 2010.

Kant, Immanuel. *Critique of Pure Reason*. Ed. Paul Guyer. Trans. Paul Guyer and Allen Wood. New York: Cambridge University Press, 1999.

———. *Critique of the Power of Judgment*. Ed. Paul Guyer. Trans. Paul Guyer and Eric Matthews. New York: Cambridge University Press, 2000.

———. *Lectures on Logic*. Ed. and trans. J. M. Young. Cambridge: Cambridge University Press, 2009.

———. *Prolegomena to Any Future Metaphysics That Will Be Able to Come Forward as Science*. Ed. Gary C. Hatfield. Rev. edition. New York: Cambridge University Press, 2004.

Katz, Leon. "The First Making of *The Making of Americans*: A Study Based on Gertrude Stein's Notebooks and Early Versions of Her Novel, 1902–1908." PhD diss., Columbia University, 1963.

Kenner, Hugh. *Samuel Beckett: A Critical Study*. London: John Calder, 1961.

Kern, Edith. "Moran-Molloy: The Hero as Author." In *Samuel Beckett*, ed. Harold Bloom. New York: Chelsea House, 1985.

Knowlson, James. *Damned to Fame: The Life of Samuel Beckett*. New York: Simon & Schuster, 1996.

Kristeva, Julia. *Le temps sensible: Proust et l'expérience littéraire*. Paris: Gallimard, 1994.

Lacoue-Labarthe, Philippe, and Jean-Luc Nancy. *The Literary Absolute: The Theory of Literature in German Romanticism*. Trans. Philip Barnard and Cheryl Lester. Albany: State University of New York Press, 1988. Originally published as *L'absolu littéraire: Théorie de la littérature du romantisme allemand*, with Anne-Marie Lang (Paris: Éditions du seuil, 1978).

Landy, Joshua. *Philosophy as Fiction: Self, Deception, and Knowledge in Proust*. New York: Oxford University Press, 2004.

Lausberg, Heinrich. *Handbook of Literary Rhetoric: A Foundation for Literary Study*. Ed. David E. Orton and R. D. Anderson. Leiden: Brill, 1998.

Lentricchia, Frank. *After the New Criticism*. Chicago: University of Chicago Press, 1980.

Lévi-Strauss, Claude. *Structural Anthropology*. Trans. Claire Jacobson and Brooke Grundfest Schoepf. New York: Basic Books, 1963.

Liu, Catherine. "Art Escapes Criticism, or Adorno's Museum." *Cultural Critique* 60 (2005): 217–44.

Lovejoy, A. O. "The Meaning of Romanticism for the Historian of Ideas." *Journal of the History of Ideas* 2 (1942): 257–78.

———. "On the Meaning of 'Romantic' in Early German Romanticism." *Modern Language Notes* 31.7 (1916): 385–96.

———. "On the Discrimination of Romanticisms." *PMLA* 39.2 (1924): 229–53.

Lukács, Georg. *Theory of the Novel: A Historico-Philosophical Essay on the Forms of Great Epic Literature.* Trans. Anna Bostock. Cambridge, MA: MIT Press, 1971.

Macherey, Pierre. "Philosophy as Operation." In *In a Materialist Way: Selected Essays.* Ed. Warren Montag. Trans. Ted Stolze. New York: Verso, 1998. Originally published as "La philosophie comme opération," *Digraphe* 42 (1987): 69–81.

———. *A Theory of Literary Production.* Trans. Geoffrey Wall. London: Routledge & Kegan Paul, 1978. Originally published as *Pour une théorie de la production littéraire* (Paris: Maspero, 1966).

Mallarmé, Stéphane. "Prose pour des Esseintes." In *Œuvres Complétes.* Paris: Gallimard, 1970.

Meillassoux, Quentin. *After Finitude.* Trans. Ray Brassier. New York: Continuum, 2008.

Meyer, Steven. Introduction to *The Making of Americans* by Gertrude Stein. Normal, IL: Dalkey Archive, 1995.

———. *Irresistible Dictation: Gertrude Stein and the Correlations of Writing and Science.* Stanford: Stanford University Press, 2001.

Millán-Zaibert, Elizabeth. *Friedrich Schlegel and the Emergence of Romantic Philosophy.* Albany: State University of New York Press, 2007.

Montaigne, Michel de. *The Complete Essays.* Trans. M. A. Screech. New York: Penguin Books, 1993.

Moretti, Franco. "History of the Novel, Theory of the Novel." *Novel: A Forum on Fiction* 43.1 (2010): 1–10.

Morier, Henri. *Dictionnaire de poétique et de rhétorique.* Paris: PUF, 1961.

Moses, Omri. "Gertrude Stein's Lively Habits." *Twentieth-Century Literature* 55.4 (2009): 445–84.

Moss, Howard. *The Magic Lantern of Marcel Proust.* New York: Macmillan, 1962.

Murphy, P. J. *Critique of Beckett Criticism: A Guide to Research in English, French, and German.* Columbia, SC: Camden House, 1994.

Nadel, Ira Bruce, and Shirley Neuman. *Gertrude Stein and the Making of Literature.* Boston: Northeastern University Press, 1988.

Ngai, Sianne. *Ugly Feelings.* Cambridge, MA: Harvard University Press, 2005.

Nietzsche, Friedrich. *On the Genealogy of Morals.* Trans. Walter Arnold Kaufmann. New York: Vintage Books, 1989.

Nordholt, Anne-Lise Schulte. *Maurice Blanchot: L'écriture comme expérience du dehors.* Geneva, Switzerland: Librairie Droz, 1995.

Novalis. "Miscellaneous Remarks." In *Classic and Romantic German Aesthetics,* ed. Jay M. Bernstein. Cambridge: Cambridge University Press, 2003.

Orlemanski, Julie. "Scales of Reading." *Exemplaria* 26.2–3 (2014): 215–33.

O'Sullivan, Simon, and Stephen Zepke. *Deleuze, Guattari and the Production of the New.* London: Continuum, 2008.

Paulhan, Jean. *The Flowers of Tarbes, Or, Terror in Literature.* Trans. Michael Syrotinski. Urbana: University of Illinois Press, 2006. Originally published as *Les fleurs de Tarbes, ou la terreur dans les lettres* (Paris: Gallimard, 1941).

Peckham, Morse. *The Triumph of Romanticism: Collected Essays.* Columbia: University of South Carolina Press, 1970.

Peden, Knox. *Spinoza contra Phenomenology: French Rationalism from Cavaillès to Deleuze.* Stanford: Stanford University Press, 2014.

Pedretti, Mark. "Late Modern Rigmarole: Boredom as Form in Samuel Beckett's Trilogy." *Studies in the Novel* 45.4 (2013): 583–602.

Pilling, John. *Samuel Beckett.* London: Routledge & Kegan Paul, 1976.

Pound, Scott. "The Difference Sound Makes: Gertrude Stein and the Poetics of Intonation." *English Studies in Canada* 33.4 (2007): 25–35.

Preston, John Hyde. "A Conversation with Gertrude Stein." In *Gertrude Stein Remembered,* ed. Linda Simon. Lincoln: University of Nebraska Press, 1994.

Proust, Marcel. *On Art and Literature, 1896–1919.* Trans. Sylvia Townsend Warner. New York: Carroll and Graf, 1984. Originally published as *Contre Sainte-Beuve* (Paris: Gallimard, 1954).

———. *Remembrance of Things Past.* Trans. C. K. Scott Moncrieff and Terence Kilmartin. 3 vols. New York: Random House, 1981. From the edition published as *A la recherche du temps perdu.* Bibliothèque de la Pléiade (Paris: Gallimard, 1999).

———. *Selected Letters.* Vol. 3. Trans. Terence Kilmartin. New York: Harper Collins. 1992. Originally published in *Choix de lettres,* ed. Philip Kolb (Paris: Plon, 1965).

———. *Selected Letters.* Vol. 4. Trans. Joanna Kilmartin. New York: Harper Collins, 2000. Originally published in *Choix de lettres,* ed. Philip Kolb (Paris: Plon, 1965).

Puttenham, George. *The Arte of English Poesie.* Teddington, Middlesex, UK: Echo Library, 2007.

Quintilian. *The Institutio Oratoria of Quintilian.* Vol. 3. Trans. H. E. Butler. London: W. Heinemann, 1943.

Rancière, Jacques. "The Aesthetic Revolution and Its Outcomes." *New Left Review* 14 (2002): 133–51.

———. *Mute Speech: Literature, Critical Theory, and Politics.* Trans. James Swenson. New York: Columbia University Press, 2011. Originally published as *La parole muette: Essai sur les contradictions de la littérature.* Paris: Hachette, 1998.

Riffaterre, Michael. "Prosopopeia." *Yale French Studies* 69 (1985): 107–23.

Robinson, Michael. *The Long Sonata of the Dead: A Study of Samuel Beckett.* New York: Grove Press, 1969.

Royce, Josiah. *The Spirit of Modern Philosophy: An Essay in the Form of Lectures.* Boston: Houghton Mifflin, 1893.

Ruddick, Lisa. *Reading Gertrude Stein: Body, Text, Gnosis.* Ithaca, NY: Cornell University Press, 1990.

Sartre, Jean-Paul. *L'imaginaire: Psychologie-phenomenologique de l'imagination.* Paris: Gallimard, 1940.

Schaeffer, Jean-Marie. *Art of the Modern Age: Philosophy of Art from Kant to Heidegger.* Trans. Steven Rendall. Princeton, NJ: Princeton University Press, 2000.

Schlegel, August. *Lectures on Dramatic Art and Literature.* Trans. John Black. N.p.: Hard Press, 2006.

Schlegel, Friedrich von. *Athenaeum Fragments.* In *Philosophical Fragments.* Trans. Peter Firchow. Minneapolis: University of Minnesota Press, 1991.

———. *Critical Fragments.* In *Philosophical Fragments.* Trans. Peter Firchow. Minneapolis: University of Minnesota Press, 1991.

———. *Dialogue on Poetry and Literary Aphorisms.* Ed. and trans. Ernst Behler and Roman Struc. University Park: Pennsylvania State University Press, 1968.

———. *Ideas.* In *Philosophical Fragments.* Trans. Peter Firchow. Minneapolis: University of Minnesota Press, 1991.

———. *Kritische Ausgabe.* Ed. Ernst Behler et al. Munich: Schöningh, 1958.

———. *Literary Notebooks, 1797–1801.* Ed. Hans Eichner. Toronto: University of Toronto Press, 1957.

———. *On the Study of Greek Poetry.* Ed. and Trans. Stuart Barnett. Albany: State University of New York Press, 2001.

Schmidt, Dennis J. *Lyrical and Ethical Subjects: Essays on the Periphery of the Word, Freedom, and History.* Albany: State University of New York Press, 2005.

Shattuck, Roger. *Marcel Proust.* Princeton, NJ: Princeton University Press, 1982.

Shaviro, Steven. "Beauty Lies in the Eye." In *A Shock to Thought: Expression after Deleuze and Guattari,* ed. Brian Massumi. New York: Routledge, 2002.

Shenker, Israel. "Moody Man of Letters: A Portrait of Samuel Beckett, Author of the Puzzling 'Waiting for Godot.'" 1956. Reprinted in *Samuel Beckett: The Critical Heritage,* ed. Lawrence Graver and Raymond Federman. Boston: Routledge & Kegan Paul, 1979.

Sibertin-Blanc, Guillaume. "L'analyse des agencements et le groupe de lutte comme expérimentateur collectif." Savoirs, Textes, Langage, February 7, 2007. http://stl.recherche.univ-lille3.fr/seminaires/philosophie/macherey/macherey20062007/sibertin07022007.html.

Simondon, Gilbert. *L'individuation à la lumière des notions de forme et d'information.* Paris: PUF, 1964.

Smith, Daniel W. *Essays on Deleuze.* Edinburgh: Edinburgh University Press, 2012.

Spinoza, Benedict de. *Collected Works.* Ed. and trans. Edwin Curley. Princeton, NJ: Princeton University Press, 1985.

———. *Theological-Political Treatise.* Trans. Samuel Shirley. Indianapolis: Hackett, 2001.

Stanivukovic, Goran V. "Mounting above the Truth: On Hyperbole in English Renaissance Literature." *Forum for Modern Language Studies* 43.1 (2007): 9–34.

Stein, Gertrude. *The Autobiography of Alice B. Toklas.* In *Selected Writings.* Ed. Carl Van Vechten. New York: Vintage Books, 1990.

———. "Composition as Explanation." In *What Are Masterpieces?* New York: Pitman, 1970.

———. *Everybody's Autobiography.* New York: Vintage Books, 1973.

———. *The Geographical History of America, or, The Relation of Human Nature to the Human Mind.* Baltimore: Johns Hopkins University Press, 1995.

———. "The Gradual Making of *The Making of Americans.*" In *Selected Writings.* Ed. Carl Van Vechten. New York: Vintage Books, 1990.

———. *The Making of Americans: Being a History of a Family's Progress.* Normal, IL: Dalkey Archive, 1995.

———. "Portraits and Repetition." In *Lectures in America.* New York: Random House, 1935.

———. *Tender Buttons.* In *Selected Writings.* Ed. Carl Van Vechten. New York: Vintage Books, 1990.

———. "A Transatlantic Interview—1946." With Robert Bartlett Haas. In *What Are Masterpieces?* New York: Pitman, 1970.

———. "What Are Masterpieces and Why Are There So Few of Them." In *What Are Masterpieces?* New York: Pitman, 1970.

Strier, Richard. "The Poetics of Surrender: An Exposition and Critique of New Critical Poetics." *Critical Inquiry* 2.1 (1975): 171–89.

Szondi, Peter. *On Textual Understanding, and Other Essays.* Trans. Harvey Mendelsohn. Minneapolis: University of Minnesota Press, 1986.

Tadié, Jean-Yves. *Marcel Proust: A Life.* Trans. Euan Cameron. New York: Penguin Books, 2000.

Taylor, Melanie. "A Poetics of Difference: *The Making of Americans* and Unreadable Subjects." *NWSA Journal* 15.3 (2003): 26–42.

Terada, Rei. *Feeling in Theory: Emotion after the "Death of the Subject."* Cambridge, MA: Harvard University Press, 2001.

Toscano, Alberto. *The Theater of Production: Philosophy and Individuation between Kant and Deleuze.* New York: Palgrave, 2006.

Toyama, Jean Yamasaki. *Beckett's Game: Self and Language in the Trilogy.* New York: Peter Lang, 1991.

Trezise, Thomas. *Into the Breach: Samuel Beckett and the Ends of Literature.* Princeton, NJ: Princeton University Press, 1990.

Ullmann, Stephen. *Language and Style.* Oxford: Blackwell, 1964.

Vico, Giambattista. *The New Science.* Trans. Thomas Goddard Bergin and Max Harold Fisch. Ithaca, NY: Cornell University Press, 1968.

Wald, Priscilla. *Constituting Americans: Cultural Anxiety and Narrative Form.* Durham, NC: Duke University Press, 1995.

Wasser, Audrey. "Deleuze's Expressionism." *Angelaki* 12.2 (2007): 49–66.

———. "How Do We Recognise Problems?" *Deleuze Studies.* Forthcoming.

———. "A Relentless Spinozism: Deleuze's Encounter with Beckett." *SubStance* 41.1 (2012): 124–36.

Watt, Ian. *Myths of Modern Individualism: Faust, Don Quixote, Don Juan, Robinson Crusoe.* New York: Cambridge University Press, 1996.

———. *The Rise of the Novel: Studies in Defoe, Richardson and Fielding.* Berkeley: University of California Press, 2001.

Watten, Barrett. "An Epic of Subjectivation: *The Making of Americans.*" *Modernism/modernity* 5.2 (1998): 95–121.

Weber, Samuel. "The Madrepore." *Modern Language Notes* 87.7 (1972): 915–61.

Wellek, René. "The Concept of Romanticism in Literary History." In *Concepts of Criticism.* New Haven, CT: Yale University Press, 1963.

———. "Literature and Its Cognates." In *Dictionary of the History of Ideas:*

*Studies of Selected Pivotal Ideas.* Vol. 4. Ed. Philip P. Wiener. Charlot-tesville, VA: Electronic Text Center at the University of Virginia Library, 2003. Online. Based on the 1974 print edition.

———. "Romanticism Re-examined." In *Concepts of Criticism.* New Haven, CT: Yale University Press, 1963.

White, Hayden. *Metahistory: The Historical Imagination in Nineteenth-Century Europe.* Baltimore: Johns Hopkins University Press, 1973.

———. "Narrative, Description, and Tropology in Proust." In *Figural Realism: Studies in the Mimesis Effect.* Baltimore: Johns Hopkins University Press, 1999.

Wilson, Edmund. *Axel's Castle: A Study in the Imaginative Literature of 1870–1930.* New York: C. Scribner's Sons, 1931.

Wimsatt, William K., Jr., and Monroe C. Beardsley. "The Intentional Fallacy." In *The Verbal Icon: Studies in the Meaning of Poetry.* Lexington: University of Kentucky Press, 1954.

Wordsworth, William. *Selected Poetry.* New York: Modern Library, 2001.

# INDEX

ACKNOWLEDGMENTS

This book has been long enough in the making that I've had ample time to reflect on the help I've received, even if I've developed scant ability to express my gratitude. I offer my thanks, then, and where they are inadequate, I hope my friends know that this book bears within it the many marks of their inspiration, support, and generosity.

This project would not have been possible from the first if I hadn't had the freedom to cultivate these ideas as a graduate student in comparative literature at Cornell University. I remain deeply grateful to Jonathan Culler, Tracy McNulty, and Bruno Bosteels, for the many ways they shaped my project as well as helped me to become the scholar capable of it. Jonathan said to me once in Zeus Café, offhandedly, "Well, you could always write your *own* theory of literature," and I decided to keep it in mind. Tracy gave me her time, affection, and support while testing my ideas in the best way; Bruno made me feel like a real writer from the moment I started working with him. Richard Klein also fostered my work and helped me improve it. Prior to my PhD, Phil Wegner and Jim Paxson at the University of Florida and Jeff Pence at Oberlin were formative influences and cherished mentors.

Intellectually vigorous and supportive graduate student communities also shaped and inspired this work. I am grateful to the Modernist Reading Group at Cornell from 2002 to 2006, the Hegel Reading Group (Cornell and Paris) in 2003–10, and the indefatigable Theory Reading Group at Cornell, 2003–10. To friends Becky Colesworthy, Bradley Depew, Aaron Hodges, Robin Sowards, and Danielle St. Hilaire I owe a special thank you. To Alan-Young Bryant, I dedicate my memories of Cornell. He fostered so many of my friendships with his warmth and wit, made them better, and offered me his own.

I brought this book nearly to fruition in the unparalleled intellectual environment of the University of Chicago, and am grateful for the support of a Harper-Schmidt Fellowship, as well as for the extraordinary collegiality and generosity of my co-fellows. Countless exchanges in the Society of Fellows inspired many ideas in this book. The Modern France Workshop, the Contemporary European Philosophy Workshop, the Society of Fellows Workshop, and the Weissbourd Conference offered me invaluable forums to present parts of this work, and I am especially grateful for feedback from Daisy Delogu, Alison James, Françoise Meltzer, Justin Steinberg, Maud Ellmann, Lisa Ruddick, and Richard Strier, and from my co-fellows Nick Gaskill, Markus Hardtmann, Ben McKean, Tim Michael, Lauren Silvers, Emily Steinlight, and Neil Verma.

Beyond institutional walls, Nathan Brown, Martin Hägglund, Anna Kornbluh, and Knox Peden offered equal parts friendship and rigorous conversation. I am indebted to Nathan and Petar Milat for inviting me to speak at Mama Multimedia Institute in Zagreb, to Anna for inviting me to the Inter-Chicago Circle for Experimental Critical Theory, and to Josh Robinson for hosting me at CRASSH at Cambridge. To Anna (again!), Gregg Flaxman, Steven Miller, and Rob Lehman, I owe a particular thank you for the care they took in reading this book in manuscript, for the insight of their suggestions, and for the examples of their own scholarship.

This project was completed at Miami University, in the vibrant scholarly community of the Department of French and Italian. I could not be more thankful for the warm welcome I have received here. The Committee on Faculty Research and the College of Arts and Science at Miami also generously offered financial support. At Fordham University Press, I am deeply appreciative to Helen Tartar for accepting this manuscript, to Tom Lay for seeing it through with care, and to the rest of the staff for their work on my behalf.

Finally, I am grateful to my family, my brothers, and especially my parents for their generosity and patience. My father taught me to ask a lot of questions when I care about something, and my mother that it is possible not just to solve problems but to reimagine them. Above all, I am indebted to my partner, Rob Lehman. The radiant intelligence and supernatural care with which he has worked with me on this manuscript has been humbling; every page of this book has been shaped by our ongoing dialogue. He has made possible every second of my writing life—and my other one, too.

A version of chapter 5 first appeared as "From Figure to Fissure: Beckett's *Molloy, Malone Dies,* and *The Unnamable*" in *Modern Philology* 109.2 (2011): 245–65; a version of chapter 6 first appeared as "Hyperbole in Proust" in *MLN* 129.4 (2014): 829–54.